Monetarism: Is There An Alternative?

JIM TOMLINSON

Basil Blackwell

© J.D. Tomlinson, 1986

First published 1986
Basil Blackwell Ltd
108 Cowley Road, Oxford OX4 1JF, UK

Basil Blackwell Inc.
432 Park Avenue South, Suite 1505,
New York, NY 10016, USA

British Library Cataloguing in Publication Data
Tomlinson, Jim
   Monetarism: Is there an alternative?
   1. Great Britain—Economic policy—1945–
   I. Title
   330.941′0858   HC256.6

   ISBN 0–631–14037–9
   ISBN 0–631–14038–7 Pbk

Library of Congress Cataloging in Publication Data
Tomlinson, Jim.
   Monetarism: Is there an alternative?
   Bibliography: p. 187
   Includes index.
   1. Great Britain—Economic policy—1945–
2. Liberal Party (Great Britain) 3. Social Democratic
Party (Great Britain) 4. Marxian economics. I. Title.
HC256.6.T66 1985 338.941 85–15084
ISBN 0–631–14037–9
ISBN 0–631–14038–7 (pbk.)

Typeset by Cambrian Typesetters, Frimley, Surrey
Printed in Great Britain by The Bath Press, Avon

116264

Contents

List of Tables

Acknowledgements

I am grateful to Alex Bowen, Stuart Burchell, David Heald, David Higham, Tom Schuller and Grahame Thompson for discussion of parts of this book. Basil Blackwell's (anonymous) reader has been unusually helpful both in general and in detail. The general approach owes a great deal to discussions over a number of years with members of the Birkbeck College 'Politics and State' seminar.

Mrs Christine Newnham and Sheila Forbes typed and retyped the manuscript with their customary speed and efficiency.

Introduction

The purpose of this book is two-fold: first, to give a comprehensive account of the economic policies proposed by the main strands of opposition to the current Conservative government; second, to offer some assessment of the plausibility of these programmes, and how far they offer a desirable and viable alternative.

I

Plainly there are any number of preferred alternatives to some or all aspects of the current repertoire of economic policies. But anyone who has taken an interest in such issues will know that the arguments of many of those oppositional statements are repetitive, and that without too much distortion they can be reduced to two or three major lines of thought. Hence the necessity, for reasons of manageability, of dividing up the policies discussed here into three groups, can also be broadly justified as catching the essence of economic argument in Britain in the early and mid-1980s.

The first strand of argument discussed in each chapter is that associated with the Liberal/Social Democratic Party (S.D.P.) Alliance.[1] Here the primary focus is on the considerable quantity of material produced by the S.D.P. This is for two reasons. First, on the major themes of economic policy the Alliance partners are, unsurprisingly, in close agreement. (As well as the 1983 election manifesto, Liberal/S.D.P., 1983, see also Liberal/S.D.P., 1982.) But, secondly, and perhaps because of its status as a new party, anxious to make a distinctive case from the 'old parties' of Labour and Conservative, the S.D.P. has been much more prolific in its production of economic policy arguments than any other party. Hence the terms Alliance and S.D.P. will be used as if they are synonymous.

However, in the case of both the Alliance and Labour parties, I have not confined discussion to those documents actually published in the name of the political parties. This would seem to impose too narrow and restrictive a definition on policy discussion. Policy discussion published in this form is often a summary (and frequently a crude one) of discussions elsewhere, and if a reasoned argument is to be made, this other material has also to be discussed. Of course this poses problems. Academic debates do not fall neatly into party political categories. Nevertheless, I believe it can be maintained that the analytic links between party positions and academic arguments are usually clear, and justify approaching academic material in this way.[2] Of course, this does not imply that any particular author is a member of the political party whose policies follow a similar line of analysis. What provides the link is analytic structure, not the political affiliation of individuals.

This extension of coverage beyond material bearing a party label is especially important in the case of the Labour Party. For, in contrast with the S.D.P., the Labour Party has not been anything like so prolific in the production of published policy documents. But on the other hand, there exists plenty of material by those sympathetic to the Labour Party which can reliably be used to look at the foundations and implications of Labour policy.

The inclusion of the Marxist Left is based on two main considerations. First, though its electoral position is very weak, at the analytical level there is a considerable weight of Marxist material on the economy which it would be inappropriate to ignore. Secondly, the influence of Marxist arguments goes beyond those who straightforwardly make the Marxist case. For many on the Left in Britain, especially in the Labour Party, Marxist arguments are taken very seriously, and often provide a major part of the context in relation to which their own position is defined. Of course, unlike S.D.P. and Labour, 'Marxist' is not the name of a political party but refers to a strand of political argument whose boundaries are both unclear and not coterminous with any organized political forces. I have used the Marxist label largely where the argument discussed labels itself as such and/or where clear Marxist themes are present. In particular, the Militant Tendency is treated as part of the Marxist Left, despite its tactic of entrism into the Labour Party, as it calls itself Marxist and uses Marxist categories.

Whilst, for the reasons given above, it seems important to include Marxist arguments in a book trying to provide a reasonably comprehensive picture of Left policies, the coverage of these arguments is generally less than the coverage of the other positions. This in a simple sense reflects the smaller volume of policy-oriented material produced by Marxists on the economy.

But this in turn relates to a broader point which it is worth briefly spelling out. The S.D.P. and the Labour Party both offer policies aimed at the better management of the British national economy, that is, a capitalist economy, however much Labour may see an eventual transformation to a different, or socialist, economy.

On the Left, the appropriateness of programmes for the better management of the national economy is the subject of considerable opposition (Hindess, 1981). This book, by its very nature, assumes that such programmes *are* appropriate for the Left. This is based on a simple political calculation. No party which does not offer a plausible programme of economic management is likely to succeed in gaining sufficient electoral support to form a government, or to stay in power long without providing some degree of success in such management. Hence all other policy proposals remain entirely Utopian if economic management is not to some degree successful.[3] In modern conditions, plausible policies of economic management by no means exhaust the policy repertoire, but they are an unavoidable condition of electoral success.

National economic management has always had an uneasy place in the Left's discussions. In large part this is because the Left is suspicious of anything 'national' in scope, seeing this as cutting across the fundamental divide between social classes. However, a commitment to national economic management does not have to mean a surrender to the rhetoric of national interest. It can be based on a combination of the political calculation outlined above, together with an acceptance that the national economy does exist, in the sense that there are reasonably well-defined instruments of policy which act largely (though never entirely) within the national state territory. At its simplest, this is because the national state does to a greater or lesser degree have the capacity to control the issue of credit, the scale and structure of state expenditure and taxation, and the general legal environment in which the economy functions. This is not to doubt the increasing international integration of the British economy (see chapter 4), but it is to assert that now, and in the foreseeable future, this integration has not rendered the national economy a redundant concept, nor its management a politically avoidable task.

A rather different view often expressed on the Left is that such issues as budgetary and monetary policy, the exchange rate and the balance of payments, are ephemeral to the 'real' economy, which is seen as the process of production. For example, Hodgson, (1984, p. 131) in a book with whose general thrust I have considerable sympathy, asserts that:

Many economic policy makers would have us believe that serious problems can be solved by a manipulation of the exchange rate, or by controlling the money supply, or merely by increasing aggregate public spending. I suspect that the public at large are sceptical of these arguments. They are right. Our problems are fundamental, and they require a major reorganization of industry, work and leisure.

But anyone who has lived in Britain over the last few years has seen how significant for the welfare of the population are movements in the exchange rate, the budget deficit and the money supply. They have very 'real' effects. Hence it is important to contest the claim that macroeconomic management is somehow peripheral to the Left's concerns. This, of course, is not to say that macro management should be seen as the most important aspect of economic policy. Whilst chapters 2–4 focus on macroeconomic policy, chapters 5 and 6 concentrate on the Left's policies for the micro economy, or the 'supply side', to use the currently fashionable term.

The general division of economic policy proposals into three strands does, of course, exaggerate the rigidity of the divisions between these packages of proposals. Whilst it may be part of the rules of the game in electoral politics to stress one's own party's distinctive stance, this often exaggerates the extent of division. In fact, the scale of policy division varies greatly in different areas – for example, it is very small in the case of short-run budgetary policy, but very large in the case of incomes policies. In outlining the policies I have tried to note the points of convergence as well as divergence, especially in the general area of macro policy where such convergence is most apparent.

II

This book, as well as outlining what the S.D.P., the Labour Party and the Marxist Left say, also attempts some assessment of these proposals. A number of points should be made to clarify what is attempted here.

First, the assessment offered tries to mix elements of what is desirable and what is feasible. This combination of criteria is inherently problematic, as, for example, what is feasible depends in part, at least, on how strongly one desires it, in other words, how much one is prepared to give up to attain one's desire. Nevertheless the distinction, if often only implicit, is important in stressing the constraints on policy action, which seems to me to be the concept to be put at the forefront of policy discussion. Only when these constraints are clarified can one attempt to reconcile the always temporary, always traducible, but always necessary reconciliation of the desirable and the feasible. Indeed, it is precisely the attempt at such reconciliation which is the very stuff, and source of intellectual interest, in any politics.

The assessment offered here is a partial one without being partisan. It is partial in the sense that it does not attempt the impossible task of an 'objective' survey. Such things must be left to the gods. However, it does try to give an honest account of the problems and possibilities of all the programmes, and it is definitely not a disguised attempt to argue for any one of the policy packages outlined. Perhaps it is appropriate for the author to state that he is a member of the Labour Party. But as will be apparent from the discussion below (and especially chapter 7) this does not mean that this book is an endorsement of that party's policies. As will be apparent, a number of Labour's policies are argued to be undesirable and, more often, unfeasible.

Finally, chapter 7 attempts to sketch some of the strategic issues. In large part, this draws together the arguments of the preceding chapters; but it also tries to indicate some of the possibilities and problems of policies to which none of the three strands of argument have given serious attention. Of course, for one person to offer a complete strategy for the future of the British economy would be a foolish pretence. All that is attempted is an outline of the main problem areas, and some more detailed discussion of areas neglected elsewhere in the book. The purpose of this chapter is partly as a summary, partly to suggest areas where Left argument might perhaps more profitably succeed.

To conclude on a rather more 'party political' point, one outstanding conclusion of this book seems to me to be the exposure of the fatuity of the common assertion on much of the Left that 'the S.D.P. has no policies'. On the contrary, the S.D.P. probably has more detailed economic policies than any other party in Britain. From the point of view of the Labour Party and other socialists, the crying need is to match the range and sophistication of the S.D.P.'s discussions by their own. Perhaps this book can make some small contribution to that task.

1

The Thatcher Years

INTRODUCTION

This chapter attempts to give a summary of the character and effects of the economic policies pursued in Britain since 1979. Such an exercise raises a number of difficulties, apart from the unavoidable compression when so much ground has to be covered in the space of a single chapter.[1]

First of all, the policy regime since 1979 has been accompanied by a radical rhetoric which attempts, amongst other things, to fix the terms of debate on economic policy. Yet clearly we should not accept this rhetoric at its face value – it is itself part of the policy, and itself requires assessment. On the other hand, it is important not to treat the rhetoric of policy as simply a blind, a disguise for what is really intended. This approach is quite common on the Left, where the argument is made that all the talk of money supply targets, Public Sector Borrowing Requirement (P.S.B.R.) and the 'supply side' is a disguise for policies deliberately aimed at generating mass unemployment, breaking the trade unions and fundamentally shifting economic power in favour of capital (e.g. Glyn and Harrison, 1980; Rowthorn, 1981).

The difficulties with such arguments would seem to be three-fold. First, they greatly exaggerate the coherence of policy since 1979, presenting this as a well-integrated, highly orchestrated strategy, and one which because its objectives were obscured, amounted to a secret conspiracy. Against this view I will argue that policy has been much more reactive and *ad hoc* than talk of 'strategy' often implies. And indeed it can be argued that national economic policy, especially in a small country with strong international links, like Britain, will always be subject to unforeseeable events which make a detailed strategy impossible to deliver.

Secondly, such a view implies a very crude notion of ideology, where this is seen as simply a disguise for 'real' intentions. This is not only an unacceptably simple general theory of ideology, reminiscent of the view attacked by Marx that 'all priests are atheists who are also liars', but fails to account for the intellectual force of monetarism as an ideology.

Finally and more specifically, the view that the Conservative government of 1979 intended by its policies to generate four million unemployed is not borne out by the evidence. It seems to have seriously believed that whilst unemployment would rise, this would be transitional and on a much smaller scale. In particular, it failed to foresee the severe effects of the exchange rate appreciation on output and employment. (All these points are dealt with in more detail in Tomlinson, 1985, ch. 10.)

This chapter therefore attempts to treat Thatcherism in its own terms rather than as simply a mendacious theory. Before doing so, however, there is one other important introductory argument. Critics of the 1979 government's policies have sometimes argued that the real turning point in economic policy came not in 1979 but back in 1975/6 under the Labour government. Occasioned by a combination of rapid inflation, increasing public-sector borrowing and a fall in the exchange rate, the senior members of that government espoused monetarist rhetoric (e.g. Callaghan, 1976), and monetary targets were installed as central features of macroeconomic policy. These changes, however, should not be exaggerated. At the level of rhetoric, much of this seems to have been linked to internal Labour Party politics and aimed at reviving financial confidence. And whilst monetary targets became important, they did not have the central status accorded to them after 1979, and were pursued alongside 'non-monetarist' measures such as the social contract. Above all, whilst policy was largely restrictive in 1975–9, it was not so in the face of a sharply deteriorating international environment as was the case after 1979. Hence, whilst some of the continuities before and after 1979 are important (a point pursued briefly in the conclusion to this chapter and elsewhere in the book), they should not be exaggerated. The differences have been appropriately summed up as between a 'monetarily-constrained Keynesianism' and 'monetarism proper' (Fforde, 1983, pp. 203–4): in other words, between continuing to try to manage the economy by macroeconomic means in the face of constraints, and essentially abandoning the idea of discretionary management of this kind.

1979 was an important turning point, and this chapter looks at policy since then in three sections. The first sets out the policy proposals of 1979 and some of the background and implications of these. This is followed by a section on the outcomes of policy since

1979. The final section attempts an overall assessment of policy over the last few years and explains why there is scope for a superior alternative.

Central to the Conservatives' economic proposals in 1979 was the view that countering inflation should be the major objective of macroeconomic policy. This relied on the views both that inflation was a major problem for the functioning of the economy, and that governments could not, over any time but the short run, affect the 'real' magnitudes in the economy, such as output and employment. The proposals also played upon the view that previous post-war policy had been too short-run in orientation, trading off unsustainable gains in employment against long-run growth of the public sector and higher inflation.

Medium Term Financial Strategy

Against this background, the policies which emerged in 1980 centred on a Medium Term Financial Strategy (M.T.F.S.) which had two target variables: the money suppy (sterling M3) and the Public Sector Borrowing Requirement.[2] The growth rate and the size of the P.S.B.R. as a proportion of Gross Domestic Product (G.D.P.) were each to be progressively reduced over a period of years (see table 1.1). (Initially, the Conservatives took over the previous Labour government's monetary targets, until the M.T.F.S. was unveiled in the spring of 1980.) A number of features of this strategy deserve comment. The strategy was clearly a monetarist one, in the sense that it envisaged a reduction in money-supply growth as both a necessary and sufficient condition for a reduction in the rate of inflation. However, the targeting of P.S.B.R. had a much less clear position in economic doctrine. The focus on this seems to have been composed of a number of elements. First, there was a belief in the financial crowding out of private investment by the public sector via the interest rates offered on government debt. Secondly, there was a belief that the public sector was in some general sense a 'bad thing', and hence should be reduced in size in all possible ways. Thirdly came the belief that there was a stable relation between P.S.B.R. and M3, so that the reduction in the former would bring a reduction in (the rate of growth of) the latter. Against such a linkage, monetarists such as Friedman argued that reductions in monetary growth and in the size of the public sector were both desirable, but had no causal relationship (Friedman, in House of Commons, 1980).

Table 1.1 Medium Term Financial Strategy, 1980

Year	£ M3 (% growth)	P.S.B.R. (% of G.D.P.)
1980/1	7–11	3¾
1981/2	6–10	3
1982/3	5–9	2¼
1983/4	4–8	1½

Source: *Financial Statement and Budget Report 1980/81*, H.M.S.O.

Another feature of this strategy was that it was explicitly pitched as 'medium term', not only because of the belief that previous macro policy had been too short-run in orientation, but because of its desired effect on expectations. The argument here was that the effects of such disinflationary policies on output and employment would depend a great deal on how far private economic agents (and especially wage bargainers) adjusted their expectations. If they continued as before, and pressed for large nominal wage and price changes, then control of the money supply would bring contraction of output and employment. Conversely, if the expectations of economic agents could be changed, then the real magnitudes would be depressed for only a short period by these policies. Hence the medium-term nature of the strategy was seen as gently altering these expectations. An alternative view was essayed (e.g. Minford, in House of Commons, 1980) which suggested that a 'short sharp shock' would be better, as the medium term would allow too much possibility for political pressure to build up to reverse the strategy. This stress on expectations allowed proponents of the M.T.F.S. to argue that it would not have the disastrous effects on output and employment suggested by its opponents, because such gloomy predictions presumed that expectations would be unchanged.

Supply-side Policies

Along with the M.T.F.S., the government proposed supply-side policies, aimed at increasing the efficiency of production in a variety of ways. In the U.S.A., where the expression 'supply side' originated, the emphasis was on tax-cutting and on deregulation of the economy. In Britain, by contrast, the emphasis was on altering the labour market (especially via anti-union measures), with a lesser role played by policies for changes in the public sector. The Conservatives were certainly strongly committed to a policy of tax cuts, but this did not have the central role in policy proposals that it had in 'Reaganomics'. This was important, because the emphasis on reduction in the P.S.B.R. in the M.T.F.S. posed the problem of what would 'give' if public expenditure were not cut to make possible cuts both in taxation and in public borrowing. In the event, in Britain, the inability of the government to cut public expenditure (see Outcomes of Conservative Policy, below) forced a choice which was resolved by increasing taxation. By contrast, in the U.S.A. taxes were cut radically, and it was public borrowing which rocketed, leading to the paradox of an alleged 'monetarist' policy with rapidly expanding public deficits.

Such difficulties led to something of a reformulation of strategy after the election victory of 1983. Much more emphasis was placed on 'privatization', that is, the sale of public-sector assets which could be presented both as a supply-side policy – increasing the efficiency in use of these assets by putting them in private hands – and at the same time would reduce the P.S.B.R. Whereas only £0·5 billion per annum had been raised by such measures under the first Thatcher government, under the second sales of £4 billion per annum were envisaged (Brittan, 1984, p. 109). As Brittan (p. 110–11) noted, 'privatisation is a partial substitute for cutting spending as a whole', and 'has emerged almost by default as the main theme of Conservative supply-side or structural policy.'

Not only was supply-side policy considerably re-oriented and strengthened after 1983, but from as early as 1981 macro policy was altering, though more slowly and subtly. For reasons which are looked at in more detail in the next section, the initial focus on sterling M3 as the appropriate monetary target has looked increasingly dubious, and has been added to by a variety of other measures of monetary policy. And, more generally, the emphasis on nominal P.S.B.R. as a target has increased in comparison with any monetary target. In other words, fiscal policy, even if of a very specific kind, has increased in importance in comparison with monetary targeting.

OUTCOMES OF CONSERVATIVE POLICY

Britain and the O.E.C.D.

A useful starting point for looking at the results of policy since 1979 is a comparison of Britain's performance with the overall performance of countries of the Organization for Economic Co-operation and Development (O.E.C.D.) (table 1.2). The reason for such a comparison is obviously to try to isolate in a simple way the specific results of British policy compared with the general pattern of activity in the world capitalist economy. This comparative approach is especially relevant given the undoubted existence of a world depression in the early 1980s, and the attempt by the Conservative government to argue that it was this depression which accounted for the large rise in unemployment.

Of course such comparative exercises can only be indicative, not conclusive. One is never comparing like with like. In particular, Britain started from a relatively weak position in the sense of low productivity levels, which could be reasonably said to make the economy more vulnerable to external pressure. On the other hand, Britain had North Sea oil which by and large should help in reducing the effects of any external shock, by aiding the balance of payments; and this would be especially so if that shock originated in a rise in the price of oil. Finally, it should be noted that the world depression cannot be treated as totally an external force for Britain. Despite its small Gross National Product (G.N.P.) relative to the total G.N.P. of the O.E.C.D., a deflationary policy pursued in Britain will have substantial impact on other countries; and in fact, Britain's pre-depression peak output was reached before that of the O.E.C.D., in the second quarter of 1979 rather than the first quarter of 1980. In other words, Britain 'helped' the

Table 1.2 Britain and the O.E.C.D., 1979–84

	1979	1980	1981	1982	1983	1984	1985 1st qu.
Inflation (consumer prices) (%)							
Britain	13.4	17.9	11.9	8.6	4.6	5.0	6.9
O.E.C.D.	9.4	13.0	10.6	7.8	5.3	5.3	4.7
Unemployment (%)							
Britain	5.7	7.3	11.3	12.3	13.1	13.0	13.3
O.E.C.D.	5.1	5.8	6.8	8.2	8.7	8.2	8.2
Output growth (%) (G.D.P.)							
Britain	1.4	–2.6	–1.3	2.3	2.5	2.0	n.a.
O.E.C.D.	3.4	1.2	1.9	–0.4	2.2	4.5	n.a.

Source: *O.E.C.D. Main Economic Indicators*

world depression get going, although this was soon greatly added to by the second oil price rise and American deflationary policies.

Anti-inflationary Policies

It is clear from the figures in table 1.2 that the unambiguous success for the Conservative policy has been the reduction in the rate of inflation. Britain in the 1970s was one of the fastest inflators in the O.E.C.D., but in the early 1980s it has become one of the slowest. This success raises two issues of assessment: how far was this outcome the result of British government policy, and how far do the benefits of such a success outweigh the costs?

A striking feature of policy since 1979 has been that whilst the intermediate targets, sterling M3 and P.S.B.R., have overshot (table 1.3), the objective of a reduction in the rate of inflation has been achieved. However, the nominal M3 and P.S.B.R. figures are misleading about the stance of policy in this period. As far as monetary policy is concerned, the rate of interest in this period suggests a very tight monetary policy (Buiter and Miller, 1981 and 1983). Tightness is also suggested by the sharp upward movement in the exchange rate in the period up to early 1981, though it is difficult to account for the scale of this appreciation solely by monetary tightness, or indeed by any other element or combination of elements (Buiter and Miller, 1983)

The P.S.B.R. target has overshot, though less significantly. Again, however, the nominal figure is misleading. In the face of an 'autonomous' movement in output and employment which would itself yield a substantial increase in P.S.B.R. (by loss of tax revenues and increased social security payments), the government

Table 1.3 Intermediate target attainment, 1980/1–1983/4

| | £M3 (% growth) | | P.S.B.R. (% of G.D.P.) | |
	Target	Outcome	Target	Outcome
1980/1	7–11	19.4	3.75	5.4
1981/2	6–10	12.8	3.0	3.4
1982/3	5–9	11.2	2.25	3.2
1983/4	4–8	9.5	1.5	3.2

Note: These are the targets of March 1980, which were revised upwards in subsequent budgets.
Source: *Financial Statement and Budget Report 1980/1*; *Midland Bank Review*, Autumn 1984

has continued with its downward pressure on public borrowing. Hence, adjusted for this decline in output, fiscal policy has been sharply deflationary (table 1.4).

The government's internal policies have therefore been part of the explanation for the decline in inflation since 1980. However, the extent to which this decline has been added to by the rise in unemployment is a matter of dispute. Beckerman (1985) has argued that the fall in inflation, which has undoubtedly been general to the O.E.C.D. countries (table 1.2), has been the consequence of the fall in commodity prices, brought about by the general deflation in all these countries. In this light, the rise in unemployment would appear as a cost of the deflationary policies, but not one which directly contributed to the fall in inflation. Such a view suggests that the Conservative success over inflation was dependent upon parallel deflationary policies elsewhere in the O.E.C.D., and that inflation is much less under the control of the British government than government statements suggest.[3]

In sum, the government's deflationary policies, both directly and by helping to inspire similar policies elsewhere, plus the truly external forces for depression, have succeeded in radically reducing the rate of inflation in the U.K. A similar pattern is apparent elsewhere in the O.E.C.D., but the particular rigour of deflation in Britain has taken the country from the top of the inflation league to close to the bottom.

This outcome is not at all surprising. Few economists doubted before 1979 that if a sharp enough bout of deflation was applied, inflation would be reduced, although the mechanisms and associated effects were matters of wide disagreement (see House of Commons, 1980). What is much more contentious is whether the costs of this success in inflation outweighed the benefits.

Table 1.4 Changes in budgetary stance (% of G.D.P.), 1980–3

Year	U.K.	O.E.C.D.
1980	0.9	0.1
1981	3.4	0.6
1982	1.2	0.0
1983	0.5	0.3

Note: These figures represent *changes* in budget deficits, and show that in Britain fiscal policy was tightened sharply despite the recession.
Source: W. H. Buiter and M. Miller (1983), 'Changing the Rules: Economic Consequences of the Thatcher Regime', *Brookings Papers in Economic Activity*, 2, p. 325

There is a substantial difficulty in assessing how far inflation is an economic problem. For a long time, until the mid-1970s, most economists saw the main evil of inflation as deriving from its redistributive effects on those on fixed money incomes. And undoubtedly there was substantial redistribution in the early period of high inflation. However, most of this redistribution arose from very specific causes – negative real interest rates, especially on building society deposits and government debt (Foster, 1976). But this can be readily corrected by policy, and in fact real interest rates have become positive since 1980, so that problem has been 'solved'.

In the mid-1970s, economists (notably Friedman, 1977) started to argue that inflation was damaging, not just because of its redistributive effects, but also because it reduced the growth of output and increased employment. The case made by Friedman is far from convincing (Higham and Tomlinson, 1982). He failed to demonstrate that inflation *per se* reduced growth, as distinct from its effects in inspiring governments to deflationary policy. Wadhwani (1984A and 1984B) has advanced a more convincing case for the harm done by inflation via its effects on company financing. Neverthelesss, some scepticism over the scale of damage done by inflation within the range experienced in Britain lately seems appropriate. If the position were one of a continually accelerating rate of inflation, such evils would seem considerable, but this was not the case in Britain in the 1970s generally, nor does it seem that such a process threatened in 1979. The surge of inflation in 1979/80 seems to have been a cyclical episode, not a harbinger of hyper-inflation. Hence, when the costs and benefits of inflation reduction are considered, the problematic nature of the harm done by inflation should be borne in mind (see chapter 3).

The major costs of the fall in inflation are the consequent falls in output and the rise in unemployment. Between the second quarter of 1979 and the fourth quarter of 1982, manufacturing production fell by 19·3 per cent, G.D.P. by 2·5 per cent. In the same period, employment fell by 10·5 per cent, and unemployment rose from 5·1 to 12 per cent. (From November 1982 the unemployment figure was massaged downwards by including only those entitled to benefits, excluding, in particular, married women who previously had registered but were ineligible for benefit. A paradoxical consequence of this from the government's point of view was that when employment began to rise in 1982, most of the newly employed were such women, and hence rising employment did not lead to a fall in the official unemployment figure.)

Table 1.2 shows how this performance compared with that of the rest of the O.E.C.D. Whilst other countries have had a similar general pattern, Britain's performance is clearly worse than most. Britain's policies measured by, for example, adjusted P.S.B.R., have been more deflationary than those of the rest of the O.E.C.D., and this has had the expected consequences for output and employment.

Apart from emphasizing the high costs of mass unemployment (e.g. Sinfield, 1981; Tomlinson, 1983B) and the irrecoverable nature of the cumulative output loss (Brittan, 1984, p. 5), two other points may be stressed. Unemployment falls very unevenly on the population: the great bulk is experienced by a small proportion of the population. Disney (1979) has calculated that, in any one year, 70 per cent of unemployment is endured by 3 per cent of the workforce. In contrast, inflation, if accompanied by indexation of financial assets, would seem likely to wreak its ill effects (whatever exactly they may be) on the population as a whole. So, if there is a trade-off between inflation and unemployment, this distributional aspect should be borne in mind.

Secondly, the fall in output has come about substantially through the closure of plant, not just lower levels of utilization. This destruction of plant may be irreversible in two senses. On the one hand, the skills of the labour force may decay and the machinery be broken up; but even more importantly, that capacity as an organizational entity will cease to exist. So the idea of infinitely malleable 'factors of production', which can be utilized or not at the drop of a hat, is inappropriate for thinking about what has happened in Britain of late. Once capacity has been destroyed, the costs of putting it back together again seem likely to be extremely high.

The Balance of Payments

On the face of it, Britain's balance of payments position may seem to have been another satisfactory outcome of the Thatcher years. The current balance (goods plus services) has been substantial and has allowed very substantial capital outflows with some accumulation of reserves, at least up to 1984. However, the crude data of the balance of payments accounts are subject to two major qualifications. Most straightforwardly, the strength of the balance of payments has itself been a reflection of the low level of output and employment, which slows the growth of imports. Simple calculations of the effect on the balance of payments of returning even to the economists' favoured 'Non-Accelerating Inflation

Rate of Unemployment' (N.A.I.R.U.), currently 6–7 per cent in the U.K. (see chapter 2) suggest that this would be enormous – a deterioration of around £14 billion in the current-account position (Williamson, 1984, p. 73). (See table 1.5.)

Table 1.5 U.K. balance of payments, 1979–84 (£ million)

Year	Visible balance	Current balance	Overseas investment
1979	−3449	− 533	+1835
1980	+1513	+3635	−1455
1981	+3652	+7251	−7351
1982	+2384	+5774	−3356
1983	−1165	+2543	−3231
1984	−4255	+ 51	−3872

Source: *Economic Trends, Financial Statistics*

More complicated than this is the position of manufacturing. In 1983, for the first time since the Industrial Revolution, Britain had a deficit on manufacturing trade. At the moment this is not a difficulty, especially because of the continuing net surplus on oil payments. However, the cause for concern may be seen in the medium term. Although cries of 'what happens when the oil runs out?' have perhaps been overdone, with the arrival of that day pushed further and further into the future, the current oil balance cannot be expected to last indefinitely. The question will then be how far the export of services can offset the import balance on manufactures. The problem is that services only provide around 30 per cent of British exports, and that even within that, only financial services provide a regular and substantial export surplus. And Britain's competitiveness in this area is far from over-whelmingly strong, its share of world exports in this area having fallen in recent years. The implication of all this is that, whilst services will undoubtedly continue to increase their share of employment, and manufacturing to decline in its share, competi-tiveness in manufacturing remains very important in Britain in the medium term (see also Smith, 1984, part one). This point is returned to in the section on Conservative industrial policy.

Public Expenditure

An important link between macro and micro policy is public expenditure. The Conservatives in 1979 were committed to a

policy of public-expenditure cuts, facilitating a cut in both
P.S.B.R. and taxes. The P.S.B.R. cut was a major plank of
macroeconomic policy, whilst the tax cuts were seen as part of the
microeconomic, supply-side policy. In addition, public-expenditure
cuts themselves were seen as increasing efficiency by reducing the
role of the state in the economy.

The first point to be noted about this policy is that public
expenditure has not been cut by the Thatcher governments. The
continued growth has been a consequence of two major causes: on
the one hand, policy commitments to increase expenditure
(defence, law and order) or maintain it (health); on the other
hand, the growth of social security expenditure as the depression
has deepened, and despite various cutting exercises such as the
ending of earnings-related supplements (see Cmnd 9189 for
details). The government has responded to the failure of its
policies in two ways. It has initiated a debate on the major
expanding area – social security. It has also accepted that public
expenditure is very difficult to cut and has therefore refocused
these objectives on a stable level of total expenditure, falling as
a share of national income as that income grows. Thus for 1985/6
the projected level of public expenditure in real terms is the same
as that planned for 1984/5, although the 1984/5 plan was exceeded
by around £1·5 billion. However, if this target were met it would
mean public expenditure falling back to 41 per cent of G.D.P.,
compared with a peak level of 43·5 in 1981/2 (see table 1.6 below).
For the latest government position, see Cmnd 9428 (1985).

Whatever may come of these discussions and proposals, the
consequence of the government's failure to reduce public expendi-

Table 1.6 Public spending, 1978/9–1985/6 (in £ billion at 1983/4
prices)

Year	£bn	Share of G.D.P. (%)
1979/80	111.7	39.5
1980/1	113.5	42
1981/2	116.5	43.5
1982/3	118.4	43
1983/4	120.3	42.5
1984/5	122.1*	42*

* Projected
Source: *Autumn Statement 1984, House of Commons Papers 12,* 1984/5, H.M.S.O.

ture and its determination to reduce public-sector borrowing, has been a rise in taxation for almost everyone in Britain except for the highest paid (Dilnot, 1984).

Leaving aside comment on the social desirability of this, the effect on supply-side policies is paradoxical; for insofar as there is any evidence of tax-cutting increasing work effort, this effect is precisely on the low paid (Jackson, 1980, pp. 72–3). Yet the only overall tax cuts have been for the high paid, for whom there is no good evidence of it having favourable economic effects.

Overall, we may say that for this government the macroeconomic aspects of public-expenditure policy have dominated the micro-economic or supply side. Here there is a very strong contrast with the U.S.A., where tax-cutting has always been at the centre of President Reagan's policies and has been vigorously pursued. The effects we well know – record budget deficits but very rapid output and employment growth in 1983 and 1984. In Britain supply-side rhetoric and especially policy has never focused as much on tax cuts, though the budget of 1985 shows some movement in this direction. The main focus on policy in this area has been trade union policy, especially under the 1979–83 government, and privatization under the government elected in 1983.

Trade Union Policy

The rationale of focusing on union reform is that the efficient functioning of the labour market is crucial to economic efficiency, and that unions are a major hindrance to such functioning. The most important reforms have been restrictions on secondary picketing (through changes in civil law), and 'democratization' measures relating to the election of union officials, the closed shop, the holding of strike ballots and the existence and use of political funds. The first reform has been carefully calculated to put the onus on individual employers to take action, rather than involving the government in likely confrontations. The other reforms have been argued on the basis of democracy, and this has put the unions very much on the defensive, as they have to try to counterpropose alternative forms of democracy to the govern-ment's own (a process hardly aided by the National Union of Mineworkers' failure to hold a national ballot in 1984).

The government and the unions have by and large assumed that the outcomes of such measures are obvious: both believe that they will weaken union militancy. Yet this is far from obvious. No doubt at the moment the workforce is largely on the defensive and not often willing to pursue 'militant' measures. However, past evidence of, for example, ballots does not suggest that this result can be guaranteed. Indeed, the Donovan Commission in the late 1960s (Donovan, 1968, conclusions) recommended against strike ballots on the grounds that they might exacerbate and prolong disputes.

Whatever the effects of these democratization measures on worker militancy, it is far from clear that they will have any substantial effect on the efficiency of the economy, as distinct from the depressed economic environment in which they are being introduced.

In a more general sense, these measures may be actively harmful. It is well known that workers in areas of collective bargaining receive higher wages than those not so covered (Stewart, 1983). Recent research, especially in the U.S.A., has suggested that this arises not from the monopoly power of unions, as traditionally argued by economists, but from their productivity-enhancing effects (Freeman and Medoff, 1979). Whatever the viability of such a view in Britain, it does highlight the positive role of unions in modern forms of production, where the unions provide a collective channel of negotiation with employers which may be an efficient form of decision-making for the enterprise. This is an extremely broad subject which cannot be discussed in detail here, but it is useful to note that the implication of government policy that union activity is a 'burden' on the economy is open to challenge, even from within a fairly narrow economists' perspective.

Privatization

As noted already, the Thatcher government in its second term of office has put more emphasis on privatization. This has partly been because of the positive effects of privatization on the size of the P.S.B.R. Again, the effects of such measures on economic efficiency are extremely unclear. There are two major points here. On the one hand the government, in order to preserve the asset value of the enterprises it wants to privatize, has not introduced much competition (for example, British Telecom, British Airways). This leads to the second point, that the traditional economists' view would broadly be that it is not ownership which is crucial, but the level of competition. This indeed is the point emphasized by the S.D.P. and its supporters in criticizing government policy (e.g. Kay and Silbertson, 1984). But this ownership versus competition dichotomy may itself oversimplify the issues. For example, the fact that the National Health Service (N.H.S.) is almost the only purchaser of drugs and doctors' services helps to lower the price of these goods, to the general public benefit. Increased competition might upset this. Privatization of ancillary services in the N.H.S. is clearly designed to drive wages down amongst the providers of those services. But in the case of British Telecom, it does not seem that privatization is likely to have such an effect. Overall, it is far from clear that privatization can be viewed as a policy with a single set of effects. And the efficiency effects depend crucially on the organizational framework which is established after privatization.

Industrial Policy

The 1979 government was committed to a general policy of retreat from 'intervention' in private industry. However, whilst policy has changed since 1979, the weight of intervention, measured at least by public expenditure in this area, has not been radically reduced. Definitions are complex here, but within the overall 'trade and industry' heading there have been big falls in expenditure on British Leyland, in regional development grants and in steel redundancy payments since 1982. However, there have been substantial increases in 'science and technology'. Broadly speaking, the government's industrial policies may be summarized as involving (a) privatization, (b) reductions of public industry subsidies, (c) more selectivity in industrial and regional subsidies and (d) a focus on the 'new' technologies (Thompson, 1985).

The focus on science and technology raises the point that industrial policy has shifted from the broad spread of manufacturing – white goods, machine tools for example – towards 'high-tech' areas. Yet this means ignoring both areas where employment and output are substantial, and areas which for the foreseeable future will be vital to Britain's competitiveness. As noted above, manufacturing competitiveness remains crucial to Britain's position, and yet has not been at the centre of the government's concerns. All the talk of the new age of technology glosses over the continuing importance of traditional manufacturing areas.

In other microeconomic areas, the government has largely continued inherited policies. Most strikingly in international trade, the government has maintained the protective environment around some industries (such as textiles and agriculture) despite its competitive rhetoric. This has led to criticism from both the S.D.P. and the Right that the government is not being true to its promises.

A big area of expansion under the Conservative governments has been various employment programmes, largely under the aegis of the Manpower Services Commission. These can partly be seen as subsidies to firms, providing a form of cheap labour. But probably they should predominantly be seen as ways of trying to reduce the numbers on the unemployment register. They also provide a link between education and industry, the gulf between which can be seen as a serious weakness in Britain (e.g. Worswick, 1984). The difficulty is, of course, that such measures can provide no substitute for higher levels of employment, and the lack of such an environment probably reduces the commitment to and hence efficiency of the programmes which do have a genuine training component.

CONCLUSIONS

The undoubted success of the Thatcher governments has been in reducing inflation. Some of the costs and benefits of such a reduction have already been noted. Whatever the balance of such costs and benefits, that reduction has undoubtedly been politically popular, both directly and because it has been seen as a sign of the general 'responsibility' of the government.

The government has also claimed as a major success the rise in productivity in industry, especially in manufacturing. In the first part of the depression, 1979 to early 1980, productivity fell, as usual during post-war downturns. This presumably reflected 'labour-hoarding' by firms as they held on to workers against the future upturn in the economy. However, from late 1980 it seems to have become clear to many manufacturing employers that an upturn was to be delayed, and that their deteriorating liquidity position required them to sack workers to remain solvent (Wren Lewis, 1984; Mendis and Muellbauer, 1983). From early 1980 productivity rose dramatically, as output bottomed out but employment continued to fall. Table 1.7 shows two versions of the productivity movements of the period. They both show a sharp upward surge in 1981, but, whereas the official figure has this continuing into 1982, the cyclically adjusted figure shows a reversion to a growth path which was in fact slower than that in the period preceding the Thatcher years.

Clearly a large part of what has happened has been a once and for all destruction of relatively inefficient production capacity, occasioned by the unprecedented squeeze on firms' liquidity. This chopped off the lower part of the distribution of firms, giving lower total output but higher productivity.[4] Plainly this is an odd way of raising the efficiency of the economy; by this logic, if all the

Table 1.7 Productivity changes, 1971–82 (annual average increase in output per person hour in manufacturing)

	Nominal % (a)	Cyclically corrected % (b)
1971.3–1979.4	2.7	1.8
1980.1–1981.1	0.3	11.0
1981.1–1982.4	5.0	1.3

Sources: (a) *Economic Trends*
(b) L. Mendis and L. Muellbauer, *Has there been a British productivity breakthrough?* Centre for Labour Economics, L.S.E. Discussion Paper, 170, p. 29

firms in the economy but the single most efficient were eliminated, this would be good for the economy. One way of reflecting this paradox is to calculate output per head of the numbers in employment in 1979 – on this basis the position is of course very much worse (Jones, 1983).

The picture since that once-and-for-all loss is much less clear. Few would doubt that there is room for substantial improvement in productivity in British firms. Equally, some of the productivity changes are unlikely to be reversed, for example in British Leyland and British Steel. But the context of these gains, apart from the depression in output, has been the rise in unemployment which has immeasurably but undoubtedly reduced resistance to changes in working practices and other productivity-enhancing measures. On the other hand, there is plenty of evidence of the possible bad effects on productivity of adverse changes in attitude, and these are likely to have affected British industry in the last few years. Overall, the position is unclear, but as Mendis and Muellbauer (1983) stress, a continuing increase in productivity above the trend of the 1970s is unlikely without a recovery of investment, and this is unlikely in the current macroeconomic climate. The initial Thatcher policy was a shock to much of British industry, and for some firms who survived, their performance may have been enhanced. But the sacrifice of the less lucky firms, the loss of goodwill in the survivors, and the lack of manufacturing investment in general (table 1.8), seems a rather limited success to record.

One theme of this chapter has been that the government's performance has not matched its rhetoric in many areas. This is perhaps hardly surprising – such a comment could be passed on almost all post-war governments. But Thatcher's government is

Table 1.8 Investment in manufacturing, 1978–84 (gross fixed investment at 1980 prices)

Year	£m
1978	7220
1979	7496
1980	6471
1981	4852
1982	4684
1983	4619
1984 (1st 3 qrs)	3931

Source: *Economic Trends*

different in putting at the forefront of its strategy the breaking-away from past policies. In some respects such a breaking-away has occurred. Above all, the government's refusal to try to manage the economy out of the slump marked a break of a substantial kind with previous policies in the post-war period. Less clear is whether it should be seen as fundamentally new. All the rhetoric of 'monetarism' has perhaps tended to conceal the striking re-semblance to a previous policy episode – that of 1920. The similarity is striking in two respects. First, on both occasions the government began highly deflationary fiscal and monetary policies almost simultaneously with the imparting of a severe deflationary shock from abroad (Howson, 1975). Secondly, the slump of 1979–81 was the worst slump in British history in the twentieth century with the exception of that of 1920–2 (when G.D.P. fell by 5 per cent). It is also of note that on both occasions the rhetoric of anti-inflation was a major contributor to the climate which made such policies politically possible.

The point of this historical parallel is to stress that the 'Thatcher experiment' was much less experimental than both proponents and opponents have commonly suggested. A sharply deflationary fiscal and monetary policy was applied and this had unsurprising effects on both real and monetary magnitudes (though of course in 1920 the latter involved an actual fall in the price level). Few economists would have expected any other result. But this does not mean that the rhetoric of monetarism was simply a blind. Fforde, in a widely quoted analysis (1983), has argued that having a medium-term financial strategy couched in nominal magnitudes rather than in real terms was politically crucial for the government's strategy. To have had simply a policy of Keynesian deflation 'would have meant disclosing objectives for, inter alia, output and employment. This would have been a very hazardous exercise and the objectives would have either been unacceptable to public opinion or else inadequate to secure a substantial reduction in the rate of inflation, or both' (Fforde, 1983, p. 207). Nevertheless this is a *post hoc* analysis, not intended to suggest that the government's espousal of monetarism was simply a cover for its nefarious designs.

A slightly different way of putting this is to say that the government decided on a policy of non-accommodation of the behaviour of some private economic agents, essentially trade unions, believing that such accommodation in the past had resulted only in increasing inflation. By its medium-term strategy the government broke away from any co-operative attempt to cope with Britain's economic problems and coupled its deflationary policies with attempts to undercut the powers of organized labour, in order to make the policy effective. In this view, the policy has been successful, in the sense that the government has stuck to its guns and the message has got home, though small groups of workers may still achieve their inflationary objectives (Buiter and Miller, 1983, pp. 361–3).

Such an analysis of policy, as a strategic 'game' between government and private economic agents, is useful in highlighting one important aspect of the Thatcher government's policies, the fact that monetarism was important not so much as a technical economic analysis, but as a political weapon to alter expectations. However, such arguments must not be used to imply that if the government had wanted to it could have delivered something close to full employment. The case against 'Thatcherism' cannot be that it deliberately created four million unemployed where otherwise full employment would have been easily possible. The underlying weaknesses of the British economy, reflected in the growth of unemployment since the end of the 1960s, makes such a case unsustainable. Rather, the case must be that the policies pursued since 1979 have exacerbated rather than mitigated the impact of the world depression and its effects on unemployment; exacerbated, both by creating their own domestic deflationary push and by example encouraging others to do likewise, and hence in part precipitating the world depression. The policies have also exacerbated the harm done by unemployment by cutting unemployment pay and failing to improve the position of those most hard hit by unemployment – the long-term unemployed, who have grown rapidly in numbers.

Clearly the room for manoeuvre in national economic management has narrowed appreciably in recent years, especially because of the enormous growth in the integration of financial markets (see chapter 4). Hence any criticism of the Conservatives must take seriously the constraints on any less deflationary macroeconomic policy. For example, governments cannot just choose the level of public-sector deficits they would like for domestic fiscal purposes, but must take into account the effects of such deficits on financial confidence and hence on the exchange rate. Nevertheless, the Thatcher government has pursued the most restrictive fiscal policies in the O.E.C.D. In other words, the government could have had substantially less deflationary policies, a higher P.S.B.R. (ignoring the feedback of higher output onto P.S.B.R.) and still maintained financial confidence. Indeed, a paradox of the politics of macroeconomic management is that Conservative governments can pursue much 'slacker' fiscal policies than more left-wing governments, because they usually have a higher threshold of loss of confidence with financial markets.

Whilst it may well be pointed out that the French attempt at a go-it-alone reflation was quickly reversed (e.g. Cobham, 1984), nevertheless, unemployment in France remains below the British level. Even relatively limited policies, which would lower British unemployment to the O.E.C.D. average, would remove the miseries of unemployment from about one and a half million people. So the issue is not continued deflation versus reflation back to full employment, but, initially, not making the position worse than is enforced by current constraints.

The fall in inflation would be counted by most people as a benefit of the government's policies. But the precise benefits of this are ill specified; the international trend has been in the same direction; and whatever benefits have accrued directly from the British policy have been purchased at a high price.

The rise in productivity, taken by itself, is welcome. But given the context of an absolute fall in manufacturing output in 1979, this seems a curious kind of success. And if the gains which have taken place have been due to a strengthening of management *vis-à-vis* unions, it is far from clear that such a change in the balance of forces could survive a substantial tightening of the labour market. Alternatively, if mass unemployment continues, such changes augur ill both for the long-run pattern of industrial relations and for the atmosphere in which production takes place.

Industrial policy since 1979 has less to be said about it, because it has changed little. Insofar as there has been a decline in support for manufacturing, and even more so a failure to devise an adequate strategy for that sector in the face of an unprecedented collapse, policy has worsened since 1979. Against this might be set some sensible if fairly limited reforms of existing regional policy, though again without any radical reform that might reduce regional disparities. Here, as with, for example, industrial finance, whatever merits policies may have had as individual elements have been overwhelmed by the general deflationary bias of macro policy.

There is a crying need for an alternative to Thatcherism, but there is no easy alternative. The powerful constraints on economic policy which partly conditioned Thatcherism in the first place, have been strengthened rather than weakened by the policies pursued since 1979.

2
Reducing Unemployment

INTRODUCTION

At the heart of all economic policy programmes of the Left is the belief that a reduction in the level of unemployment should be the top priority. It is right, therefore, to begin an assessment of these programmes with the Left's proposals for reducing unemployment. The emphasis here is very much on the macroeconomic aspects of the unemployment debate: issues which are more microeconomic and long-term in nature are left to later chapters. This chapter does not address the question of whether the Left's focus on reductions in unemployment is in any sense 'correct'.[1] The objective is taken for granted,[2] and the question discussed here is the feasibility of the proposed measures.

One major difficulty, touched on in the introduction, but particularly serious in this chapter, is how far it is useful to offer a detailed commentary on the particular proposals offered (at least by the S.D.P. and the Labour Party) at the time of the 1983 election. On the one hand, it is important to be specific about the programmes offered by the groups under discussion. On the other hand, those programmes have to be viewed in context, and it would be unhelpful to treat them as the last word on policy by the parties. This dilemma is resolved by offering a fairly detailed summary of the proposals of the groups c.1982–3, with some commentary, but leaving most of the analysis to the end. This analysis is organized around the issue of the causes of unemployment, and the adequacy of the programmes offered to deal with these causes. In this way the major elements of the policy programmes are discussed without being tied too much to statements made in very specific circumstances which have since changed.

The final section of this chapter offers some brief comments on the recent French policies designed to reduce unemployment. The failures and successes of these have some lessons for British policy.

THE S.D.P. AND UNEMPLOYMENT

The S.D.P. policy starts from the premise that macroeconomic policy should concern itself directly with the real objectives of output, employment and prices, not intermediate targets like those of the current government for P.S.B.R. and money supply. These objectives should be balanced against each other, but the 'principal objective is to turn the tide of our national economic decline and get the jobless back to work' (S.D.P., 1983A, p. 1).

The policy proposed is a reflationary one, but one at the same time designed to keep down costs and prices as far as possible. This leads to proposals for increases in public spending, coupled with reductions in Value Added Tax (V.A.T.), indirect taxes and moderation in public-sector pricing. But these measures are said to be slow in their effects, and they are therefore coupled with 'a crash programme of special short-term measures, designed to act quickly and targeted on the most needy groups, especially the long-term and the young' (1983A, p. 2).

These policies would be accompanied eventually by an exchange-rate policy to maintain competitiveness, and an incomes policy to control inflation. But the starting points of the employment strategy are the fiscal boost and the employment subsidy measures. These were seen in 1983 as reducing unemployment by, respectively, 400,000 and 600,000 over a two-year period. Thus it was hoped that the measures would reduce unemployment by about one million, from the figure of just over three million where it stood when the proposals were made. Other proposals in the area of industrial policy and industrial relations policy could be pursued to reduce unemployment beyond this target, with their effects coming mainly over a longer time period.

The scale of fiscal-induced expansion envisaged by the S.D.P. is, then, rather limited in relation to the scale of the unemployment problem. Partly this is an effect on the perceived constraints on a faster rate of expansion (see below). But equally it reflects the view that firms will not rapidly expand employment in the face of increasing demand. Because of under-utilization of their existing labour force, and the effects of lack of confidence on the desire to incur the costs of employing more people, the initial response by many firms will be to increase overtime working. This provides the rationale for special employment measures, as a way of reducing unemployment quickly (pp. 15–17).

Such measures would include schemes for 'useful' employment for the long-term unemployed who would be paid a small amount above social security levels to do jobs in the community. Secondly, there would be subsidies to private-sector firms to retain or hire more workers. Thirdly, especially to help women, there should be an expansion of some labour-intensive public services. In part, such policies would be an expansion of existing schemes run by the Manpower Services Commission. They would be explicitly temporary measures: 'a sensible programme to provide jobs where so much needs to be done, and to pay people for being employed rather than unemployed . . . due to be phased out as the economy expands and other jobs become available' (p. 17).

These measures are in part just like any other fiscal expansion, although they are targeted on what may be politically favoured groups. The trouble with such proposals is that if they are targeted on particular groups, this may simply mean those groups replace alternative, unsubsidized, kinds of labour – unless the increase in demand is sufficient to generate a net employment expansion, or the subsidy aids international competitiveness. This consideration has led some sympathetic commentators to suggest that the major effort of such policies go into public-sector schemes which do not compete with private-sector employment – the classic kind of pump-priming schemes, that is, schemes whose main effect is to stimulate indirectly private activity (Miller *et al.* in Matthews and Sargent, 1983, pp. 66–7).

More fundamental to the S.D.P. programme are the notions of constraints in which the policy proposals are embedded. As already noted, the S.D.P. criticizes the current strategy for focusing on P.S.B.R. and money supply targets. It offers a wide-ranging critique of the nominal P.S.B.R. as a sensible intermediate policy target. It points out that because of inflation the real addition to the public debt has been negative in the early 1980s; that the national debt:national income ratio is historically low; that much of the P.S.B.R. goes to finance worthwhile investment projects; that variations in the P.S.B.R. are an effective means of countering the economic cycle; and that interest rates are not determined mainly by the size of the P.S.B.R. (S.D.P., 1983A, pp. 9–10). All these points are standard for critics of the government.[3] What is of especial interest is the implication drawn by the S.D.P.

> It is not possible entirely to disregard the P.S.B.R., because of present market views about it. But proper presentation of the

arguments stated here could affect market views. And in handling market sentiment much depends on the broad view which is taken of the government's economic stance. If it is clear that the government of the day is paying little regard to the inflationary consequences of its plans, then a rise in the P.S.B.R. will certainly provoke a rise in interest rates. If on the other hand it is clear that expansion is being promoted within a framework designed to keep inflation under control, then the reaction would be different. (1983A, pp. 10–11)

The S.D.P.'s arguments may, then, be seen as Keynesian in two quite different senses. On the one hand, the S.D.P. adheres to Keynesian economic theory in believing that with mass unemployment the appropriate policies are ones involving a reflation of demand, led by fiscal policy and with monetary and exchange rate policy playing an accommodating role. Such policies are seen as generating a substantial increase in employment and output, though it is strongly argued that there are serious constraints, on the supply side and of inflation, which will require to be addressed if a successful reflation is to be maintained. But the supply-side policies advocated have little in common with those of the current government (except, perhaps, with respect to trade unions – see chapter 3), and overall, at the theoretical level, the S.D.P. makes remarkably few concessions to currently fashionable economic nostrums.

The S.D.P. position is also Keynesian in the sense that it views rational policy as inhibited by the irrationality of other economic agents, notably financial markets.[4] Unfortunately, despite their irrationality, these have to be taken seriously because of their capacity to affect the success of policy.

> Market perversity about the P.S.B.R., like inflation and wage expectations, compounds the problem of policy-making, and it cannot be ignored. This is one of the reasons why reflationary fiscal packages have to be moderate and why advantages attach to measures (like special employment measures) that do not increase the P.S.B.R. too much. (Matthews and Sargent, 1983, p. 9)

These perversities of market sentiment should not be taken as given: they are not immutable, and to some extent at least, they can be persuaded towards a path of greater rationality.

This 'double Keynesianism' helps to explain a seeming paradox in S.D.P. policy. On the one hand, it provides rigorous and well-founded critiques of the theoretical foundations of the whole edifice of current government macroeconomic policy. On the other hand, it proposes measures of reflation which, in relation to the size of the unemployment problem, are modest. This is really only a paradox if one believes that economic policy is simply a matter of putting economic theory into motion. But the S.D.P.'s important point is that, irrespective of theoretical views about the economy's functioning, its management requires constraints on policy to be taken seriously. This point is crucial in talking about macroeconomic policy, and will be returned to in the discussion of other Left programmes.

The other notable feature of the S.D.P.'s perception of the constraints imposed by financial market sentiment, is that this constraint is not to be directly attacked by policy measures. Financial markets may be talked into a more sensible attitude, but their leverage over policy is to be largely accepted. Contrast this with the other 'irrationality' which constrains policy – inflationary expectations. These expectations are to be attacked not just by trying to persuade wage bargainers to see the error of their ways, but by wide-ranging reforms to make such expectations ineffectual in the outcomes of wage bargains. No explanation is given for the contrast between radical policy measures on the one hand, and rather optimistic calls to rationality on the other.[5]

THE LABOUR PARTY AND UNEMPLOYMENT

In 1983 the S.D.P. hoped, if its policies were followed, to reduce unemployment to 5 per cent over the lifetime of a parliament. This would be the consequence of the fiscal measures discussed above, plus other policies (S.D.P., 1983A, p. 4). The Labour Party offered a slightly more optimistic target of reducing unemployment below one million (about 4 per cent) in five years (Labour Party, 1983A, p. 8). Where the S.D.P. offers a quantified package for at least part of this expansion, the Labour Party programme for 1982 (1982B) is much less specific. Whilst over fifty pages of this document are given over to outlining 'Labour's Plan for Jobs', this plan is extremely diffuse and is not summarized into a macro-economic schema.

It may be argued that such quantifications give a spurious exactitude to policy proposals. As the S.D.P. itself points out (1983A, p. 4) 'In economics it is notoriously difficult to judge in advance the effect of a particular set of measures. So much is a matter of confidence and a great deal is anyway outside the control of U.K. policy makers.' Nevertheless, quantification does allow some 'feel' for the order of magnitudes involved to be created, and failure to quantify inhibits rational policy discussion.

The Trades Union Congress (T.U.C.) has in the past put numbers to its proposals, and in 1981, for example, proposed a five-year, £24 billion investment programme (T.U.C., 1981). The T.U.C. itself expected this to reduce unemployment by only 500,000, and a sympathetic analysis of the programme has suggested that 300,000 would have been closer to the actual outcome (Barker, 1982, p. 34). These figures are contentious, and obviously the context has changed since 1981, but nevertheless they serve to illustrate both the scale of the problem of unemployment, and the usefulness of trying some form of quantification of policy proposals.

Like the S.D.P., the Labour Party offered, as the first stage of its employment creation programme, a reflationary fiscal package. 'The next Labour government will, therefore, introduce a substantial reflationary programme of additional public spending and selective tax reductions, financed by public sector borrowing' (Labour Party, 1982B, p. 18). Within this fiscal stimulus, the focus was to be on increased spending, which was emphasized both because 'it has a more direct impact on demand for home produced goods and services' (1982B, p. 18), and because this spending could readily be used to reflect Labour's economic and social priorities. The initial emphasis would be on public-sector investment and current spending in the labour-intensive public services (see also Labour Party, 1982C, pp. 12–14).

On the first aspect, it is important to note that whilst such a view is borne out by most if not all analyses of the impact of fiscal changes on the economy (Laury *et al.*, 1978; Brooks and Harvey, 1984; Huhne, 1984), it is related to comparisons of *repeated* tax cuts versus *repeated* spending increases. If the changes are once and for all, the first-round effects will be as this analysis suggests, but thereafter there will be little difference. In other words, whilst increased spending on public investment and public-service wages may have high multipliers because of the low import content and the low savings ratio respectively, these characteristics will disappear as the money is spent and received by other economic agents.

Secondly, the Labour Party programme tries to reconcile the employment-creating and socially desirable aspects of public spending, but does not take on board the problem of inflation. This is in contrast to the S.D.P., which explicitly tries to formulate measures which will expand the economy whilst not having too great an inflationary impact. As it seems clear that inflation is a weak point in Labour Party proposals (see chapter 3) this aspect of reflationary packages needs to be incorporated. This means that the different and potentially conflicting demands of the reflationary package have to be spelt out and then reconciled, not simply assumed to be readily compatible with each other.

Like those of the S.D.P., the Labour Party proposals accept the case for an increase, though an unquantified one, in the P.S.B.R. They reject the use of targets for public-sector borrowing as a guide to policy (Labour Party, 1982B, p. 20). No elaborate case against the P.S.B.R. is offered, but this case has been made elsewhere. The best presentation of the 'Alternative Economic Strategy', which the Labour Party broadly follows in its proposals, makes almost the same case against the P.S.B.R. as the S.D.P. (C.S.E./L.W.G., 1980, pp. 42–4). But unlike the S.D.P., this theoretical case against the P.S.B.R. is not coupled to any appreciation of its effectiveness as a constraint because of its impact on financial markets (though see below). Fairly typically on the Left, the current government's concern with the P.S.B.R. is treated as simply an ideological smokescreen for its desired policies of cuts in public spending and an increase in the role of the market (see, for more discussion, Tomlinson, 1985, ch. 10).

A similar rejection of money supply targets is stated by the Labour Party:

> Labour will have nothing to do with monetarism. We accept, of course, that tax and spending policies have monetary implications; and that the money supply – through interest rates, the exchange rate and the availability of credit – has an impact on the real economy. Our financial policy will recognise these effects. But we believe that announced, rigid targets for the growth in money supply are entirely misconceived. Nonetheless, a Labour government must be concerned about the rate of growth of credit and its allocation between different activities. (Labour Party, 1982B, p. 19).

This is a very curious position. On the one hand it accepts that the money supply does have effects (though not in the simple way the government's rhetoric suggests); on the other hand it disavows 'announced, rigid' targets. But if it is accepted that the money supply cannot be ignored, does this mean the government will have unannounced and flexible targets, and if so does this create a more desirable framework for policy? Unannounced monetary targets seem to have little to recommend them, as this would forgo whatever beneficial effects such targets might have on financial markets and on price and wage setting (however much such effects have been exaggerated in Conservative policy). And whilst wholly rigid monetary targets may be undesirable, 'flexible targets', if taken to their logical conclusion, are no targets at all – though of course periodically adjusted, rolling targets are necessary, in recognition of the difficulties of reaching targets in this area.

The difficulty here would seem to arise from the Labour Party's correct perception that monetary targets are the sign under which Conservative deflation has been pursued, but at the same time these targets have not been successfully achieved. On the first point, it is clear that the Labour Party accepts that money supply targets do not necessarily equal monetarist policies, even if the implications of this appear to be avoided in the quotation given above. On the second point, the Left has rightly stressed the difficulties of money supply control against the idea which many Conservatives seem to have had in 1979/80, that the money supply was akin to a tap that could simply be turned off and on. Against this view, Aaronovich (1981, p.23) has stressed that the money supply is 'hard to define, even harder to actually measure, and much harder still to control'. This is true, but exactly the same point could be made about other instruments of policy – this statement would be equally accurate about public expenditure, for example. Of course there are issues of the effectiveness of control of the money supply as an instrument of policy, but the necessary imperfection of any policy instrument has to be accepted in this assessment.

The Labour Party thus denounces absolutely P.S.B.R. targets and is ambivalent about money supply targets. This posture is in part the consequence of not making a clear separation between theoretical positions (such as the effects of an increase in P.S.B.R. on output and employment), and constraints on policy (for example, the effect which an increase in P.S.B.R. would have on the perceptions of economic agents, such that these theoretical effects might be undermined).

As noted above, the S.D.P. discussion of the P.S.B.R. makes this distinction very clearly. However, what it does not do is suggest any institutional reform to reduce the leverage of purchasers of government debt, only the hope of persuading them to act more rationally. Interestingly, the Labour Party does suggest the need for such reforms, though the case is not properly made. It is asserted that Labour will

> continue to expand National Savings as a means of funding Government debt;
> continue to make use of index-linked stock to finance borrowing;
> secure the necessary funding of the public debt by the financial institutions, without resorting to damaging and abrupt changes in interest rates. (Labour Party, 1982B, p. 20)

The first two points mark a continuation of existing policy, and the third remains a somewhat pious hope. Nevertheless they do signal an appropriate approach to the P.S.B.R.: an acceptance that, whatever the theoretical arguments about the effects of changes in its size, its scale and financing have to be treated as constraints on policy. In similar vein, money supply targets cannot be regarded as simply Thatcherite instruments, but as a very difficult-to-avoid component of economic management under current conditions. This argument stresses the expectational aspect of money supply targets. In addition, the instrumental aspect – whether the money supply is an effective instrument of control – is also important. Here, as argued in chapter 3, the exchange rate may be a more sensible target, with the use of interest rates as a short-run means of trying to attain such targets. These points are much more fundamental as a starting point for discussion of reflationary policies than the precise mix of spending increases, tax cuts and so on, in any reflationary package, important as these are.

THE MARXIST LEFT AND UNEMPLOYMENT

The strength of Marxist arguments is the emphasis they place on profitability as a crucial aspect of the functioning of a capitalist economy.[6] This means, for example, that Marxist writers emphasize the importance of the favourable conditions for profitable production in bringing about the long boom, and hence low unemployment, of the 1950s and 1960s (e.g. Glyn and Harrison, 1980; Armstrong *et al.*, 1984). Such an approach is rightly sensitive, therefore, to the existence of constraints on a simple reflationary policy posed by the level of profitability. But the general usefulness of this viewpoint is greatly undermined by the manner of its deployment in policy discussions.

In the Marxist view, the current level of unemployment reflects the low profitability of investment and the measures taken to restore that profitability. The current deflationary policies aim to restore the profitability of production, and this is the 'hidden agenda' behind the rhetoric of money supply policy and public-sector cuts (Glyn and Harrison, 1980, pp. 138–47). The strategy might succeed, but apart from political opposition, it faces an internal contradiction. Successful capitalist production requires not only that profits be made (by exploiting the worker) but that they be realized, that is, the goods must be sold. Thatcherism may provide the possibility of the first of these, but only by undermining the likelihood of the second.

In contrast, a reflationary policy such as the Alternative Economic Strategy is said to focus on the 'realization' aspect at the expense of profitability in production. This means that reflationary policy is a snare and delusion. By itself it will fail because it would raise worker living standards and:

> Higher pay means lower potential surplus value. Profitability might initially be maintained, or even rise a little, as capacity utilisation rose and actual surplus value approach potential. But this development would prove short-lived. Capital would not undertake the substantial productive investment required to raise productivity and maintain the impetus of the boom because potential surplus value would be inadequate. (Glyn and Harrison, 1980, p. 151).

From this view the appropriate Marxist conclusion can be drawn: full employment capitalism is an impossibility. Either one has mass unemployment to maintain profits, or a fall in living standards so that the share of profits in national income rises, or one has to find an alternative form of economic organization where the profit criterion no longer dominates.

Analytically, such a view rests on the belief that both on a world, but particularly on a British, scale there is no possibility of combining full employment with profitable economic activity. In a simple sense this is clearly untrue; some capitalist countries have maintained close to full employment and without large falls in living standards, for example Austria, Norway, Sweden. These countries have not seen the profitability issue in a 'zero-sum' fashion, meaning that either profits or living standards must fall. Instead, they have found mechanisms to make more or less compatible profitability and consumption standards.

More specifically, this kind of analysis assumes that mass unemployment increases profitability by lowering real wages. But in Britain this has not been the case. Real wages of those in work have not been radically reduced under the Conservative government since 1979. As the figures in table 2.1 suggest, though, there has been considerable dispersal within this average. Secondly, what matters for profitability is not real wages *per se*, but those wages relative to productivity, and as already argued in chapter 1, there has been no productivity miracle in the British economy since 1979. Finally, profits have recovered sharply since 1980/1 but this movement is largely cyclical, reflecting a sharp recovery from an unprecedented low point (B.E.Q.B., September 1984). (See table 2.2.)

Overall, Thatcherism has not shifted resources from labour to capital in a fundamental way. Equally, there is no reason to

Table 2.1 Real earnings, 1979–83

Year	Manual workers	Non-manual workers	All workers
1979	100	100	100
1983 (using output price deflator)	110	119	117
1983 (using Tax and Price Index*)	106	114	112

* This figure reflects the tax increases over the period.
Source: D. Metcalf and S. Nickell, 'Jobs and Pay', *Midland Bank Review*, Spring 1985, Table 3

Table 2.2 Profits, 1978–84 (gross trading profits of companies as proportion of G.N.P.)

Year	Profit (%)
1978	13.5
1979	14.6
1980	12.6
1981	11.7
1982	12.2
1983	13.5
1984 (1st 3 qrs)	14.9

Source: *Monthly Digest of Statistics*

suppose that a reflationary policy would necessarily cut profitability; this would, of course depend very much on the other policies pursued simultaneously.

As suggested at the beginning of this section, the general emphasis on profitability by Marxists is important, given that other Left discussions tend to underplay this aspect. But the follow-up to this starting point is unhelpful. Points which might be drawn out are not. First, in Britain the share of national income going to investment is very low compared with most other O.E.C.D. countries, and the share going to consumption very high. Economists are well aware of this, but its implications for economic policy are not usually spelt out. It means that if the conditions for rapid growth are not available, and there is a policy of radically raising the level of investment, consumption standards of those in work may have to fall. And this may well take place in a context where, with economic expansion, profits are rising (even if a substantial part of the investment is in some sense socialized).

I have already suggested above that there is no necessarily zero-sum character to the relation between profits and private consumption, and the same applies to investment and consumption. It all depends on what is happening to overall national income. But the point here is that the kind of scale of increase in investment which might be required in Britain, and the unpropitious external circumstances which might accompany an expansion, might make a fall in living standards and a parallel rise in profits inescapable. From the Marxist point of view this represents a demonstration of the unacceptable aspects of capitalism, and an argument that the system cannot go on.

Such a stance treats the level of profits and the movement of real wages as the crucial signs of the real character of economic policy. A rise in profits shows a policy to be 'reactionary', a fall in real wages likewise (e.g. Glyn, 1982). But in the conditions suggested above, these signs may be inappropriate. Under such conditions, the problem would be how to make sure that the increased profits were used for investment, rather than lamenting their existence. Only under such conditions would a fall in real wages look likely to be politically acceptable. (These issues are returned to in chapters 3 and 7.)

Apart from this emphasis on profits, the Marxist Left would appear to have little to offer discussions on unemployment. In part this arises from the point that the Marxists are not interested in offering programmes of reform, but in demonstrating that any reform will fail without a full-scale transformation of the economy to 'socialism' (nationalization plus worker control). In particular, Marxists do not accept that it is a concern of theirs to offer programmes for the better management of the national economy. This is linked to a political argument which has already been briefly discussed in the introduction. Its more directly economic aspects are set out most appropriately in the chapter on the international aspects of economic policy (chapter 4).

THE CAUSES AND CURES FOR UNEMPLOYMENT

All policy programmes of the Left assume that a substantial proportion of current unemployment could be eradicated by a reflation of demand. Most economists' work on unemployment

offers an answer to the plausibility of such an assumption by trying
to calculate a 'Non-Accelerating Inflation Rate of Unemployment'
(N.A.I.R.U.) As its name implies, this is the rate of unemployment which can be maintained by macroeconomic measures
without causing accelerating inflation. Total unemployment can
therefore be split into demand deficient (or 'Keynesian') unemployment and those forces, essentially microeconomic, which
raise unemployment for a given level of aggregate demand.

The most intensive studies of the causes of the current
unemployment have two clear conclusions. First, the N.A.I.R.U.
has moved up persistently since the late 1960s, and accounted for
most of the rise in unemployment which took place from 1967 to
1979. Secondly, the great bulk of the increase in unemployment
since 1979 has arisen from changes in demand factors (Layard and
Nickell, 1984, table 7, p. 71 and table 11, p. 99; Nickell, 1982).

The main contributions to this demand deficiency have been (in
ascending order of importance) real interest rates, slow-down of
growth of world trade, fiscal stance and competitiveness. This
analysis broadly accords with the thrust of the Left's programme,
with its emphasis on domestic macroeconomic policy and a
competitive exchange rate, though it perhaps emphasizes the latter
somewhat more than is common, certainly amongst non-
economists.

In relation to the current government's restrictive policies, this
emphasis on the level of demand is obviously crucial, and central
to the economic case against such policies. However, in the
context of discussing the plausibility of programmes such as the
Labour Party's and the S.D.P.'s, which talk about a reduction of
unemployment to 4 or 5 per cent, the implications of these
analyses are much less straightforward. If much of the unemployment rise since 1979 can be ascribed to demand factors, it is
equally clear that the rise from 1967 to 1979 cannot be so ascribed,
and that even since 1979 the upward trend in N.A.I.R.U. has
continued. Thus in the middle of 1984 the unemployment rate
stood at 14·5 per cent (old definition),[7] and the N.A.I.R.U.
around 9 per cent, according to Layard *et al.* (1984).

Taking these figures at their face value would mean that fiscal
reflation without substantial inflationary effects might be able to
reduce unemployment to around 9 per cent (coincidentally, close
to the O.E.C.D. average rate). But policies aimed at reducing it
further would lead to very substantial inflationary pressures. In
Layard and Nickell's (1984, see also their 1985) analysis, the only
period when N.A.I.R.U. was substantially above the actual rate of
unemployment was 1975–9. They suggest, though without statis-

tical support, that this was possible because of the incomes policies of that period (1984, p. 72). Hence for these authors, incomes policy is central to a feasible reduction in unemployment, given the upward movement of the N.A.I.R.U. (pp. 97–8). However, the whole issue of incomes policy is so central to the political programmes of the Left that it is best dealt with in detail separately (chapter 3). Here the focus is on the reasons why N.A.I.R.U. has risen, on the assumption that any feasible unemployment strategy will at least have to take these reasons into account.

Why Has Unemployment Risen?

Some of the reasons canvassed for the rise in N.A.I.R.U. can be dealt with very summarily here. The suggestion that the level of unemployment benefit is crucial has been most enthusiastically essayed by Minford (1983), but has found little or no support on the Left.

Mainstream neo-classical economists are not opposed in principle to the idea that the level of unemployment pay may affect the level of unemployment, given that they view labour supply as determined in wholly instrumental fashion by a trade-off between the pains of working and the financial benefits of receiving a wage (e.g. Nickell, 1979). But empirically this factor is argued to be unimportant, certainly in the 1970s and 1980s. Nickell (1984) strongly criticizes Minford's arguments on theoretical grounds, also pointing out that it is difficult plausibly to link the rise in unemployment over the last decade with the stability of the benefit:wage ratio over that period.

The Technological Revolution An explanation of unemployment which finds rather more sympathy on the Left is that of 'the technological revolution'. The precise meaning of this theory is far from clear, but the broad argument is usually that a greater capital intensity of production has caused a big increase in productivity which has reduced the demand for labour. Let us leave aside the issue of why demand has not expanded at the same time (for example, by lower prices), and why, if it has not, the problem should be seen as technological rather than as a problem of demand. Even making these large concessions to the case for technological unemployment, the story still does not seem to hold up. Whilst productivity rose rapidly for a while in 1980/1, as already argued in chapter 1, there is no clear evidence of an upward shift in the trend growth of productivity. Indeed, over the last decade there has been a clear slow-down in the growth of productivity across most of the Western world including Britain (e.g. Matthews, 1982).

For these reasons, it would seem important for the Left to counteract rather than reinforce the very widespread view that current unemployment is due to unavoidable technological imperatives. Whilst in certain respects the pattern of employment is no doubt undergoing rapid changes, it is, as always, the case that technological changes both create and destroy jobs. In the absence of clear evidence that more jobs are being destroyed than are being created, emphasis on technological unemployment misfocuses the policy debate, and in particular tends to let governments off the hook of responsibility for proper national economic management.

Unemployment Strategies

Education and Training A great deal of emphasis in both S.D.P. (1981A, pp. 15–16) and Labour Party (1982B, pp. 26–31) policy is on the need for a large expansion of the training programme. If this means increased public spending, then this will act similarly to any other act of reflation. If it is seen as alleviating the consequences of unemployment by 'targeting' a particular unemployed group, this seems a good way of allocating that extra spending. But as a means of reducing unemployment in the medium term such policies seem more problematic. Education and training would have a vital role to play in reducing unemployment if there was a clear mismatch between the skills of the unemployed and the skills demanded by potential employers. The evidence on the very poor levels and types of educational performance in Britain compared with those in other O.E.C.D. countries would certainly seem to make such a mismatch plausible (e.g. Worswick, 1984).

However, it is one of the most striking results of recent empirical work on unemployment in Britain that the increase in the N.A.I.R.U. does not seem to have been related to any increase in the mismatch. This is true whether the mismatch is analysed by skill, industry or region (Layard and Nickell, 1984, pp. 86–8). As the authors themselves note, this is not based on an ideal measure of mismatch (empirical work never is). But nevertheless it seems fairly conclusive. The point here is not that this argument means that education and training are unimportant; but it must be clear that the employment benefits of such policies are likely to be long-term via effects on efficiency, not directly by improving the 'employability' of the unemployed. It is important to stress this when so much public rhetoric, both on Left and Right, seems to suggest that the unemployed are a group left behind by techno-logical changes which have made their skills redundant. There is no good evidence of such a process, and it casts a very misleading light on the unemployment problem.

Wages policies The programmes of the Left find no space in their analyses of unemployment for any role for reductions in wages, and have reacted strongly to the current government's suggestions that such reductions are crucial to any future fall in unemployment. A number of points need to be disentangled in these arguments. First, the argument from the government is about real, not nominal, wages. Nominal wages may well have an impact on unemployment via their effects on inflation and hence the government's macroeconomic stance; but this is an issue more appropriately dealt with in the discussion of inflation in chapter 3.

The stress on real wages by the Treasury is in contradiction to the Left's view in playing down the effect of falls in real wages on the level of demand. The standard view of the Left is that, following one interpretation of Keynes,[8] the effects of real-wage cuts would decrease the level of aggregate demand with depressing effects, which would outweigh any expansionary effects from individual firms facing lower labour costs. The assumption is that initially, the lower real wage leads to higher profits from a given output, of which a larger proportion than wages is saved. Subsequently, the lower level of demand leads to lower output and hence lower wages and profits.

The Treasury's answer to this seems to fall into two parts. On the one hand is an argument that firms' investment will react positively to higher profits, and hence not lead to a fall in demand (H.M.S.O., 1984). In addition, it is argued, lower-real wage growth may reduce inflation, leading to a 'real wealth effect'; in other words, because savings lose their real value more slowly with lower inflation, consumers' expenditure as a share of income increases. Secondly, at a given exchange rate, the lower the level of inflation, the cheaper goods abroad will be (Treasury, 1985).

In many ways, there is no objection to these arguments as principles. The idea that investment will be in part a function of profit levels and not demand *per se* is hardly revolutionary. Equally, the argument that lower inflation with a fixed exchange rate will increase exports seems jejune rather than startlingly radical. Neither of these points is tied to any serious discussion of whether these theoretical possibilities account for any substantial part of the current level of unemployment. On the issue of international competitiveness, it is plain that the great problem of 1980/1 was the rise in the nominal exchange rate, against which any rise in wage costs at that time pales into insignificance (chapter 1 above). No one on the Left denies the need to maintain the exchange rate at a competitive level, so the issue is not one of contention here. (The issue is discussed in chapter 4).

Much more important for the Left and its programme is the direct effect of real wages on employment. The best starting point for looking at this is the work of Layard and Nickell (1984). In their model, real wages are crucial to employment, but so also is the level of autonomous demand. They argue that a 1 per cent rise in real product wages, other things being equal, raises unemployment by an equivalent percentage. (Though Wadhwani's (1985) estimate is much lower – around 0·2 per cent.) This by itself is very much in accord with the arguments of supporters of the current policies, such as Minford and Beenstock. However, the implications of this for policy are far from straightforward.

First, what matters to employers is the total cost of employing a person relative to the output they will produce. This is the real product wage. For the employer, the costs of employment include not only the take-home pay of the worker, but also the taxes associated with employment – income tax and National Insurance payments – plus the indirect costs associated with measures of employment protection.

Income tax and employees' National Insurance contributions reduce take-home pay for any given real product wage, and an increase in them will in part lead to upward pressure on that wage to claw back the previous level of take-home pay. More direct in effect is the employer's National Insurance contribution. This second factor has been very important in raising unemployment since the late 1960s, whereas the first has had a fairly trivial role (Layard and Nickell, 1984, pp. 90–1). Employment protection on the other hand has a two-sided effect, reducing both employment (reduced hiring) and unemployment (reduced firing), and Nickell (1982) suggests the net effect may have been to reduce unemployment slightly.

Secondly, of course, the real product wage is affected by the level of productivity. As the rate of growth of productivity in Britain and other O.E.C.D. countries has slowed over the last decade, it could be that wage expectations have not adjusted to this, and that therefore N.A.I.R.U. has been raised. (Note that this presumably would be used to account for unemployment rising across the O.E.C.D. area, not just in Britain.) Layard and Nickell question the truth of this argument (1984, pp. 92–3).

Elsewhere it has been given more credence (Grubb *et al.*, 1982). These authors emphasize that 'the prime source of difficulty is that people are *trying* to achieve too high real wages. It is this that raises the N.A.I.R.U., and the fact that real wages become too high is a consequence rather than a prime cause of the difficulty'. Certainly the rhetoric of collective bargaining would suggest that it is not generally accepted that the recent slow-down in productivity growth should reduce expectations of real wage growth.

The important points in discussing future possible policy which derive from the issue of real wages would seem to be twofold. On the one hand, an acceptance of some trade-off between real product wages and employment is emphatically not a rationale for a programme of wage-cutting. Layard and Nickell's own analysis (1984) emphasizes the role of taxes in raising the real product wage, so any reflationary programme based on such an analysis would put considerable weight on cutting those types of taxes, as does that of the S.D.P. (see the S.D.P. and Unemployment, above).

Secondly, an emphasis on the real product wage and its effects on unemployment would be another reason for stressing the importance of increasing productivity, as a way of reducing the gap between productivity growth and expected real-wage increases.

On the other hand, should real take-home pay be treated as inviolable by the Left? As already noted, there is no good case at the moment for seeing direct attempts to reduce take-home pay as a way of generating employment. Increases in fiscal stimulus via (amongst other things) cuts in employers' taxes make much more sense. Nevertheless, it is important to grasp the nettle and to say that it is not impossible that in the future a fall in real take-home pay might be a means of reducing unemployment. Such a view runs counter to all the Left's attitudes, and in many ways rightly so. But if such a stark possibility is raised, it is not clear why such wage cuts should be ruled out under all conditions. Much of the political discussion of unemployment is dominated by a fatuous rhetoric about 'who really cares'. If the Left 'really cares', it must face the possibility of such unpalatable possibilities. (This issue is returned to in chapters 3 and 7.)

The Role of the Unions The question of wage levels leads naturally to the role of the unions. It has been well known for a long time that employment in areas covered by collective agreements seems to be associated with higher real wages than in areas not so covered. (Though it is not clear if wages in non-unionized sections are lower than they would otherwise be.) For a long time, however, the appropriate word was very much 'associated', because industries covered by collective agreements were often very different from those not covered other than in respect of union membership. Recently, Stewart (1983) has shown that, comparing individual with individual, the union 'mark-up' is only about 7–8 per cent, much lower than many previous estimates. Nevertheless, if the elasticity of employment with respect to real wages is approximately unity, such a differential or rather, changes in its size, could have a substantial effect on unemployment. Such a view seems to be reflected in much S.D.P. writing on the unions, which treats them as simply monopolistic elements, on a par with any other monopoly.

However, the idea that collective bargaining should be seen as a kind of bargaining between monopolies has recently come under attack, notably in American literature. There is a growing acceptance that collective agreements may be functional to enhanced efficiency, reducing labour turnover, improving morale, and generally improving the atmosphere in which production is carried out (Freeman and Medoff, 1979). In that context, unions have a more positive general role to play rather than a large role in raising real product wages by an unsustainable amount. Layard and Nickell (1984, p. 3, pp. 89–90) display some ambivalence on this issue. They suggest that an increase in union militancy may have raised unemployment by 1·25 per cent points over the post-war period. But they also suggest that the American literature on efficiency wages may be relevant to Britain.

The chapter has taken the N.A.I.R.U. type of analysis very much for granted. It certainly seems the best available framework available at the moment. However, one clear issue which it raises is the long-run rise in the level of N.A.I.R.U., roughly in line with the *actual* level of unemployment. Now this parallel movement may be explained by simply saying (Metcalf, 1984, p. 62) that, as governments do not want accelerating inflation, they will pursue policies which, one way or another, keep the actual rate close to the N.A.I.R.U. (except in 1975–9).

Another mechanism may be at work, which is referred to by Layard and Nickell as a decrease in the intensity of job search (1984, pp. 88–9). They give some limited credence to this feature in raising the level of N.A.I.R.U. One could argue that this reflects a perfectly plausible and rational response to mass unemployment. If no jobs appear after months of unemployment, it is commensurate with what we know about the psychological effects of unemployment (Jahoda, 1982) that less effort will be wasted on search for a job. Hence actual unemployment may feed back on the N.A.I.R.U.

CONCLUSIONS

Advocates of alternative employment strategies in Britain have to steer between two unacceptable poles of argument. On the one hand they have to resist the temptation to reduce the problem to one of will: if the government had the political will to reduce unemployment, then the battle would be all but won. This is the position which some advocates of an alternative economic strategy get close to when they declare that 'the obstacles to full employment are primarily political' (C.S.E./L.W.G., 1980, p. 33). Of course the current government has drawn what political advantage it could from mass unemployment, but that is far from the same as asserting that such unemployment has arisen simply from an economically unconstrained act of political malevolence.

On the other hand, it is commonly suggested that full employment is now a chimera; Marxists claim this because of the incompatibility of profitability with full employment, others because of the imperatives of technology. With knowing looks, one is told that full employment is 'really' impossible, though the reasons remain obscure. One can sympathize with the view that we should be realistic about the pace at which unemployment can be reduced, and hence think seriously about aiding those who will remain unemployed for a long time. But this is not at all the same as the belief that mass unemployment is permanently ineradicable.

More specifically, the arguments of those who have seriously studied the unemployment problem point to the complexities that any employment policy must take into account. In the short run, the undoubted employment-generating advantages of public-expenditure increases over income tax cuts, should not be allowed to obscure the benefits of cuts in 'taxes on jobs', notably the employers' National Insurance contribution. More generally, this points to the importance of thinking through the impact of policies on employers' demand for labour. This is definitely not a reason, for example, for reducing the level of employment protection and the costs this imposes on employers. But it does mean thinking about tax changes in particular, not just as fiscal instruments, but as affecting the calculations of employers about the level of employment.

This is related to the point made above about the Marxist Left. The Marxists rightly stress that profitability is crucial to the employers' employment decision, and this is really only the other side of the issue of real wages discussed in the previous section. Again, the general point is to guard against viewing employment policy as solely about the level of aggregate demand, and not also about affecting the ways in which companies will respond to that increased demand.

Metacalf (1984A) has addressed the issue of 'where will the new jobs come from?' There seems to be a general consensus that there is little scope for expansion of employment (though not output) in manufacturing. The scope for expansion in private services appears limited. Hence it is difficult to see where, if not in public services, the jobs can come. But if this is the case, it does require a major discussion of the ways of organizing and paying for such employment, neither of which issues the Left seems to be facing up to in their published programme. This is of vital importance. On the level of 'how organized' it is a crucial challenge to Left (and perhaps especially Labour Party) policy to demonstrate that the public sector can be run in a manner which as a minimum retains the consent of the majority of the populace. The question of 'how paid for' raises not only the issue of taxation (chapter 6), but the even more general issue of how movement back to full employment can be managed if it involves a shift of resources from the consumption of those at work both to the unemployed and to investment. In the short run, reflationary policy might raise profitability via spreading costs over a larger output. But in the medium term, the forces making for low profits in Britain would have to be addressed in a manner which allowed for higher levels of investment to be financed. The issue of who controls that investment is rightly central to the Left's discussion; but it cannot be allowed to obscure the fact that it must be financed, with the implications that has for the distribution of the national income.

Finally, the trade unions. As noted above, the traditional economists' view of unions as simple monopolists, who thus drive up real wages and increase unemployment, has come under some challenge even in the mainstream literature. What seems to be more helpful is to stress the role of unions in forming wage expectations, with the consequences of that for possible reflationary strategies. Unions may in this way play an important role in determining the shape of the inflation/unemployment trade-off. But the whole issue of unions seems best left to the discussion of inflation in the next chapter.

LEARNING FROM THE FRENCH?

In the summer of 1981 the newly elected socialist government in France launched a reflationary programme somewhat akin to that advocated by the Left in Britain. The policies had an initial success, in that French growth was above that of most O.E.C.D. countries in 1982 and unemployment, which had been rising sharply, ceased to do so in July 1982. However, growth was heavily concentrated in consumption, whilst investment fell in both 1981 and 1982. The budget deficit rose sharply, inflation did not fall as in other O.E.C.D. countries, and probably most importantly, the balance of payments deteriorated sharply (Cobham, 1984, p. 42).

From spring 1982 the policy was reined back, a further devaluation followed that of December 1981; but the pressure on the franc continued, and in spring 1983 macroeconomic policy was thrown into reverse. Hence it may be argued that the French experiment of 1981–2 demonstrates the impossibility of a reflationary strategy as advocated by the British Left.

Certainly the French experience does offer a useful corrective to any naïve view about the possibility of reflation in current conditions. But equally, as Barker *et al.* (1984, p. 82) have argued, 'the failure of policy in France was not due to reflation as such but to the whole policy mix being introduced at the time.'

The policy mix included not only the standard Keynesian macroeconomic elements of increased public expenditure and public deficits, but also increases in the minimum wage of 10 per cent, and in social security benefits of 20–5 per cent (though employers were relieved of part of the cost of these increases). The working week was reduced and annual leave entitlements increased (Barker *et al.*, 1984, p. 78). At the same time, the government was rapidly expanding the nationalized sector of the economy (Mansen, 1984).

Hence the policy pursued was one which combined a fiscal reflation with measures which sharply increased real product wages and acted to discourage investment. Plainly any Left government may face a problem of private investment being reduced (though public investment also fell in France), but the French policies seem more or less to have ignored the problem. Secondly, the government seems to have been unprepared for the pressure its policies would exert on the franc, so that devaluations of the franc mainly came after the event rather than being an integral part of the strategy. No doubt the French were unfortunate in that their expansionary attempt coincided with deflationary measures in most O.E.C.D. countries; but as Cobham (1984, pp. 45–6) points out, this international deflation was not an unforeseen event, but already apparent by the spring of 1981.

Overall, the French policy (for understandable political reasons) tried to do too many things too quickly. If reflation is the priority, then this is likely to be undermined if accompanied by measures which sharply increase wages costs. Unfortunate as it may be, policies geared to rapid employment creation may not in the short run be made easily compatible with desirable longer run changes in the distribution of income and taxation.

3
Controlling Inflation

INTRODUCTION

A traditional difference between the Left and the Right in economic policy debates has been the relative priorities accorded to inflation and unemployment. As already noted, the Left sees the current priority as very much that of reducing unemployment. This is coupled with an acceptance that inflation, too, is important, but not of overriding significance, as it has become for the modern Conservative Party.

A case can be made that the economic damage done by inflation is extremely uncertain and probably exaggerated in much political debate. A few economists have stressed the lack of evidence about the serious harm done by inflation, at least within the range experienced in Britain in recent years (e.g. Hahn, 1980;[1] but see Wadhwani, 1984A and 1984B). However, political parties, including those on the Left, seem to recognize that public opinion does worry about inflation, whatever some economists may argue, and that therefore a party looking for public support must offer policies at least partly geared to its suppression. This kind of political calculation on inflation seems to be most strongly implied by the Labour Party: 'In four successive general elections the electorate has judged the major parties on the credibility of their policies to control inflation' (Labour Party, 1982B, p. 23).

The starting point for those in opposition to the current government's policies on inflation is, then, that the government puts too high a priority on this policy objective, and has paid much too high a price for its success in this area. The alternative is to find policies which will reduce unemployment without a major impetus being given to inflation. How this is to be done is a major, perhaps the major, point of contention on economic policy within the Left.

THE S.D.P. AND INFLATION

The Liberal/S.D.P. Alliance is an uncompromising advocate of incomes policy: 'combining expansion with adequate control of inflation is the central problem. It must be said quite plainly that there is no hope of keeping unemployment on a downward trend without an effective incomes policy' (S.D.P., 1983A, p. 3). Incomes policy is politically crucial to the Alliance stance, which argues that 'Unlike other parties, the Alliance will seek a specific mandate from the electorate in support of an incomes policy' (Liberal/S.D.P., 1983, p. 337).

The crux of the S.D.P. position is that incomes policy is not required directly to hold down inflation, but as a means of combining low inflation and reduction in unemployment. The analysis is one which has come to be called 'New-Keynesian' and is given a full exposition in Meade (1982; see also Meade, 1981). The central argument here is that the 'traditional' Keynesian view that fiscal and monetary policy would be used to regulate the level of employment, and incomes policy the level of inflation, is no longer viable. Above all, it is no longer viable because the claims on real output now exceed that output, and in such conditions full employment can only be maintained by higher inflation. The best policy is therefore to 'turn Keynes on his head', by expanding money demand by a given proportion each year, and having an incomes policy so that this expansion in demand is not taken out simply in the form of higher wages and prices, but at least in part in higher employment.

Such an approach fits in with two crucial aspects of the S.D.P.'s views on the economy. It accepts the need to take seriously the views of powerful economic agents whose actions may be crucial to the attainment of policy objectives. It also chimes in with the S.D.P. view of trade unions and collective bargaining.

On the first aspect, Meade's 'New Keynesianism' fits in with the S.D.P.'s recognition (chapter 2) of the constraints on policy imposed by the need to maintain international financial confidence. 'The financial community has to be pursuaded that a less rigid approach to monetary and fiscal policy is not the same as financial irresponsibility. It is important to avoid attempting to expand so rapidly as to threaten a rekindling of inflationary pressures. Incomes policy is a key element in this strategy' (Liberal/S.D.P., 1982, p. 13).

Secondly, the policy makes it clear that the government will not simply 'validate' whatever level of money wage settlements emerges from the system of collective bargaining. At the same time, it does not involve a fixed, centralized, process of wage-fixing but leaves unions and employers still able to make their own bargains, though subject to a new set of incentives guiding their behaviour.

A slightly different way of putting this approach is to say that it means re-assigning policy instruments to policy goals. Hence, in the Liberal/S.D.P. paper (1982, pp. 14–15) monetary policy is assigned the goal of securing an appropriate degree of competitiveness, that is, an exchange rate target. Fiscal policy is seen as the main instrument for controlling the overall level of money demand. Incomes policy would be geared towards 'preventing the re-emergence of a competitive scramble by powerful groups aimed at avoiding their fair share of the restraint that is collectively essential if expansion is to be achieved'.

Meade's own policy for the institution of incomes policy is one of 'not-quite compulsory arbitration' (1982, ch. VIII), such that, in the case of employers and unions failing to agree, there would be an arbitrating body which would make an award on the basis of maximizing employment.[2] Strikes or lockouts against its awards would not be criminal, but would incur penalties falling short of fines or imprisonment. Such a process would not necessarily lead to acceptance of the employer's offer, depending upon the arbitrator's view of labour supply to the firms involved in the wage bargaining.

This approach has not been accepted by the S.D.P., which instead advocates a counter-inflation tax as the long-run structure in the private sector, possibly following an initial 'freeze' immediately after the Alliance comes to power. Whilst the counter-inflation tax is played down and seen as rather a last resort in the Alliance manifesto of 1983 (Liberal/S.D.P., 1983, p. 337), there is no doubt that for many in the S.D.P. the counter-inflation tax is the centrepiece of their macroeconomic proposals.[3] Other components of the proposed incomes policy are a 'national forum' for discussion of macroeconomic policy between the main economic interest groups, but not a 'social contract' like that of the 1970s, and with the government keeping the right to pursue its policies if no agreement is possible. In the non-market public sector, the S.D.P. advocates great use of comparability in determining pay, and in nationalized industries the use of external financing limits to certain inflationary settlements (S.D.P., 1983A, pp. 22–4).

However, the main focus here is on the proposed counter-inflation tax which would work by taxing employers where the growth of hourly wages of their employees exceeded some norm.

The advantages of this are spelt out by its major advocate, Layard (1982, p. 6), as follows:

> First, there is no absolute compulsion on anybody. Free collective bargaining continues. Firms and workers can agree on pay rises above the norm, but they are discouraged from going too far by the tax. If a group is paid above the norm, the policy has not broken down, nor is the policy of the government discredited. The tax can be imposed without the agreement of the unions. Though the government would discuss policy with the unions, it could if necessary impose it without their agreement. So we have a policy that can be permanent. Second, the adjustment of relativities is determined in a decentralized manner through collective bargaining, and not by a central pay body.

The S.D.P. is very sensitive about maintaining the efficient functioning of the labour market (a point returned to below) and hence faces up to one of the perennial problems of past incomes policies, that of productivity. Many past policies have allowed increased productivity as a reason for exceeding the norm, but many such productivity increases appear to have been bogus. Hence the S.D.P. argues that this exception to the norm should be allowed, but only retrospectively, when the productivity improvement has actually been delivered. Secondly, the S.D.P. argues that the higher income generated in this way should be distributed not as wages, but 'through the distribution of shares which are not immediately marketable' (Liberal/S.D.P., 1983, p. 337). Thus the incomes policy is neatly tied to another plank of Alliance policy, worker share ownership.

The proposal for a counter-inflation tax as a centrepiece of a policy for combining low inflation and low unemployment can be discussed in terms of both macroeconomic and microeconomic aspects. On the macroeconomic side, the S.D.P.'s argument rests a good deal on Meade's work. This focuses on the inflationary consequences of any reflationary policy unaccompanied by any reform of the wage bargaining system. Whilst the reduction of inflation is an inescapable part of an electorally tenable political programme, one does not have to base an argument of this type only on such a political calculation. Rather, as suggested in chapters 2 and 4, one can see as necessary a restraint on the growth of money demand because of the constraints on economic policy. The constraints are especially powerful via scrutiny of the P.S.B.R. and money supply growth by international finance, and the ability of that finance to undermine any policy via flight from a country's currency.

Of course, a focus on the growth of money demand can be seen as just monetarism under a new guise. But such a view can only rest on a willingness to ignore the constraints on expansion, as noted above. In any case, it is clear that Meade's (and the S.D.P.'s) proposals are seen as expansionary, unlike the policies pursued since 1979.

More explicit criticism of Meade's macroeconomic arguments have been made by Cambridge Economic Policy Group (C.E.P.G.) authors (Tarling and Wilkinson, 1982). They criticize Meade's view that low profits and low investment are due to excessive increases in money wages. Against this they suggest that firms generally pass wage increases on into prices, and that the main causes of low profits are recession of demand, when price mark-ups become inadequate to cover the higher ratio of overhead costs to sales revenue, and overvaluation of the exchange rate which forces exporters to reduce profit margins. Whilst the first of these factors does operate, it seems inadequate to account for the fall in profits in Britain, which began in the 'long boom', before the recession of the 1970s (King, 1975). The Left generally seems to exaggerate the fall in costs brought about simply by expansion, as a corollary of an excessive emphasis on the non-price competitive nature of product markets. On overvaluation of the currency, a similar general point seems appropriate; this undoubtedly had its effects, especially at the beginning of the 1980s, but was only a temporary phase which cannot easily be used to explain a long-run problem. Tarling and Williamson also criticize Meade's discussion of the exchange rate, perhaps with more force, an issue discussed in chapter 4.

More complex are the microeconomic issues raised by a counter-inflation tax. First, the proposals are classically Keynesian in seeing a clear distinction between macro and micro spheres: the former is where government action is imperative, and the latter where it should be avoided as far as possible. In other words, the approach to the labour market is a neo-classical one, with competitive processes seen as necessary to maximize welfare. One very important policy consequence of this approach is that the redistribution of income, especially via minimum statutory wage levels, is seen as nothing to do with incomes policy, but as the preserve of the tax and social security system. Redistribution would hinder the competitive function of labour markets (Layard, 1980 and 1982, ch. 8).

Such a theory rests on arguments both about poverty and about labour markets. On poverty, much of the evidence used derives from Layard *et al.*, 1978 (data related to 1975). This shows that if one looks at the bottom 10 per cent of the income distribution (by household) only one in five of these households has a 'head' whose pay falls in the bottom 10 per cent of the pay distribution. In other words

> It is not true that the workers in the poorest families are mostly low paid, nor that low paid workers are mainly in the poorest families . . . most of those on low hourly wages are married women, and married women workers are not usually in the poorest families. The poorest families are mostly ones in which there are a number of children and only one earner. (Layard, 1980, pp. 123, 125).

A number of comments may be made on this argument. First, it is based on households not individuals. This implies that if a low-paid woman is in a household with an average-paid man there is no problem, a view which has rightly been contested by feminists. Secondly, it is clear that the number of one-parent families is increasing (and the great bulk of these parents are women) so that the numbers falling into poverty because of women's low pay are likely to have been increasing.

Further, the effect of a minimum wage policy depends, of course, on the level of that wage – a 'two-thirds of average' minumum, for example, would raise the pay of nearly half the workers in the poorest families (1980, p. 125).

Whatever the benefits of wage minima in terms of the effects on poverty, Layard argues that these would be offset by the effects on employment, the higher wages leading to a fall in demand for labour. However, as his own account suggests, the evidence on the relation between wage minima and employment in the U.S.A., where such policies are common, is extremely mixed, except perhaps in the case of youths (p. 125). The fact that the evidence is mixed does not mean that minimum wages are unlikely to have any employment effects, nor that such effects can be ignored. But it is a pointer towards the complexity of the issue, which advocates of minimum wages need to take seriously (see Neuberger, 1984).

The approach to minimum wages and employment by Layard and the S.D.P. is symptomatic of their general neo-classical approach to the labour market. This stresses the efficiency properties of freely functioning labour markets, and the need, therefore, to minimize interference with such markets. In such an approach, unions logically appear as monopolists, who disrupt the free play of markets. This is very much the approach of Meade (esp. 1982, ch. V). This does not, however, lead him to advocate strong anti-union measures, mainly for 'social' reasons (1981, pp. 92–5).

Whilst less explicit, the *economic* analysis of unions by the S.D.P. is very similar to that of Meade. Thus Layard's defence of his counter-inflation tax proposal, against the view that unions should be directly confronted, is answered by saying (a) such institutional reform would take too long, and (b) collective organization and the right to strike are 'basic ideas of human dignity' (S.D.P., 1982, p. 26). Again the analysis is one where unions are seen as monopolies, but where their destructive powers are to be circumvented rather than attacked directly. Hence the S.D.P. policy on trade unions (S.D.P., 1983C) is mainly one of democratization, rather than destruction.[4] Only the proposals on restrictions on secondary action and picketing can be seen as clearly restrictive of trade union capacities for action. (Though measures on political funds can be seen as restructuring the unions' political role.)

Such an approach to unions also fits in with the S.D.P. approach to industrial democracy. Such democracy is a central plank of S.D.P. policy (S.D.P., 1982A), but it is based on the idea of an extension of democratic rights to the workplace, not on the extension of collective bargaining, as many on the Left see industrial democracy. This is a major reason why the S.D.P. stresses that unions will not have a privileged place in such schemes of democracy, which will be based on an 'equality of citizenship' within the workplace.

Fundamental to the 'monopolist' approach to trade unions is the view that variations in relative wages are central to the efficient allocation of labour, and that labour monopolies, like producer monopolies in product markets, threaten such efficient allocation. Whilst the S.D.P. neither advocates nor sees as realistic the frictionless, atomistic labour markets of the basic textbooks, it does use these as the implicit measure of the actual performance of labour markets.

Two issues may be separated here. Do labour markets work in anything like the manner suggested by such analyses? Secondly, would it be a good thing if they did?

On the first issue, the evidence is mixed. Pissarides's (1978) econometric work is commonly cited in support of the view that relative wages do play a part in the allocation of labour, though not, according to his evidence, a very large part. Looking at the same issue in a rather different way, Daniel (1981) and Daniel and Milward (1983, ch. X) attempted to see how far wages varied in relation to various indices of performance by firms; in other words, how far efficient, expanding firms attracted labour by paying higher wages than the less efficient and contracting firms.

Their evidence suggests strongly that wages depend on such 'structural' factors as the size of establishment, and the composition of the labour force, rather than on performance indices. In part, but only in part, these elements correlate with levels of unionization, so it is difficult to argue that relative performance would determine relative pay if only union monopolies did not exist.

A more thorough-going attack on the neo-classical approach to the labour market is made by Tarling and Wilkinson (1982). They argue not only that the labour market is highly segmented into non-competing sections, but that this segmentation is in many respects a positive aspect for efficiency. Above all this is so because 'the present limitation of competition provides the stability of employment and income required by both workers and employers if the highly specialised division of labour characteristics of modern production is to be a success. Unnecessary job movements would involve a great waste of experience and skill' (Tarling and Wilkinson, 1982, p. 42).

One might add also that the obstacles to movements in relative wages seem to be embedded not only in the collective bargaining process, but in popular attitudes to wage relativities, which see them grounded in some moral imperatives, even if this moral system does not generate a national consensus on the pay of all jobs (Wootton, 1962; Willman, 1982). Hence the often-observed stability of the overall wages structure, even in the highly inflationary 1970s, does not suggest that rigidity in relative pay is simply the product of trade union monopoly power, which has fluctuated a great deal over the years. (For the long-run see Routh, 1980; for the 1970s, Saunders, 1980.)

These points are not made to suggest that all is well in the functioning of the labour market. For example, the segmentation of the market is probably highly unfavourable for those in the less well-paid 'segments'. Equally, it is not to suggest that there are no mechanisms of redistribution in the labour market – but these mechanisms are mainly not relative wage differences.[5] The central point is that approaching the labour market with a picture of a simple neo-classical model as an ideal may be very unhelpful. Indeed, it is symptomatic of the open-ended nature of neo-classical theorizing that in different ways economists within that school are starting to look at unions in a new and more positive light, rather than as simply monopolists.[6]

The above discussion of the S.D.P.'s arguments can be briefly summarized. Incomes policy is vital if a reflationary package is to be sustainable. The constraints on macro policy are such that a relatively slow expansion of money demand is all that is feasible,

and to translate that expansion into a substantial fall in unemployment requires an incomes policy. This should take a form which
retains as far as possible the efficiency characteristics of the labour
market, and the best possible format to achieve that objective is a
counter-inflation tax. The microeconomic case for such a policy is
open to considerable economic objections (and the rejection of
any redistributive role for the policy makes it looks politically
problematic). But it is not obvious that, even if the critical points
made above on the microeconomic aspects are accepted, this
would strongly qualify the case for such a policy. The macroeconomic case is strong, and the microeconomic analysis may be
seen as not in itself crucial to the advocacy of such policies (a point
returned to in chapter 7).

THE LABOUR PARTY AND INFLATION

For the Labour Party the control of inflation is seen as an electoral
necessity, but an objective which should not take priority over
economic growth and high employment. A set of policies to defeat
inflation is propounded explicitly excluding any role for monetary
policy. 'We cannot accept that monetary control is either
appropriate or effective as a means of restraining prices' (Labour
Party, 1982B, p. 23.)

The policies proposed are six-fold. First, the very fact of
expansion is seen as a cost-cutting (capacity effects) and hence
anti-inflationary, and in the long run industrial planning will
increase productivity with similar effects. Secondly, direct
measures of price restraint would be used in the initial reflationary
package, for example a cut in V.A.T. and subsidies on basic
products. Thirdly, the Labour Party would stop the use of
nationalized industry and local-authority charges as a form of
disguised taxation. Fourthly, there was in 1983 (though now
effectively abandoned) a clear commitment to leaving the European
Economic Community (E.E.C.); it was believed that this would
aid the reduction of inflation by giving Britain access to cheaper
food at world market prices. Fifthly, Labour proposed 'a flexible
but comprehensive' system of price controls, with investigative
capacities to make sure firms were not raising prices without good
reason.

Finally, and most ambiguously, there was the advocacy of a
'national economic assessment', a negotiation between the T.U.C.,
government and employers aimed at assessing the

use of resources between personal consumption, public and private investment, public services and the balance of trade. Such an assessment, to be comprehensive, has to embrace such issues as the share of the national income going to profits, to earnings from employment, to rents, to social benefits, and to other incomes. It has also to take a view on the movement in costs and prices which will support and sustain expansion and will be compatible with our economic and social objectives. (1982B, p. 24).

The details of this assessment were spelt out more fully in a joint document with the T.U.C. (Labour Party, 1983B, esp. section III). The argument here is that within a National Planning Council the unions will extend both the powers and the responsibilities of collective bargaining to the sphere of national economic policy. This bargaining, it is argued, will have clear priorities: first, job creation; secondly, improving the living standards of those on pensions and benefits, and the low paid; and only thirdly, improving the living standards of the majority of those in work. But the context of all this is seen as one where 'the growth in output and activity that we can generate will accommodate a real growth in living standards, including the social wage' (1983B, para. 30).

The document also asserts that 'Policy on pay has been from time to time isolated and elevated in importance above all other considerations and at the expense of our real long term objectives' (para. 19). Hence the policy is not a pay policy, but it is hoped that it will influence wage bargaining: 'The National Economic Assessment will form the background to bargaining on pay . . . that bargaining can take place in an atmosphere of wider recognition of what is needed for national economic success' (para. 29).

But any notion of pay norms is anathema, and this is unambiguous in almost all Labour Party discussions, despite some slight signs of a shift as the threat of a third Thatcher term approaches (see Jones, 1984). The reasons for this are not extensively spelt out. For example, *Labour's Programme 1982* simply says 'such policies cannot be maintained for any length of time without putting intolerable strains upon industrial relations and threatening to perpetuate all the anomalies and injustices in the present framework of pay differentials' (Labour Party, 1982B, p. 24).

The first point to be made in any assessment of the Labour Party's anti-inflationary programme is that the complete rejection of monetary policy seems to be based on a theoretical argument about money, rather than on the constraints imposed on monetary policy by the operation of financial markets. In other words, the powerful anti-monetarist theoretical case that can be made is the basis of policy proposals, whereas it can be argued that largely irrespective of economic theory, if financial markets take a particular view of the conduct of policy (such as the growth of the money supply), then, for the time being at least, they have ways of making their views cut across government policy. Thus Labour's attitude to the money supply and inflation is part of the approach discussed in chapter 2, in which there is an inadequate concept of the constraints on macroeconomic policy.

More specifically, some brief comments may be made on the other elements in the Labour Party package. As suggested above, the Left has commonly put great faith in the cost-reducing effects of fuller capacity utilization. Direct evidence on this appears to be absent, but what we know of economies of scale does not suggest that such effects are likely to be large in relation to the total costs of a firm.[7]

Direct measures of price restraint such as a cut in V.A.T. are plainly effective, but, as accepted by the Labour Party, are only relevant to the initial reflation, and cannot be repeated over a long period. And it is precisely policies for the long period which are at issue in the debate on inflation. A similar point can be made about nationalized industry prices. If other policy objectives (for example, conservation of natural gas supplies) are forgone, such policies can reduce price increases, but only over a relatively limited period.

Price controls are in many ways a more substantial issue. The Labour proposal is that such controls should be closely linked to the proposed system of industrial planning, so linking prices to profit margins, productivity and investment. However, as the Labour document recognizes, the main effect of price controls as an anti-inflationary weapon depends upon their effects on profits. 'For price controls are effectively a form of profit control and, as such, help us to intervene in the conflict over distribution of income by restraining the share claimed by profits' (Labour Party, 1982B, p. 24). But if the overall strategy is based on large increases in investment, a squeeze on aggregate profits is likely to be counter-productive, and hence this is not a plausible counter-inflationary policy. This is not to argue that price controls in something like the form of the Price Commission of the late 1970s might not be a useful agency. But the most important role of that Commission was not to hold down the rate of inflation, but to apply a form of 'compulsory management consultancy' to firms who sought price increases (Tomlinson, 1983A). Such an agency might be part of the regulatory regime that a Left government could construct, its purpose being to raise the efficiency of firms (see chapter 7).

The Labour Party accepts that any inflation policy must look at costs. This is where the national economic assessment fits into policy. But as already noted, this explicitly excludes any kind of incomes policy. The inescapable issue is what would be done where groups of workers rejected the norms suggested by the national economic assessment. The stated reasons for such an important policy stance are extremely summary: the argument that such policies strain industrial relations rather begs the question whether a superior kind of policy might not have this consequence. And the argument that incomes policies will perpetuate the anomalies and injustices of existing differentials is rather curious, both because those differentials are themselves the consequence of a system of 'free collective bargaining', but more broadly because such a position totally evades the question of any policy on wage differentials. Gill (1981, pp. 185–7) is typically disingenuous, arguing against incomes policies that they do not help the low paid, but also that they do not preserve necessary differentials.

The cynical will assert that Labour's hostility to incomes policy is not grounded on any clear principle, but on 'the dictates of its union paymasters' (Liberal/S.D.P., 1983, p. 336). Whilst the political and financial role of the unions in the Labour Party is obviously important, this view of why Labour is opposed to incomes policy is wholly inadequate. Such opposition is founded on arguments which any discussion of this topic must take seriously.

Except in periods of severe crisis, coupled usually with the desire to help a Labour government in office, British unions and many in the Labour Party have opposed incomes policies, because they cut across the central commitment of British unions, the commitment to free collective bargaining.

In looking at this, it perhaps needs to be stressed that the meaning of free collective bargaining is extremly ambiguous. It would seem best understood in a negative sense as a hostility to any role of the state in wage bargaining, most especially to any role of the courts. In many ways advocacy of free collective bargaining is analytically parallel to the advocacy of market forces in the economy more generally. The positive content of market forces in general is extremely vague, separate from the specification of the forms of calculation, objectives and constraints on economic agents. What such advocacy usually involves is simply hostility to government's role in the economy. The parallel with free collective bargaining is not just an analytic one, because advocating such bargaining is rather like being in favour of allowing market forces to work in the labour market, subject to one of the agents in the labour market being able to bargain collectively rather than individually. Thus the state should only have a role 'as the second best alternative to the development by employed people themselves of the organisation, the competence, the representative capacity to bargain and to achieve for themselves satisfactory terms and conditions of employment' (T.U.C., 1967, para. 90; see also paras 174–5).[8]

Advocacy of free collective bargaining is, then, partly based on the *laissez-faire* political tradition. As Flanders (1979, p. 101) has pointed out:

> The moral defence of the voluntary character of our system has always been conducted in the name of freedom. In spite of some mutual inconsistencies, its basic elements of freedom of contract, freedom of association, freedom to strike (and to lock out) and, above all, *free* collective bargaining, have been the ultimate rationale for rejecting outside, notably government, intervention in industrial relations. Trade unions may only have flourished at the expense of extreme versions of laissez-faire, but they sought for workers a collective freedom that was not at variance with the prevailing ethos.

Such an argument should not be pushed too far (see Currie, 1979). This adherence to free collective bargaining has not been a historical constant, and it is clear that support for it gained enormously as a result of its perceived success in the 1950s and 1960s in achieving sustained increases in real incomes for the mass of workers. In the inter-war period it was much less prominent, the focus of trade union activity then being on national rates, as a defence against local bargaining weaknesses (Flanders, 1979, p. 109).

Nevertheless, it is important to note that support for free collective bargaining is not just because of its perceived financial benefits to trade unionists but is also based on a more general doctrine about freedom. In other words, free collective bargaining is seen as a crucial element in the overall freedom of society, on a par with freedom of speech and of assembly (see, e.g. Currie, 1979, p. 212; T.U.C., 1967, para. 515).

Insofar as such a position is based on an assessment of the role of the courts in industrial relations, it has much to be said for it. Throughout the period since unions began they have been hampered and constrained not so much by legislation as by judge-made law. (Much of the trade union legislation of the early 1980s seems to be giving such law legislative basis for the first time.)

However, the more general belief that the unions' strength is largely a function of their own efforts is clearly a myth. Except in the case of a few craft unions, most union growth in Britain has been strongly dependent upon the role of the state, notably in the two world wars. So the general picture of a homogeneous state as an inhibitor of trade union activity in Britain cannot be sustained.

Also, the idea that free collective bargaining over wages and conditions is on a par with freedom of speech and of meeting as a fundamental freedom is difficult to accept. This conflation of trade unionism with free collective bargaining is common (e.g. Tarling and Wilkinson, 1977, pp. 408–9), but whilst the right of organization by unions can be given such a status, the wage bargaining process itself does not deserve it. Clearly, other democratic freedoms have proved robust in countries where free collective bargaining over wages in the British sense has been severely attenuated, for example in Austria and much of Scandinavia.

Much more powerful as an argument for free collective bargaining is the view that, in Britain at least, such bargaining over wages in the *raison d'être* of trade unionism, and that without such a role trade unions would wither and die. This is not unambiguously the case – many people seem to join unions for protective reasons as much as for participation in bargaining (e.g. Daniel, 1981). Nevertheless, bargaining over wages does provide the major dynamic of trade unionism, and many other issues are in trade union practice translated into wage questions (e.g. Daniel and Milward, 1983, ch. 8).

The small band of people on the Left who have supported both strong trade unions and incomes policy have sometimes argued that the way to make these compatible is by a shift in trade union orientation away from wage bargaining towards radically extended forms of industrial democracy (e.g. Purdy, 1980 and 1981; Hirst, 1980). As a broad strategy such a position has much to commend it to the Left, but it raises a number of difficult issues, not least the form of incomes policy most compatible with such a system of industrial democracy. These issues are returned to in chapter 7.

Another objection to incomes policy common in the Labour Party is that relating to the effects of such policies on real wages. Critics of incomes policies stress that past policies of this kind in Britain have been accompanied by a fall (in the rate of growth) of real wages (e.g. Tarling and Wilkinson, 1977, pp. 402–3; Ormerod, 1981, p. 186). As incomes policy has usually been introduced as a response to crisis, it is perhaps not surprising that real wage growth has also slowed, and this may not be solely due to incomes policies. For example the big fall (and subsequent rise) in real wages under the social contract, 1975–8, owed much more to changes in the terms of trade than to the incomes policy. Nevertheless, many on the Left treat a reduction of real wages as a touchstone of policy desirability.

However, as already noted in chapter 2, if an increase in real wages has been secured *de facto* at the expense of the growth of unemployment, this makes the use of such a touchstone extremely problematic if the reduction of unemployment is a serious policy goal.

Secondly, external events such as a deterioration in the terms of trade may make a decline in real wages unavoidable (especially given the tiny proportion of profits in national income in the U.K. – see table 2.2). In the context of such a shift, an incomes policy may be the best way of managing a decline in real incomes, rather than in any sense a cause of that decline.

Thirdly, one of the striking features of the U.K. economy is the high level of consumption/low level of investment relative to output. Now it might well be that a progressive government would argue for a reduction in consumption levels secured by a fall in real wages as a necessary condition for the revival of the economy. It would seem difficult to rule this out on principle as sensible socialist policy.

These points are not made to deny the argument that incomes policies in the United Kingdom have often been simply wage control and nothing else, and have sometimes led to (short-term) falls in real wages with little clear offsetting benefit. But it is important to deny that the path of real wages should always be used as a clear guide to the acceptability of a policy to socialists.

In sum, common Labour Party arguments against incomes policy appear weak, except that which stresses how wage bargaining has come to be the *raison d'être* of British trade unionism. Even here, the Labour argument in defence of strong trade unions is usually vague and inexplicit, and the presumption is that on the Left the case does not have to be made. But, it may be argued that what is lacking is precisely any specifically socialist politics of trade unionism.

The S.D.P. (1983C, p. 1) makes a strong case for trade unions as follows:

> Trade Unions have a vital role to play in a social democratic society. They are the only effective tool in the hands of working people to ensure their rights of work: the right to fair treatment; the right to the representation of their grievances; the right to a full say in

determining their pay and conditions. Without trade unions, none of this would be possible. However generous and fair the pay and conditions granted by a particular employer may be, in the absence of a union, they are merely concessions that can be withdrawn as easily as they are granted.

This is unobjectionable as far as it goes, but from a socialist perspective what it clearly lacks is any political role for unions. Yet for the Labour Party the political aspects are crucial: first, that unions have always been a prime source of recruitment into Labour Party and socialist politics; secondly, that unions are (at least potentially) mass democratic organizations, and possible agencies for forms of democracy in industry. They are the only bodies, in the foreseeable future, with any chance of offering corporate strategies in the context of industrial democracy.

The pertinence of these points in the current context is that the weakness of Labour on incomes policy is partly because of the lack of a clear doctrine about unions and their role, which is one of the most paradoxical of Labour's doctrinal shortcomings. Of course, such doctrinal issues are not all important – policy-making is never simply doctrine set in motion – but in this area the lack of a clear doctrine is a crippling weakness, especially when trade unionism is politically so much on the defensive.

THE MARXIST LEFT AND INFLATION

It is far from clear that there is any distinctive Marxist position on inflation. Most Marxist writing sees inflation as a consequence of distributional struggles (e.g. Rowthorn, 1977; Aaronovitch *et al.*, 1981, pp. 178, 362–4). Typical is the latter's summary of the acceleration of British inflation in the 1970s: 'It was the result of intensifying conflict between workers and capitalists over the distribution of resources that were themselves coming under pressure from the state and foreign-sectors' (1981, p. 362). Of itself such a position is not very different from some mainstream positions, which emphasize worker bargaining over a target real wage. But Marxists draw the particular conclusion from such conflict, that anti-inflationary policies as pursued by, for example, the Thatcher government, are really a disguise for shifting the distribution of income (and power) from workers to capitalists (see chapter 1).

Such an approach has little room for the role of the money supply in affecting inflation, though some more complex versions do argue for an indirect effect of money on inflation, via its effect on the distributive struggle (Rowthorn, 1977). Equally unsurprisingly, such analyses tend to see incomes policy as simply a way of resolving this distributive struggle in a manner unfavourable to workers, and thus parallel to the kinds of anti-incomes policy arguments of the Labour Party. Glyn and Harrison (1980, p. 153) use this distributive struggle as another means to argue the impossibility of capitalism resolving its contradictions. Incomes policies will be unsuccessful if they do not shift income towards profits, but such a policy would rouse the justified hostility of the working class.

Analytically more interesting are the arguments about corporatism which have been deployed by Marxists, and find considerable sympathy elsewhere on the Left.[9] The Marxist version of the corporatism argument has been propounded by Panitch, who in a whole series of pieces (especially 1976, more recently 1982) has argued that incomes policies are clear signs of the pressure towards 'incorporation' of the working class into capitalism, by means of their subordination to policies misleadingly labelled 'in the national interest'. Thus the history of Labour governments' attempts at incomes policies in the post-war period is a history of attempts by those governments to subordinate working-class interests to those of capitalists, because the national interest is really the capitalist interest.

The difficulty with this argument is that it presumes that workers' 'real' interests are secured by free collective bargaining. Yet this surely cannot be stated unconditionally. In conditions of relatively fast output growth it may be true that free collective bargaining maintains or even increases the wage share in output with few adverse side effects. However, it is far from clear that free collective bargaining has secured an income distribution which should be in any sense desirable to socialists. A striking feature of the wage distribution in the post-war period has been its immunity from most equalizing pressures – and it is not at all certain that collective bargaining is such a pressure.

In the early post-war years, support for incomes policy was quite widespread on the Left. In the 1950s and 1960s this position was eroded by the apparent success of free collective bargaining in securing substantial real wage increases. But the conditions of such success – sustained national income growth, absence of inflation – have been eroded.

Secondly, the corporatism argument treats any discussion on national policy as merely obfuscating the real interests of workers. Yet, as noted in the introduction to this book, it is surely apparent that the material interests of workers are partly conditioned by the management of the national economy. To say so is not to endorse any notion of a transcendental national interest and the rhetoric which surrounds such notions. It is merely to assert that there *is* a national economy, differentially constructed rather than given, subject to severe qualifications in its management, but nevertheless not just a figment of the bourgeois imagination. Its management matters to all those engaged in economic activity within its boundaries.

Thirdly, the Marxist version of corporatism decries the common consequences of incomes policy in giving a large role to national trade union leadership, especially the T.U.C. The dislike of such a role is based on the view that such leadership is inherently more reactionary than the 'rank and file' and will pursue policies inimical to that rank and file. This is based on the view that, at least in part, rank and file trade union militancy is intrinsically socialist (albeit imperfectly so).

'dissatisfaction with existing social relations is inherent in wage claims of 25, 30 or 40 per cent . . . in occupations of factories shut down in accordance with the law of profits . . . in the large number of strikes challenging managerial prerogatives' (Panitch, 1976, p. 253). Such an argument is based on the notion of a consciousness created by the experience of capitalism which propels workers towards socialist ideology. Apart from the theoretical difficulties of such notions as 'experience' and 'consciousness' (on which see, e.g., Hirst, 1979), such a position totally avoids any issues of policy formation and political calculation. In other words, it treats the interests of the working class as transparent, as not needing any specific policies or means of strategic action. As such it can play only a negative role in any discussion of political programmes for identifiable and attainable reforms. A good example is the debate over the Bullock report on industrial democracy in the late 1970s. As is well known (Lloyd, 1978) proposals for worker directors were pushed mainly by a few trade union and T.U.C. leaders, where many rank and file trade union leaders were opposed to such policies. There are very serious political arguments about the effects of such policies, but they are precisely arguments about *where* the interests of workers lie, and the issue cannot even be discussed if it is presumed that those interests are transparently given in capitalist relations of production, simply the consequence of ownership or non-ownership of the means of production.

None of these points is intended to suggest that an incomes policy which concentrated all decision-making in the hands of the T.U.C. and trade union leaders would be an ideal; far from it. But there is no reason to suppose that negotiations between T.U.C.

and government which fixed (an enforceable) national norm for wage bargaining would be incompatible with continuing trade union activity at rank and file level. Indeed, such a combination could be seen as precisely the objective of a well-constructed incomes policy.

CONCLUSIONS

The macroeconomic aspects of 'New-Keynesianism' provide a radical challenge to the Left's economic policies. If the constraints on national economic management are severe, as this book argues they are, then the case for accepting the limited scope of possible reflation of money demand is very powerful. In such a case, anyone who takes seriously the objective of reducing unemployment must face up to the need for an incomes policy to translate that money demand into as much employment as possible.

The pressures for any future Labour government to pursue an incomes policy will arise not only from its own objectives but also, as in the past, from external events. Such a government is likely to face a run on the pound which will be a very serious impetus to some kind of incomes policy. It is important not to be too glib about dismissing the experience of past incomes policies to deal with such a situation: that of 1975–9 was quite successful until its last stages. Nevertheless, the current period should provide an opportunity to devise policies which are not simply a reaction to crises, but try also to embody appropriate political principles.

In this chapter, the argument has been that the starting point for discussion of incomes policy should be unemployment, which, in rhetoric at least, is very much given pride of place amongst the Left's concerns. But as argued above, much of the Left's hostility to incomes policy appears ill-founded anyway, an intellectual baggage used to avoid facing up to serious economic, ideological and political questions.

If the Left's doctrine on trade unions is as ill-developed as suggested above, so also is its discussion of wages. The Labour Party in particular has failed to develop any clear view of how the labour market works, and what reform of the wages structure might be desirable and attainable. Thus, for example, a 'solidaristic' wages policy as pursued in Sweden with some considerable success, seems never even to have appeared on the agenda for discussion. Yet so many other areas of potential reform – social security, corporate management, unemployment – as well as inflation, are linked to wages.

4

The Balance of Payments and the Exchange Rate

INTRODUCTION

By contrast with policy discussion on employment and inflation, that relating to the balance of payments and the exchange rate is notably diffuse. Whilst, other things being equal, nearly everyone can agree that less unemployment is better than more, and lower inflation better than higher, there is no such clear measure of policy preference and performance in the case of the balance of payments and the exchange rate. On the Right of the political spectrum, a popular view is that any talk of active policy in this area is inappropriate. Given appropriate institutional conditions, especially free capital movement, flexible exchange rates and appropriate monetary policy, very strong balancing forces will obviate any need for government action. The current government has tended to such views, though it encouraged and welcomed, for example, the rise in the exchange rate in 1979–81 as aiding its anti-inflationary objectives, and in early 1985, intervened against the fall in sterling, though arguing that this was not an attempt to alter the long-run trend of the exchange rate.

On the Left, such views have never found much favour, and there has been a much greater tendency to see both the balance of payments and the exchange rate as requiring policy consideration. Broadly speaking, the Left has stressed the constraints imposed on the pursuit of its other policy goals by the international aspects of the British economy, but has seen these constraints not as inescapable 'facts of life', as the Right tends to do, but as things about which something can and should be done. However, especially beyond the time horizon of a short-run reflation of the economy, there is little agreement on how these constraints should be seen, let alone how they should be tackled.

THE S.D.P.

S.D.P. policy proposals in this area are largely in the short-term context of the party's programme of reflation. Within this context, the S.D.P. argues for a positive policy on the exchange rate, aimed at maintaining the competitiveness of British exports. The object would be to use monetary policy to maintain a roughly fixed degree of competitiveness, as measured by a 'competitiveness index', in the form, for example, of an index of Britain's labour costs relative to those of other countries. The overall objective would be to prevent the party's reflationary policy being aborted by an inappropriate movement of the exchange rate (S.D.P., 1983A, p. 18). The context of these proposals was originally a sterling exchange rate substantially higher than that considered compatible with such expansionary policies, so that the expectation was that the policy would involve a fall in the exchange rate: the precise level (reasonably enough) was not specified, though reference was made to 1976 as an acceptable base level, before the effects of North Sea oil. Even with the subsequent fall of the dollar exchange rate through 1984 and into early 1985, this policy would require a further fall in the exchange rate, essentially against other European countries. More importantly, such policies involve clear downgrading of monetary goals, and a move to the use of monetary policy as an instrument to attain a desired exchange rate.

Such a policy is seen by the S.D.P. as the appropriate one for the medium term. It is also argues that in the short run the problem might be an excessive depreciation of the pound, leading to unacceptable inflation, caused by two factors. On the one hand there is the 'J-curve effect', whereby the initial effect of a currency devaluation is to weaken the balance of trade by worsening the price ratio of imports and exports before the volume adjustment to these new prices. On the other hand, according to the well-known characteristic of a period of reflation, is the fact that imports for stock-building initially rise more quickly than any export expansion (1983A, p. 19).

In response to such pressures, controls might be needed. 'Social Democrats are disinclined in principle to use exchange controls or general import controls, but would not absolutely rule out temporary measures if expansion was threatened by an upsurge of imports' (pp. 2–3). But the emphasis here is very much on the temporary nature of such policies, and the S.D.P. strongly and specifically criticizes the Labour Party proposals for any long-run policies on import controls (p. 8).

In long-run stance, the S.D.P.'s view of trade policy, as of other policies, is similar to that of the mainstream of economics in Britain. This sees free trade as, with few exceptions, the 'first best' policy[1] (Henderson, 1984). However, it is of interest to note that such a position views the current *ad hoc* system of trade discriminations as analytically indefensible, whereas a general protectionist policy of the Cambridge Economic Policy Group style (see further below) is seen as based on 'subtle argument' and, analytically, if not practically, more defensible (Henderson, 1984, p. 16).

As noted in chapter 2, on unemployment policy, the S.D.P. stresses the constraints on unilateral expansion in the U.K. This in turn leads to an emphasis on the desirability of multilateral, especially European, co-operation in policies of expansion. As Artis and Posner (1984, p. 15) argue, 'Parallelism in recovery reduces the balance of payments, exchange rate and inflation risks for each individual country, as against the go-it-alone option and by the same token affords greater credibility.'

Such a view, and the general pro-E.E.C. stance of the S.D.P., predisposes it to a favourable view of the European Monetary System, which links together the exchange rates of the other E.E.C. members. Strictly speaking, Britain is a member of the E.M.S., but does not participate in its exchange rate mechanism, the current government having a 'wait and see' attitude to Britain's full participation. The advantages of full E.M.S. membership would, in the S.D.P. view, be to provide an appropriate framework for pursuing an exchange rate policy, providing participants with access to greater resources to deploy in foreign exchange markets, and generally creating a zone of currency stability, at least with Britain's major trading partners.

In sum, the general characteristics of the S.D.P.'s attitude to Britain's international economic policy are continued support for the principles of free trade and free capital movements, coupled with a belief that adherence to these principles may be justifiably broken for short-term, macroeconomic reasons. Thus the S.D.P. sees no 'structural' disadvantages for Britain in full participation in the international economy, and views the constraints imposed on British policy by such participation as reasons for greater international co-operation, not for reducing the level of participation. Finally, international capital movements are seen as significant for their balance of payments' implications only, not as important for the long-run development of the British economy.

THE LABOUR PARTY

Like the S.D.P., the Labour Party starts from the argument that its policies of reflation would quickly lead to a balance of payments deficit. 'Such a deficit would leave us exposed to external pressures and to speculation against the pound, as well as draining away spending power and curbing expansion' (Labour Party, 1982B, p. 20). But whereas the S.D.P. policy focuses on movements in the exchange rate as the major way of dealing with such problems, the Labour Party stresses the need for direct controls over trade. The policy would involve drawing up 'import penetration ceilings on an industry-by-industry basis across a broad range of sectors' (1982B, p. 21). The objectives here would be two-fold: first, 'to ensure that the overall level of imports does not grow substantially faster than our exports – and to do this without a depreciation of the pound on a scale which would entail huge costs'; secondly, 'to provide a breathing space for our industries to recover and invest. We must check, and in some cases reverse, the rapid growth in import penetration of recent years . . .' (pp. 20–1). The role of changes in the exchange rate is played down in relation to direct controls over trade; the need to adjust the value of the pound for competitiveness is accepted, but it is argued that 'many other factors besides price affect competitiveness, and even in the case of price competitiveness, the exchange rate is not the only factor' (p. 22).

The advocacy of import controls raises extremely sensitive issues on the Left, and the Labour Party is well aware of, and tries to counter, some of these. In particular, the document stresses that 'The object of trade policy is not to cut the overall level of imports but to ensure a controlled growth of trade' (p. 23). It is emphasized that current policies restrict trade by deflation, and that Labour's proposed alternative is aimed at raising the level of growth of the economy and hence both exports and imports, even thought the latter are now tied to the rate of expansion of exports. But whilst this is the general thrust of the policy, it is accepted that within this overall increase 'imports in certain sectors will have to be held back or even cut back where this is necessary for particular industries to recover' (p. 23).

The dangers of retaliation are also recognized, and it is argued that the expansionary intent of the policy makes it compatible with adherence to the General Agreement on Tariffs and Trade (G.A.T.T.). Such intent is also seen as the basis for the argument against retaliation.

Coupled with trade controls, the Labour Party sees a central role for exchange controls. Such controls would not simply involve a reversion to those controls abolished by the Conservatives in 1979, but would be much wider in purpose 'so that capital flows are regulated with regard to their industrial implications as well as their immediate financial impact' (p. 22).

This argument is indeed central to the Labour Party's attitude to the world economy. The broad thrust of this is that Britain's participation in an international economy based on free trade and capital movement is fundamentally disadvantageous, and that the problems go far beyond those of short-run pressures accompanying a reflation as emphasized by the S.D.P. Free trade is seen as making it impossible to revive Britain's manufacturing capacity, and therefore long-term controls over the level of import penetration are advocated. The free international movement of capital is seen as damaging to Britain, broadly because of the excessively international orientation of the British financial system and the very large role played by multinationals in the British economy. Both of these are seen as facilitating excessive outflows of investment funds from Britain, especially since the abolition of exchange controls.

In addition, it is argued that Britain has become locked into an unfavourable trade pattern, 'trapped in exports of traditional goods with low value added and low technology input – and these are precisely the markets which have not expanded' (C.S.E./L.W.G., 1980, p. 93). Taken together, such arguments make a general case for long-run policies which see a reduction in Britain's level of integration with the world economy as an important policy objective, though this is not often explicitly argued for (but see 1980, p. 93).

The Labour Party pronounces in favour of an orderly growth of world trade and international monetary co-operation. But it does not couple this with advocacy of Britain's membership of the E.M.S. Essentially, the attitude here mirrors that of the Labour Party towards European Community institutions generally: they restrict Britain's freedom of action, and hence are disadvantageous. Thus 'we believe that Britain should, as far as practicable, determine its own exchange rate policy, in the light of Labour's policies for expansion. Labour will not therefore join the European Monetary System' (Labour Party, 1982B, p. 22).

The policies currently proposed by the Labour Party in the area of the international economy have shifted quite notably in recent years. Whilst the emphasis on restricting overseas investment is a long-standing one, the focus on trade controls is relatively new.

Traditionally, the dominant view in the Labour Party (if not always of Labour governments) was that Britain, under City pressure, had been committed to an overvalued exchange rate which benefited 'finance' at the expense of industry. Such views are still present (Gould *et al.*, 1981; Labour Economic Policy Group, 1982), but as the above outline of Labour Party policy makes clear, import controls are now seen as much more crucial than exchange-rate policy.

In part, this no doubt reflects what has happened to the exchange rate since floating in 1972 (see table 4.1). Whilst by most criteria overvalued for some of the period since then (especially 1979–82), it has also fallen to low values without providing any indication of being a panacea for Britain's trade problems. This general impression seems to have been reinforced by two quite separate developments in economic arguments.

Table 4.1 Effective exchange rate of sterling, 1975–85.* (1975 = 100)

Year	Rate
1975	100.0
1976	85.7
1977	81.5
1979	87.3
1980	96.1
1981	95.3
1982	90.7
1983	83.3
1984	75.8
1985 (Jan.)	71.5
1985 (Apr.)	78.0

* the value of the pound relative to other currencies weighted by their importance in international trade. (Note that gyrations against the dollar have been even more severe.)

Source: *Economic Trends*

Best known of these is undoubtedly the work of the Cambridge Economic Policy Group. If the Clare Group may be seen in many ways as the S.D.P. in academia (an exaggeration, but not an absurd one) the C.E.P.G. have played something of a similar role for the Labour Party (though qualifications to this are given below).

The central thrust of C.E.P.G. policy pronouncements (see the *Cambridge Economic Policy Reviews*, 1975–82; for a summary, Ward, 1981) is that the major constraint on Britain's successful economic performance is the level of import penetration, which creates a vicious circle of low demand, low investment, uncompetitiveness and consequent further worsening of the trade balance. The circle should be cut by a system of *general* import controls, raising the level of demand, the incentive to invest and the competitiveness of the British economy. (The general background to C.E.P.G. proposals is very powerfully outlined in Singh, 1977; see also Neild, 1979; Lal, 1979.)

Whilst the Labour Party has undoubtedly drawn a great deal on the C.E.P.G.'s work, there are noticeable differences. These can be briefly summarized from the Labour Party viewpoint as the C.E.P.G. exaggerating the efficacy of import controls alone as a cure for Britain's economic problems, and in particular 'a reluctance to go beyond macroeconomic aggregates to look at the implications for industry and the kind of industrial policies which would be necessary' (C.S.E./L.W.G., 1980, p. 95).

Hence Labour policy places much more emphasis on industrial planning than the C.E.P.G., though the latter is not necessarily opposed to such policies. The members of the C.E.P.G. are, in their own eccentric way, Keynesians in their emphasis on the demand-side, macroeconomic, aspects of import controls. The Labour Party plays down this aspect, in favour of more selectivity in the working of such controls, but coupled with a view that there is a general problem of too high a level of import penetration. One might say that the Labour Party would tend to see the appropriate place to break into the vicious circle of Britain's economic decline in the area of investment rather than imports. (In this very limited sense the Labour Party is closer to the present government than to the C.E.P.G.)

One other source of the Labour Party's decreased emphasis on the exchange rate as a means of easing balance of payments problems can be more briefly dealt with. This is the literature which emphasizes the non-price elements in competitiveness – elements such as quality, reliability, after-sales service etc. One of the best-known examples of this is the study by the National Economic Development Office (N.E.D.O.) in 1977, which shows quite clearly how successive exchange rate falls in post-war Britain kept export prices competitive, but did not prevent loss of competitiveness as evidenced by actual trade performance. Whilst such arguments have no necessary relation to import control policies, they clearly can and have been used to turn discussion away from the exchange rate as the answer to trade competitiveness problems.

The general thrust of Labour Party policy in this area is, then, quite distinct from that of the S.D.P. Whilst both parties start from the need for policies to cope with the likely consequence of their domestic reflationary stance, beyond that there is little similarity. S.D.P. policy focuses on the exchange rate and sees policy as largely conducted with the traditional instruments of macro-economic policy, that is, monetary policy, with little scope for trade or exchange controls. The Labour Party puts the emphasis on such controls, with exchange rate management mattering but not being crucial. Beyond these short-term issues the positions diverge more sharply. For the Labour Party, the mechanisms of economic integration with the rest of the world are largely seen in a negative light. In particular, the flow of foreign investment out of Britain is seen as part of the reason for the low level of investment in domestic industry, thus fitting in with the general Labour Party emphasis on low investment as central to Britain's economic problems (see chapter 5).

THE MARXIST LEFT

The Marxist view of national economic management as an inappropriate concern of the Left is nowhere more apparent than in the discussion of international economic policy. The Militant Tendency, for example, has been quite prolific by its own standards in its discussion of the issue of import controls.

These discussions have been a central part of the criticisms by Militant of the Alternative Economic Strategy of the Labour Party and other Left groups. Some of these criticisms are the fairly standard ones about the efficacy of such import controls – the problems of retaliation, the likely effects on the standard of living, the possibility that they will simply lead to protected inefficiency in British industry (Militant, 1981A, pp. 9–10; Glyn, 1978, pp. 36–41). But above and beyond those reasons, such policies should not be supported, 'Because they imply a national solution, import controls are essentially anti-working class and anti-socialist' (Militant, 1981B, p.12). The reason why these policies are anti-socialist is not that they might be said to export unemployment. (In principle anyway, as already noted, Labour Party policies aim at increasing the level of imports and hence foreign employment in the medium term.) Rather, it needs to be emphasized, the argument is that any national policy compromises the inescapably international character of the class struggle.

> So the demand for import controls must be recognised as being nationalistic – an attempt to preserve the interests of the 'British nation', workers and capitalists alike, and on this basis there would be no possibility of British workers appealing to the labour movement abroad to oppose the retaliatory response of their capitalists. A class approach, by contrast, sees the only solution to the problems faced by workers in all the capitalist countries in a common struggle against the capitalist system which is the source of these problems. So any measure which sets workers in this country against workers in other countries must be rejected. It weakens the struggle for socialism by strengthening one of the strongest ideological weapons in the hands of the capitalist class – the appeal to workers to make sacrifices in the name of a national interest being threatened by actions of foreigners. (Glyn, 1978, p. 39).

Clearly such a view leaves little room for policy programmes for the balance of payments and the exchange rate. The essential element is the belief that prior to 'socialism' (in other words, widespread nationalization) any national policy will reflect the interests of the capitalist class, though under 'socialism' such policies would be acceptable 'as a necessary part of a socialist plan to control the economy in society's interests' (1978, p. 40).

One other aspect of Militant's arguments in this area is worthy of note. Criticism is made of the Left's views that controls on outward foreign investment would of themselves bring higher levels of investment in domestic manufacturing. 'Rather than additional productive capacity, they always have the alternative of investing in government bonds or other financial assets and this would happen if stiffer controls on capital export were introduced' (p. 43). This fits in with the general thrust of Militant's argument, that the problem is not one of institutions, and hence subject to possible reform, but one of the central mechanisms of capitalism, which leads to investment going to where profits are highest. The conclusion drawn from this is that there is no solution to Britain's economic problems short of the abolition of capitalism.

It must be said that whilst in other areas Marxists have important points to make on policy issues, in this area their contribution is very small. In part this no doubt arises from the complexity of the issues in this area, without any obvious links between standard policy issues such as the exchange rate and the balance of payments, and the Marxist concern with issues such as wages and employment. But more generally, it reflects the fact that international economic issues are unavoidably pitched at the level of national economic management, which the Marxist Left rejects as an appropriate issue.

SHORT-RUN POLICIES

Whilst both the S.D.P. and the Labour Party see the balance of payments and the exchange rate as problems for their short-run reflationary strategies, they differ sharply on how to cope with these. The S.D.P. expects that its objective of exchange rate management to maintain competitiveness will only in emergency have to be accompanied by exchange and trade controls, whilst the Labour Party sees such controls as an integral part of the strategy.

Reflation

It is extremely difficult to predict what the response of buyers and sellers of foreign exchange would be to a reflationary policy in Britain (Coutts *et al.*, 1982, p. 12). Much would depend on the stated scope of the reflationary package and the international context in which it was being pursued. (The reaction to the French reflation was affected both by the ambition of the strategy and the fact that other large countries were simultaneously pursuing deflationary policies.) It might also depend on the political context, in the sense that reaction to a Labour Party programme might be greater than to an S.D.P./Alliance one of equivalent reflationary scope. Even given the most favourable context, it is likely that some form of exchange control would be needed to prevent the exchange rate falling too fast. Joining the E.M.S. may or may not be sensible (see below) but it is difficult to see this as much help in the context of a short-run crisis likely to occur even before a reflationary government took office.

Devaluation

Slightly more determinate would be the effects of a fall in exchange rate. Here very much depends on the time scale. There is now an almost unanimous belief that a fall in the exchange rate cannot bring any permanent competitive advantage, the area of dispute being how quickly any such advantage would be dissipated (and the mechanisms of such dissipation) (see, for example, 'Report of the Discussion' in Major, 1979).

Winters (1982) has estimated that a 10 per cent devaluation will improve competitiveness for up to four years, though domestic prices will make half the adjustment to the new exchange rate within about a year. However, central to such analyses is the effect of devaluation on wages. In Winters's account, the 10 per cent devaluation reduces real wages by 1·5 per cent; the other side of this is an increase in profits. In terms of policy, therefore, the effects of devaluation would depend a great deal on what happened to wages at the time when the devaluation was occurring. Winters adopts the quite common view amongst (Keynesian) economists that depreciation of the currency is a relatively easy way of moving the economy to a superior equilibrium, by bringing about a fall in the real wage: 'by raising prices it allows real wages to fall merely by ensuring that nominal wages increase less rapidly than prices' (1982, p. 103).

As noted in chapter 2, such a view is not popular on the Left, and indeed none of the political parties advocated depreciation for this reason. (The Conservatives advocate a fall in the real wage, but are precluded from advocating a fall in the exchange rate as a means to this, both because they see exchange rates as affecting only the rate of inflation, not real variables, and because, in any case, the exchange rate should be left to be determined by 'market forces'.) However, others on the Left have not been so reticent. Artis (1982, qs 584–7) argues that a devaluation would lead to an initial cut in the real wage and that incomes policy should be used to maintain that cut: 'I was not suggesting the whole of the devaluation of 30 per cent should immediately be an equivalent cut in real wages, but if you put it to the labour movement that this was the price of removing upwards of 1½ million from the unemployment register perhaps you would get some co-operation' (q. 586).

This seems to be a powerful argument, although the political obstacles in this area are immense, as discussed in chapter 3. Perhaps here it suffices to say that if devaluation is to be used in this way, then it is important to make this explicit, and not engage in the disillusioning Wilsonian rhetoric about 'the pound in your pocket' not being devalued, as in 1967.

Exchange Rate Targets

Both the S.D.P. and the Labour Party support the idea of an exchange rate target, geared to some measure of competitiveness. In the short run two issues arise from this, one rather technical, one much more general. The technical issue arises from the S.D.P.'s advocacy of such a target and its simultaneous adherence to the E.M.S. Adherence to the E.M.S. means having an 'effective exchange rate' target, that is, one geared to the values of the basket of the currencies of the other members of the system. But such a target may not be readily compatible with a target based on competitiveness, based, for example, on some measure of relative labour costs. Whilst it may be that in the long run the effective exchange rate will conform reasonably closely to movements in relative competitiveness this is far from true in the short run. In particular, short-term capital flows may make this divergence substantial. This may be seen as either a further argument against joining the E.M.S., or as a reason to some extent compromising the 'competitiveness' target if the other gains of joining the E.M.S. are seen as very large.

The much more general issue which arises is that of exchange rate targets as a central feature of policy. The current government has always refused to own up to having such a target, but since 1982 has explicitly taken the rate into account when deciding on the appropriate monetary stance. Artis and Currie (1981) have argued that in a technical sense if the major effect of money supply policy operates via the exchange rate, then it makes sense to cut one link in the chain of causation, and have an exchange rate target directly. (Though they do not argue that such targets should be adhered to in all circumstances.) The Labour Party and the S.D.P. make it clear that an exchange rate target means abandoning monetary targets, using monetary policy (amongst other things) as a means of regulating the exchange rate. The issue this raises is whether such an abandonment of monetary targets is likely to be a major cause of loss of international confidence, given that such targets seem to have become a widespread index of financial responsibility. However, the really significant question is what is actually done with the exchange-rate target. If the attempt is made at a very rapid and very large devaluation, this will be seen as extremely inflationary and likely to lead to adverse reaction. However, if the depreciation is relatively slow and not over ambitious, then it is not obvious that financial markets will act so adversely. In other words, whilst financial markets are likely to react unsympathetically to any reflationary package, there seems no good reason to suppose that the reaction will be affected by the index the British government is using to guide the degree of reflation it is trying to engineer.

THE LONGER RUN

The S.D.P., as well as seeing an exchange rate target as appropriate in the context of a reflationary package, sees such targeting as desirable in the longer term. This is part of a broader perspective on the world economy and Britain's place within it, a perspective which conflicts sharply with that of the Labour Party and others on the Left.

E.M.S.

The S.D.P. broadly supports the dominant view amongst economists that free trade and free flows of capital are desirable. Hence its emphasis on exchange and trade controls as, at most, temporary measures to overcome short-term problems (S.D.P., 1983A, pp. 2–3). This stance goes along with a recognition of the interdependence of the British and the world economies which leads to an emphasis on the need for international co-operation in economic matters. This particularly means co-operation within the E.E.C. Such vague aspirations are made much firmer by the commitment to join the E.M.S. This commitment, as well as being part of a general sympathy with Britain's E.E.C. membership, also rests on the view that membership of the E.M.S. will help the objective of exchange rate management. The case for the E.M.S. is briefly summarized by Artis (1982, p. 155).[2]

> E.M.S. membership would certainly enhance the U.K.'s ability to maintain a credible exchange rate target. Second . . . it has provided a corner of comparative exchange rate stability; third, E.M.S. members have grown in importance for U.K. trade and fixity with respect to E.M.S. members' rates contributes significantly towards fixity in the U.K.'s effective exchange rate. Fourth, the E.M.S. is dominated by a low inflation country (West Germany) and insofar as full membership of the E.M.S. would imply West German inflation rates, this would be a considerable success.

Finally, Artis suggests that a fixed exchange rate looks more plausible if part of the E.M.S. might be seen as useful against inflation. But Artis also points to arguments against Britain's membership: Britain's trade with members of the E.M.S. is less than that of other members; there is no common policy *vis-à-vis* the U.S.A., the success of E.M.S. has been accidental; it does not permit gliding parities; it sees pressure for membership as leading to policy convergence, rather than vice versa. (These points lead Artis to 'scepticism' on membership.)

These arguments against E.M.S. membership have considerable force. However, Britain's share of trade with E.M.S. members is growing. The absence of a policy on the dollar is serious; but this seems to be a reason for joining and trying to develop such a policy, rather than for not joining. The problem of 'gliding parities' refers back to the issue of the incompatibility between parities based on indices of competitiveness and effective exchange rates as in the current E.M.S. system. Whether some reform of the E.M.S. is possible in the direction of such indices is a question which never seems to have been addressed. The final point of Artis's objections is in many ways the most imponderable. If membership of the E.M.S. were part and parcel of a co-operative reflationary effort by its members, then this objection would have much less force; proponents of Britain's E.M.S. membership see the two things going together: each country reflating whilst protected from international repercussions partly by parallel reflation in major trading partners, partly by mutual assistance against strong pressures on the exchange rate originating outside the system. This, interestingly, is the kind of scenario outlined by members of the C.E.P.G. (Cripps and Ward, 1983) who argue that a policy of reflation might be achieved 'through a radically reformed and greatly reinforced E.M.S., designed to support rather than obstruct reflation' (1983, p. 93). They accept that such membership might be used to exert deflationary pressures, but believe that these are unlikely to be worse than current policies (p. 93).

Such an outlook is undoubtedly an optimistic one. The likelihood of such a situation occurring is no doubt small, but ultimately imponderable. What can usefully be done is to compare it as an approach to Britain's role in the international economy with that of the Labour Party. In order to do this it is useful to look at the common ground between the two parties.

Exchange Rate Management

Both the S.D.P. and the Labour Party, as already noted, see an exchange rate target as part of their policy, although it is much less central for the latter. Such consensus does not, of course, mean that this is a good policy. There are two issues here. First, would greater rigidity of exchange rates be a good thing? Second, is it realistic to aim at greater rigidity?

On the first issue, it is very difficult to make a clear cost–benefit analysis of floating rates. As Artis (1982, p. 152) points out, however, what does seem clear is that in the period since generalized floating began in 1973, several countries have had to make very painful adjustments to changes in the exchange rate, which have tended to 'overshoot' in response to variations in the attractiveness of different currencies. This was Britain's problem in 1979–81. As long as monetary authorities concentrate on monetary targets and not on the exchange rate, this pattern is likely. This is because any disturbance to the system will bring a very rapid response in capital flows, but only a slow one in the prices of goods, services and wages (Currie, 1982, p. 233). In addition, floating may have been inflationary, in removing one weapon in the hands of government to be used in bargaining over wages (see also Brooks, 1979).

But these kinds of arguments presuppose a comparison with a largely fixed rate regime, and it may be argued that such a regime is no longer possible, which is why it ceased to exist in the early 1970s. But what is really at stake is not some 'return to Bretton Woods' that is, to a structure of exchange rates fixed for long periods, but the desirability of more emphasis on, and formality in, exchange rate policy, where many governments already pursue some level of intervention. Ultimately, the plausibility of having an exchange rate target seems to be one of degree. For example, for a British government to have resisted all upward pressure on the pound in the period 1976–80 would have been useless, because of North Sea oil. But it would have been possible both to pursue different domestic macroeconomic policies, and perhaps to use instruments such as taxes on inward capital flows to prevent the upward pressure pushing the pound to the absurd heights attained in 1980.[3] To go entirely against market sentiment is impossible; for example, total E.M.S. reserves are only about one-fifth to one-sixth of total Euro-currency deposits, to give just one measure of the weakness of governments *vis-à-vis* private holders of foreign exchange. But as Cairncross has pointed out, (1982, questions 805–9) fixed exchange rate systems have survived in the past with such unfavourable ratios. As Currie (1982, p. 237) argues, 'There is, therefore, scope for exerting a short- to medium-term influence on the real exchange rate. But the scope . . . to influence the long-run real exchange rate is probably quite limited.'

If one grants that greater exchange rate stability is desirable, and that, within limits, it is not impossible to attain it, what policies are most likely to deliver such attainment? The Labour Party's approach is quite unambiguous. 'We believe that Britain should, as far as is practicable, determine its own exchange rate policy, in the light of Labour's policies for expansion. Labour will not therefore join the European Monetary System' (Labour Party, 1982B, p. 22).

Such a position reflects a general paradox of the Labour Party's approach to the E.E.C. On the one hand, there is the acceptance of the vulnerability of the British economy to international influences; on the other hand, a rejection of the only supranational governmental body which might provide a framework which would be used to regulate some of these international influences. Of course this is done in the name of a 'wider internationalism', but this seems largely rhetorical in the absence of institutional underpinnings.

In the case of control over the exchange rate, the Labour Party argument implies that Britain, by the use of exchange controls, can determine the sterling exchange rate. But whilst exchange controls may be a useful adjunct to other policies (for example, in the context of a reflationary package) it is difficult to see them as, in the long run, as powerful a weapon as is suggested by a 'go-it-alone' policy. In Vernon's words, 'When restrictions are placed on capital movements, especially in the more highly developed countries, the people who are determined to move their funds into other countries can often still find a way' (1972, p. 53). Other policies for exchange rate management, such as multiple exchange rate systems, have been discussed on the Left (e.g. Currie, 1982) but not in Labour Party literature. Currie's discussion makes clear that, whilst plenty of things might be done to affect the exchange rate over a relatively short period, there is no obvious way of making such policies effective over the long run.

Hattersley (1985) has more recently argued that a return to general exchange controls is implausible. In their place he proposes that the outflow of funds be stemmed by rigging the fiscal privileges of institutional investors against too large a commitment to foreign assets. This proposal is linked to the Labour Party idea of a National Investment Bank, and indeed is probably best considered as part of the Labour Party's policies for investment rather than for the exchange rate. Whatever the merits or otherwise of changing the portfolios of the major fundamental institutions, this is only one element determining international capital flows and hence the exchange rate (see further below).

So far in this chapter it has been suggested that if the policy proposed is one of exchange rate management, then trying to move to full membership of the E.M.S. makes sense, as long as this does not too greatly compromise reflationary objectives (and in the best of all worlds, membership would aid such objectives).

Such a focus on exchange rate management is in some respects appropriate for Britain, given the gyrations of the exchange rate recently experienced and its effects, especially in the first years of the Conservative government. (For the effects of this on competitiveness, see table 4.2.) However, both the S.D.P. and the Labour Party accept that whilst bad exchange rate policy can be harmful, its capacity for positive benefit is limited. In other words, other policies have to be pursued, alongside exchange rate management, to increase the international competitiveness of the British economy. For the S.D.P., such other policies involve a more successful participation in the international economy, broadly as currently constituted. They see no 'structural' inhibition to Britain becoming a more competitive producer in the current arrangements of the world economy. Policy should therefore focus on long-run supply-side programmes to increase efficiency; and indeed, central to such a policy for the S.D.P. is enhanced competition, including that from imports (see also chapter 5).

Table 4.2 Competitiveness of the British economy, 1975–84. Relative normalized unit labour costs in manufacturing.* (1980 = 100)

Year	Costs
1975	74.2
1976	68.7
1977	65.9
1978	70.0
1979	80.9
1980	100.0
1981	107.8
1982	104.6
1983	100.6
1984	95.3

* British labour costs relative to other major countries expressed in a common currency.

Source: *Economic Trends*

In contrast, the Labour Party sees the current structure of Britain's participation in the world economy as inherently un-favourable to a British recovery. Thus, fundamental to their approach to the international economy is a desire to 'dis-integrate' to some degree from that international economy. They therefore propose widespread import controls as a long-run policy. In addition, they propose controls over capital movements. The major emphasis here is not the desire to control the exchange rate, but the desire to control investment. The basic thrust of the argument is that as a result of the decisions of financial institutions and multinationals, Britain is losing investment funds which can and should be invested in Britain.

IMPORT CONTROLS

The proposal to impose widespread import controls in Britain derives a great deal of its intellectual support from the arguments of the Cambridge Economic Policy Group. So, although the Labour Party proposals are not the same as those of the C.E.P.G., and the differences are significant, some discussion of the C.E.P.G. arguments is very relevant to the Labour Party's general strategy of reducing the level of integration between Britain and the world economy.

The C.E.P.G. Model

The starting point of the C.E.P.G. analysis is the notion that the decline of U.K. industry relative to that of its competitors is a 'cumulative, interlocking process, in which a weak balance of trade has caused slow growth of aggregate demand, resulting in low investment and limiting opportunities for development of new products and increased productivity' (Moore *et al.*, 1978, p. 29). Thus the analysis is Keynesian in focusing on the demand problems caused by increasing import penetration, and the disincentive this provides to investment. Hence the central need is for policy to improve the trade balance and thereby increase demand, as the first step to reviving investment. Desiring a rapid and substantial improvement in the trade balance, the C.E.P.G. was critical of the cautious policies of the Labour government 1974–9, and even more sceptical about the supply-side policies of the present government. This leads to a choice between devaluation and general import controls as means of quickly altering the trade balance as employment expands.

Analytically, the two policies are similar, but the C.E.P.G. is known for its sustained view about the superiority of the import control policy. Fundamental to this preference is the assumption made about wages. In the C.E.P.G. model there is a target real wage which is determined essentially outside the economy, by indeterminate political processes. In the case of devaluation, the effect of this wage-setting process is that the devaluation feeds through into prices quite rapidly and hence into the rate of inflation (only partly offset by the fall in costs induced by higher capacity utilization). In contrast, the presumption is that with import controls, prices will not rise as real wages are not affected by the imposition of such controls.

As Hare (1980, p. 192), has noted:

this comparison is only so clear cut because of the model's implicit supposition that real wage targets held by workers are independent of government policy, which is surely neither rational nor plausible. For if workers anticipate that a policy of import controls will make the country (and presumably, therefore, themselves) better off, why should they fail to take that into account in their wage bargaining, for example, by anticipating a stronger demand for labour?

The other side of this coin is the presumption that, unlike under devaluation, workers would not have their real incomes squeezed by higher import prices; rather, it assumes that they are 'willing at prevailing prices to substitute back into domestic products when import controls are imposed' (1980, p. 195). This latter presumption seems to have been modified in more recent discussion, with the idea that the rise in prices caused by tariffs could be offset by tax cuts, financed by tariff revenues and higher taxes on the higher level of domestic incomes. (Indeed, the sharp preference for import controls over devaluation appears to have been modified in more recent discussions; see, e.g. Coutts *et al.*, 1982.)

Nevertheless, the heart of the C.E.P.G. programme still seems to be notions about real wages: that these are more or less immutable, and that they *should* be, at least in a downwards direction. This is logically coupled with either scepticism or hostility to incomes policies (see Tarling and Wilkinson, 1977 and 1982; Meade, 1981). This returns us directly to the issues discussed in chapter 3.

Purdy (1980) has offered a number of other pertinent criticisms of an import control strategy from a socialist viewpoint. He argues that whilst the C.E.P.G. (and the Labour Party, 1982B, p. 21) have stressed that the objective of such controls is not to cut the total level of imports, but to permit a planned growth, this is not an adequate response to those who say that such a strategy invites retaliation. First, it is too rationalistic, in assuming that in the context of discussions of trade barriers such a justification would carry much weight: 'Rationality would not necessarily prevail in the jostling for international advantage that would be likely to follow any major unilateral protectionist move by the U.K.' (Purdy, 1980, p. 68). In addition, even if *total* imports were to rise under such a strategy, some countries would be disadvantaged, and therefore likely to retaliate.

Given this, Purdy suggests that any policy of import controls would best be pursued via negotiation, which would inevitably be a slow process, rather than by the overnight erection of a protective shield around the British economy. He links this to the argument that general import controls involve a danger of shoring up industries which cannot be justified on their present scale; hence the need to start with a view of which industries are to be protected, then to see how far such protection can be negotiated, rather than starting from general import controls (a point returned to below).

Finally, Purdy (1980, p. 72) gives a useful twist to the standard welfare argument for free trade. Simply put, this says that consumer welfare will be maximized where consumers can buy from the cheapest source, thus pressing resources into their most efficient allocation. Such a view may well be heavily qualified in its practical application (though not out of existence), but it is undeniable that many consumers in Britain do perceive their ability freely to purchase imported manufactured goods as an important part of their welfare. This may not be a decisive argument against import controls, but it is an important warning against too cavalier an attitude to the consequences of an import control policy.

The Labour Approach

As already suggested, the Labour Party approach to import controls is not simply derived from the C.E.P.G. In particular, it stresses much more the causative role of low investment in Britain's economic decline, and hence emphasizes policy measures to raise the level of investment. Whilst the C.E.P.G. have assumed industrial policy, they have seen this essentially as supporting the import control policy. The problem which arises is that a focus on the supply side (investment) poses the issue of which sectors to expand, an issue not relevant where the focus is largely on the demand side. Labour policy is a rather uneasy amalgam of general import controls for balance of payments purposes and to provide a 'breathing space' for domestic expansion, with an acceptance of the need to discriminate between sectors in determining the degree of protection (Labour Party, 1982B, pp. 20–1). If, as suggested above, general import controls pose severe difficulties, does this mean that the emphasis should move to a more selective approach? As a broad perspective this seems to be right, but it faces at least two difficulties.

First, even those who have started from the view that selective controls are appropriate, such as the T.U.C., have been led to such a broad definition of those to be selected that very few are excluded (C.S.E./L.W.G., 1980, p. 97). This is not just a problem of the T.U.C. It indicates the general point that once selective controls are accepted as a principle of policy, there will be very strong pressures from a whole number of industries which for different reasons will be able to make a case for protection of their industry. There is no magic wand which will make this problem go away, but it must be emphasized that if a selective import controls strategy is to work, it must make hard choices about where the selectivity is to operate.

The second point is one derived from the literature of trade theory. This argues that if there is a case for protecting an industry to allow it to grow, this is best done by subsidy rather than by tariff or quota. There are two reasons for this. A subsidy has an explicit cost, unlike a tariff, the cost of which is always difficult to calculate. Socialists who are interested in public accountability and rational economic policy should take this point very seriously. Secondly, all of the cost of a tariff falls on the purchasers of the tariff-protected goods (they either pay the new higher price or buy an inferior substitute). However, if it is public policy to protect industry X, then there is no good reason why the costs of this should fall on consumers of industry X's products. A subsidy rather than a tariff will mean that the costs fall on all taxpayers instead.

Overall, the arguments on import controls may be summarized as follows. The C.E.P.G. was right to stress the limitations of devaluation as a means of altering the trade balance. Whilst sharp appreciations of the exchange rate may do great (and perhaps irreparable) damage, persistent devaluations will not act as a cure-all. Thus it is quite wrong to argue that 'a competitive exchange rate would also deal successfully with the group of difficulties which are sometimes described as "supply-side" problems' (Gould *et al.*, 1981, p. 193). Indeed, there is evidence that devaluation may exacerbate the problems in this regard, by sustaining and reinforcing Britain's emphasis on low-quality products (Brech and Stout, 1981).

However, the advantages of general import controls over devaluation seem to have been exaggerated, and their dificulties understated. Whilst C.E.P.G. advocacy of such a strategy was never as crude as some free-traders alleged, import controls came to have something of the panacea about them, and were used to divert attention from the more complex and lengthy problems of trying to improve Britain's capacity to compete in international markets. Improving trade competitiveness may well involve much more *dirigiste* policies than envisaged by the S.D.P., and include some import controls, but it seems difficult to justify giving them pride of place in the policy.

CONTROL OF CAPITAL FLOWS

For the Labour Party and the Left more generally (although not the S.D.P.), the advocacy of exchange controls is based on a much broader argument than simply a desire to manage the exchange rate (Labour Party 1982B, pp. 22–3, 44–5 and 1982D, pp. 21–2). Exchange controls are seen as part of a strategy to prevent capital outflows which are thought to be damaging to Britain's domestic level of investment. As Purdy notes (1980, p. 71), the argument that Britain's interests are being sacrificed on the altar of finance capital has a long, radical pedigree dating back to Hobson at the end of the nineteenth century. But this argument has been reinforced of late by three factors: first, the acceleration of Britain's economic decline and the Left's view that central to this has been the low level of investment (this general diagnosis is discussed in chapters 5 and 7); secondly, the abolition of exchange controls in 1979 and the subsequent outflows of funds (see table 4.3); thirdly, the growth of multinationals as agencies for this outflow of funds.

In the context of these kinds of arguments, Coakley and Harris (1983) have made a number of useful points. First, they make the vital distinction between the international flow of funds, and the process of real investment. In discussions of international invest-ment the focus is usually on financial flows which do not necessarily bear any relation at all to whether plant and equipment is constructed in the U.K. or abroad. Linked to this is the point that the balance of payments consequences of foreign investment may well be favourable, as the only, if rather dated, study of this question suggested (Reddaway, 1968).

Secondly, Coakley and Harris point out the important distinction between direct investment, such as I.C.I. constructing a chemical plant in West Germany, and portfolio investment, such as a pension fund acquiring already issued shares in a West German chemical company. These types of flow raise rather different issues. In the first case, it may be possible to argue that this investment decision could be undesirable for employment reasons (though see below) but that the capacity for alter such decisions may be very limited, given the abilities of multinationals to move funds around in pursuit of their global strategies. In any case, over the long term the vast bulk of funds for such investments is likely to be raised in the host country, West Germany, rather than in the home country, in which case the capacity of the home country to regulate is especially constrained.[4]

Table 4.3 Capital flows, 1973-83

	1973	1974	1975	1976	1977	1978	1979	1980	1981	1982	1983
Total overseas investment in U.K. (£m)	1,497	2,204	1,514	2,091	4,399	1,877	4,283	5,206	3,458	3,425	5,455
Total U.K. private investment overseas (£m)	1,760	1,148	1,367	2,269	2,334	4,604	6,802	8,033	10,660	10,724	10,560

Source: U.K. Balance of Payments (Pink Book), 1984

In the case of portfolio investment, the problem is rather different. Certainly, since the lifting of exchange controls in 1979 such investments have increased sharply. In the case of pension funds, whereas in 1979 8·7 per cent of acquisitions were overseas, in 1982 the figure was 28·5 per cent; for insurance companies the comparable figures were 6 per cent and 22 per cent (Coakley and Harris, 1983, p. 39).[5] The Bank of England has suggested that this is probably a once-and-for-all adjustment of portfolios to the desired domestic/foreign mix (B.E.Q.B., 1981). Even if this is not the case, the central issue remains whether such investments have significant impact on the domestic level of investment. In the simple sense of comparing behaviour before and after the abolition of exchange control the answer would seem that they do not. Before 1979 most institutional money went into property, government debt and already issued securities, so it is far from clear that the acquisition of foreign financial assets has in any straightforward way deprived British industry of funds which could be invested. The abolition of exchange controls may have had some small effect in raising the cost of funds to U.K. industry (Labour Party, 1982D, p. 21), but this is likely to have been marginal, given all the other forces acting on the interest rate, and in turn played a very small role in determining the level of investment.

Hattersley's (1985) proposal is for a greater proportion of institutional funds to be used for domestic investment via a National Investment Bank. As argued at greater length in chapter 7, such a bank may have a role as a support to an industrial policy which can generate projects requiring finance. In such circumstances, forms of capital market segregation such as this may be helpful, in reducing the costs of the subsidy paid by government for private-sector finance. But obviously such a view does not see the change in pension funds and insurance companies portfolios as the major cause of higher investment.

Coakley and Harris (1983, p. 43) make the important point that the flow of capital is in both directions, into and out of the British economy. Indeed between 1971 and 1977 the net flow was inwards. As they stress, the international flow of capital implies the increasing interconnection of the Western economies, within which multinationals are key institutions.

Multinational companies are the demons in many recent Left discussions of the economy (e g Holland, 1975, ch. 3; C.S.E./ L.W.G., 1980, pp. 104–8; Labour Party, 1977). I have argued elsewhere that these accounts tend to exaggerate the powers of multinationals, in the sense of overemphasizing both their capacity to attain global objectives and their power to inhibit government policy (Tomlinson, 1982, ch. 6). This response is based on the view that private companies have always been powerful *vis-à-vis* national governments, and whilst multinationality adds a new dimension to this, it does not create problems of a wholly new order. On the other hand, these arguments are not intended to imply that multinationals do not pose policy problems, even if the Left would seem commonly to exaggerate these.

Against the common tone of discussion on the Left about multinationals, it needs to be asserted that their activities can have positive as well as negative aspects. It is striking in the C.S.E./ L.W.G. book that when it is suggested that some of those who are employed by multinational companies might gain thereby, this is said to be because 'surplus value is transferred to monopoly capital from other sectors of the economy, enabling these companies to afford wage increases and remain profitable at the same time' (1980, p. 107). What such arguments notably fail to recognize is that, for Britain in particular, multinational companies represent a source of superior managerial organization and technologies, which can significantly raise the efficiency of production in the U.K. economy; they can also generate overall gains in efficiency by their international pattern of operations. The Left's failure to accept this seems to stem both from a general approach to capitalist enterprises which treats them as largely sites of the class struggle, in which any actual output appears as rather a by-product, and more specifically from a lack of concern with questions of managerial organization.[6] This latter is the other side of the coin to the focus on investment as the only apparent determinate of productive efficiency.

Multinationals are not, then, just agencies for sending British money abroad and playing off one national government against one another. On the first point, the positive aspects of some outward foreign investment are sometimes given grudging recognition (e.g. Labour Party, 1977, pp. 16–17; T.U.C., 1979, para. 86 and 1982), but these tend to get played down in general policy discussions, and the positive aspects of inward foreign investment are ignored.[7]

Clearly, multinationals do pose problems for national economic policy, in their capacity to relocate activity and to play off one government against another. The rapidity and ease of the first of these aspects should not be overstressed: 'overnight' departure of a multinational is extremely unusual (Labour Party, 1977, p. 37). The second aspect leads to the problem of trying to find supra-national bodies to regulate multinationals so as to reduce their capacity to do such things.

The Labour Party has always had a severe difficulty in this area, in that the one body which looks remotely likely to perform such a function is the E.E.C., yet the Labour Party has been hostile to this institution (although some movement is apparent on this since the general election of 1983). In 1977 the Labour Party pointed to the Treaty of Rome with its free-market philosophy as likely to prevent any role for the E.E.C. in regulating multinationals (Labour Party, 1977, pp. 75–6). But as subsequent events have shown, the Treaty was not brought down on tablets of stone, and the E.E.C. Commission has provided a number of initiatives which have been more 'interventionist' than the conservative national governments of the Community would like. In particular, the Commission has proposed policies on information disclosure by companies and employee involvement in their management which would provide a starting point for Labour's policies on the corporate sector, and which have been strongly resisted by multinational and other companies (D.E./D.T.I., 1983).

Unfortunately, Labour support for such proposals has hardly been vociferous. The Labour Party accepts the need for 'concerted international action', but the only practical proposal is that 'every assistance will be given to trade unions in their attempts to organise on an international basis' (Labour Party 1982B, p. 45). Whilst international trade union co-ordination is desirable and important, it cannot replace the need for an enforceable regulatory framework for multinationals which is most likely to be attained (though not easily) by working through the E.E.C.

Such points are not made to challenge the case for a Foreign Investment Unit to monitor inward and outward investment, as proposed by the Labour Party (Labour Party, 1977, p. 52; 1982B, p. 44). It is perfectly sensible to monitor and attempt to regulate some aspects of the activities of multinationals and of course to make them subject to whatever policies are applied to purely British companies. Some things can be done at the national level, but much more could be done to bring about international action, especially within the E.E.C. The crucial point argued here is that it is of no help in such policies either to exaggerate the powers of multinationals or to treat them as having wholly negative consequences for the domestic economy.

CONCLUSIONS

The starting point for most Left discussion of Britain's inter-national economic policy is the need to regenerate British industry and especially British manufacturing. This point is powerfully made by the C.E.P.G. (Coutts *et al.*, 1982, p. 2).

> The loss of traditional industries has already made Britain a depressed and divided country. If manufacturing continues to be squeezed out of both home and overseas markets at anything like the past rate, there is no plausible growth rate of earnings from the export of services and technology that will rescue Britain from severe recession within the next two decades. On the contrary the trends imply that the living standards of a growing fraction of the population will deteriorate, the more so in the 1990s when offshore oil and gas production eventually goes into decline.

Whilst one may disagree with some of the analysis of the C.E.P.G., their supposedly pessimistic prognoses have largely been justified in the past, and on current policies this one looks likely to be equally correct.

In responding to this situation, it would be possible to divide the Left's policies into three stark choices. The first would be broadly to maintain the character of Britain's participation in the world economy, but in the short run to reflate, and in the longer run to pursue policies to raise British efficiency (S.D.P.).

The second choice would be to reflate but at the same time move towards dis-integrating Britain from the world economy by extensive capital and trade controls (Labour Party). Thirdly, one could argue that nothing can be done to improve things until the arrival of socialism (some Marxists).

Leaving aside the third approach, the difference between the S.D.P. and the Labour Party is probably posed too sharply. It is perfectly possible to combine a broad continuation of the current kind of economic integration (in the sense of generally free trade and regulated but substantial movement of capital) with quite radical measures to improve the performance of the British economy within that context.

At the same time, in looking at the international economy, and especially international capital flows, it is useful to try to differentiate between policies aimed directly at the current balance of payments and those intended, for example, to affect the level of productive investment. The days when a sharp line could be drawn between speculative short-term capital flows and long-term investment are now gone. But the distinction still has some validity in the sense that some measures can be aimed to regulate the former, some the latter. An interest equalization tax, for example, is a possible way of trying to deter too much short-term capital movement. As Currie (1982, pp. 239–40) points out, such policies would hardly be new in the international economy, but they do have the unpalatable implication that if operated to hold the currency up as well as down, both foreign and domestic holders of sterling would have to be compensated for the interest forgone in holding foreign deposits. In any case, such policies need to be sharply distinguished from the role of a foreign investment unit set up to monitor multinational investment in real assets.

One further conclusion emerges from the arguments of this chapter. For good or ill, Britain now appears inevitably to be a member of the E.E.C. The recognition of this should be coupled with a realistic but positive assessment of the possibilities this affords British policy. In particular, it provides a framework for international economic co-operation which, at the very least, would make any of the Left's plans enormously easier to attain.

On a rather different plane is the argument about what to do 'when the oil runs out'. Here is an area where it is likely that the dangers of the current *laissez-faire* attitudes will be exposed. North Sea oil has, over the last decade, shielded the balance of payments, and hence the standard of living, from the consequences of the continuing decline in manufacturing competitiveness (as well as playing a small part in the exacerbation of that decline) (see table 4.4). Here the government's view seems to be that exchange rate movements will deal with any problems unsolved by their own policies for improved competitiveness. (On this issue, see Smith, 1984, especially ch. 5).

Table 4.4 The importance of North Sea oil to the balance of payments (£million)

	Mid-1970s (average of 1974/5/6)	1983
Visible balance (including oil)	−4204	− 716
Invisible balance	+2325	+3632
Net imports (−) or exports (+) of oil	−2435	+6875

Source: *U.K. Balance of Payments* (Pink Book)

Plainly, this problem must be taken seriously by any political party aiming to govern Britain in the late 1980s and the 1990s. It involves specific problems, such as how an exchange rate target is to be adjusted under such circumstances. But more generally, it gives an urgency to debates in the area of international economic policy (as well as, of course, policies on efficiency) which, this chapter suggests, are a long way from clear formulation, let alone resolution, for most people on the Left.

5
The Left and the Supply Side

INTRODUCTION

Accompanying the monetarism of the Thatcher government has been an emphasis on reforming the 'supply side' of the economy. This derives from the belief that the performance of the 'real' economy in the long run cannot be affected by macroeconomic policies, but only by measures which increase the efficiency with which labour and capital are mobilized and used.[1] For the Conservative government this has meant a particular focus on making the labour market work more efficiently, and on privatizing various kinds of economic activity, as a way of making product and capital markets function with greater efficiency. Even if the Conservatives' dismissal of demand management is rejected, and it is believed that governments both can and should have policies affecting the level of output and employment, this does not mean that emphasis on the supply side can be dismissed out of hand. The case for macroeconomic management is not that it provides all the conditions necessary for efficient economic activity, let alone other economic goals that might exist. Equally, because Thatcher's supply-side policies have had very particular emphases, with which the Left has little sympathy, this does not mean that other supply side policies have not been advocated and to some extent pursued by the Left.

'Supply side' is a very ambiguous term, and can be used to describe radically different kinds of policies. On the Left, as on the Right, these policies derive in part from perceptions of the shortcomings of demand management. Most radically, for many Marxists, the whole of the notion of demand management in a capitalist economy is mistaken, changes in the rate of profit rather than government policy fundamentally determining the path of the economy (e.g. Glyn and Harrison, 1980; Militant, 1981, pp. 10–

11; Glyn, 1978, ch. 1). In contrast, the S.D.P., whilst remaining a strong advocate of demand management, has also stressed the constraints on such management and the need for additional policies (S.D.P., 1983A). However in this area (unlike in macro policy) the S.D.P. policies are closer to Thatcher policies than to others further to the Left. The emphasis is on competition, both in product and labour markets (though with notably more emphasis on retraining than the Conservatives). In fact, one can say that the S.D.P. is committed to a more radical pro-competition industrial policy than the Conservatives have actually carried out. Because of their desire to massage the P.S.B.R. downwards, the Conservatives have privatized industries, sometimes at the expense of enhancing competition (Cairncross *et al.*, 1982). In addition, the S.D.P. is more sceptical about centralized government industrial policy of the kind commonly advocated elsewhere on the Left, the policies put forward being notably less 'interventionist' than those of the Labour Party (S.D.P., 1983B, 1984; see also chapter 7).

In contrast, the Labour Party's policies have been characterized by a belief both that capitalism can be tamed by the state, and that the state can successfully pursue policies on the supply side. The overall character of these policies is well summarized by the title of a major recent Labour Party document in this area, *Economic Planning and Industrial Democracy* (Labour Party, 1982A). The policies attempt to combine two elements, the first being the traditional Left focus on an enhanced state role, putting forward planning instead of workings of the market. On the other hand, it is seen as necessary to respond to the criticism advanced against traditional state planning and nationalization – that it is undemocratic. Thus 'planning and democracy' attempts to combine increased state, rather than market, allocation of resources, with accountability, both to society in general, but especially to the workforce in enterprises.

Such policies have, in a very limited sense, been put into action by local authorities in recent years, and some discussion of this is offered below. Overall, this chapter will give most attention to the Labour Party proposals, both because they have, on this limited scale, been translated into action, but also more generally, because they are the most fully developed alternative programmes to Thatcherism (unlike in macroeconomic policy, where the S.D.P. has the most detailed programme). First of all, however, the chapter looks in more detail at the Marxist and S.D.P. arguments and proposals.

MARXISM AND THE SUPPLY SIDE

For Marxists, the problems of the British economy derive essentially from the general problems of capitalism. For Glyn and Harrison (1980), for example, the fundamental problem is one of 'over-accumulation' in relation to the supply of labour. In other words, capital accumulation requires wages to be high enough to provide an outlet for industry's products, but not so high as to threaten profits (Glyn and Harrison, 1980, pp. 27–8). For Glyn and Harrison this delicate balance was upset from the late 1960s across the whole world economy, and developed into the economic crises of the 1970s. Thus, the central economic problem is the relative strength of class forces (capitalists and workers) and the effects of this balance on profitability and hence investment, productivity and growth.

As so often in Marxist economic discussion, Glyn and Harrison jump from extremely broad concepts about capitalism in general, to highly specific features of national economies, with little to explain how these very different kinds of analysis are to be linked. There is a particular problem for such analyses when they address Britain's economic decline. The whole framework suggests the worldwide nature of the slow-down in capitalist economies, but the authors have to link to this the very particular character of Britain's relative decline. Thus, after putting forward a rather *ad hoc* list of factors which may have affected Britain's competitiveness since 1945, they conclude lamely that 'It is impossible to disentangle the various factors discussed above, or to gauge the relative importance of these contributions to the decline of U.K. competitiveness' (1980, p. 51). This is coupled with the argument that once a pattern of low growth became established 'it developed its own dynamic' (p. 51), which hardly takes the argument forward.

Militant (1981A, pp. 3–7) similarly offers a number of *ad hoc* factors in a rather different list emphasizing, for example, arms expenditure in Britain. Glyn (1978) is more single-minded in focusing on the fall in profitability as the cause of Britain's problems, but then (rightly) points out that the fall in profits has been general to the capitalist economies since the mid-1960s. Thus, this factor can serve as an explanation for the general problems of the world economy, but not as an explanation for Britain' peculiar difficulties.

The solutions offered for Britain's economic problems follow the diagnosis, in being essentially attuned to a 'general capitalist crisis', rather than closely linked to specific British conditions. The standard Marxist solution is nationalization, planning and workers' democracy, though with most emphasis on the planning aspect. Planning is seen as essentially a technical process (Glyn and Harrison, pp. 166–7; Glyn, 1978, pp. 23–4). In the Marxist view, it is technically possible for an economy to be planned from the centre, with implementation then passed on to committees of worker and other representatives at enterprise level (Glyn and Harrison, pp. 167–8; Glyn, pp. 67–71). These arguments are staggeringly naïve.

Whatever other lessons may be drawn from past attempts at comprehensive planning, notably the Soviet experiences, it seems clear that a (if not the) major lesson is that planning can never be treated as a purely technical exercise (e.g. Nove, 1983, part II). It is not just that setting planning targets involves inherently political arguments over priorities, but the actual implementation is a political process. Planning is, in fact, never simply directive, but always involves a greater or lesser degree of negotiation 'up and down' the planning hierarchy. This is inescapable where production units have *any* automony, and a complex economy without such autonomy is inconceivable. Hence, planning must always involve problems of bargaining, arguments over the content and use of information, divergent sites of decision-making etc. This is not to argue that planning is always a chimera. Directed to specific problems (such as large-scale resource transfers), planning is undoubtedly a powerful weapon. But to present it as a technical device and panacea for all economic problems is absurd. (On planning in Britain, see chapter 7).

Equally naïve is the view that workers' democracy would straightforwardly contribute to a rise in productivity (1980, p. 170). Again, worker's democracy is not seen as setting up a whole series of new political arenas, where different policies would be fought over and only messily and temporarily resolved, as it is argued it should be, in chapter 7. Rather, workers' democracy represents, in effect, the means by which the consensus that socialism is assumed to bring about can be registered. This is a highly apolitical view of democracy, which appears to ignore all the complexities of attempting to establish greater economic democracy, (as, for example, in Yugoslavia, see Lydall, 1984). It also makes huge assumptions about the consensus that would emerge simply from the process of nationalization and the construction of mechanisms of workers' control.

Plainly, this kind of analysis is linked to the whole Leninist analysis of politics, which fails to take seriously the mechanisms of democracy. Indeed, the analysis of workers' democracy by Marxists often has the same Utopianism as Lenin's analysis of political democracy (Hindess, 1983; Polan, 1984).

THE S.D.P. AND THE SUPPLY SIDE

The S.D.P. position is compounded of a highly political analysis of Britain's present economic difficulties, and some very orthodox economic analysis. The highly political component is a stress on the damaging effects of the two-party system and its ties to the unions and big business. This is seen as having generated both seesaw government policies and excessively conflictual industrial relations, both harmful to economic performance. (Though see Cairncross *et al.*, 1982, p. 13, who explicitly deny such a seesaw in industrial policy.)

The two-party system is obviously the 'mould' which the S.D.P. aims to break, especially via the introduction of proportional representation. But on the more specific question of policies designed to enhance economic performance, these can broadly be divided into two – more competition, and industrial democracy (S.D.P., 1983B).

More competition is seen as important in both product and labour markets. For product markets, the arguments derive from the traditional Keynesian economic view that if demand management is used to maintain the fullest possible use of resources, the market mechanism provides the best means of allocation of resources. This market mechanism is said to have been undermined both by government intervention and regulation, and by the growth of private monopoly and restrictive practices. Hence the S.D.P. wants both public and private sectors to be subject to much greater competition. The negative side of this is a quite strong hostility to the kinds of directive industrial policies that pre-Thatcher governments of either political party have pursued.

What may be criticized in the S.D.P. approach is its postulate of a contradiction between greater competition and an enhanced state role. It may be argued that there is a case for both. The point about market competition is that its existence is not a 'natural' phenomenon, ever-present unless governments or others prevent it. It can be the objective of government policy to create competition, and indeed such a policy (via, for example, a much strengthened Monopolies Commission) would have plain advantages in Britain's highly concentrated industrial structures.

Equally, a strong case can be made for industrial policy in the sense of attempting to formulate (loose) strategies for which industrial sectors should be expanded (and which contracted) and how this can be done. There is no necessary contradiction between these two policies. Focusing on particular sectors, and, say, providing government aid to such sectors, has no necessary implications for competition in that sector, and may well enhance competition if it means building up British companies against monopolistic foreign suppliers.

The S.D.P. is equally keen on increased competition in labour markets, and this has led it to support much of the legislation on unions under the Thatcher government. As already noted, the conceptual basis of this policy is the idea that the unions are essentially monopolies, and like corporate monopolies, prevent the best allocation of resources, in their case of labour. This is obviously a very traditional economists' analysis of unions. What it fails to recognize is that unions not only impinge on the allocation of labour, but, more importantly, they impinge on its organization within production processes. In other words, unions are supported by management in many cases because they offer a means of organizing the consent of workers to production proccesses, provide forums for negotiation that any production process requires, and generally play a positive, as well as sometimes a negative role, in the efficient organization of the modern enterprise.

Thus the S.D.P. has a partial and unbalanced view of the role of the unions in the economy. In addition, even in terms of the allocation of labour, it is very doubtful if the labour market functions like the 'ideal market', whether or not unions exist. For example, the allocation of labour seems to be much less affected by relative wage rates than such mechanism would imply. (e.g. Routh, 1980, p. 184; see also discussion in chapter 3). Hence the effects of unions, even if they acted as the S.D.P. suggests, would be far less than implied.

The other plank of the S.D.P. programme is industrial democracy (S.D.P., 1983D and 1982A). Here an explicit objective of the policy is to undercut Britain's excessively class-bound and conflict-ridden industrial relations, effectively by legitimizing management; this would be achieved by giving workers new democratic rights in the enterprise. The enterprise is conceived in a 'unitary'[2] fashion, with industrial democracy as a means of reducing obstruction to existing management practices put up by obdurate workforces. Leaving aside any question about whether this deserves the name democracy, an issue raised in chapter 7, it means an acceptance that existing management would, if allowed to, pursue the best possible policies, although this should be done in less authoritarian, more participatory, fashion. This seems to run against the evidence that existing management strategies and practices are at least part of the problem of the British economy and need themselves to be reformed. These comments are not intended to suggest that there are any easy solutions to the design and implementation of industrial democracy strategies in Britain (a point returned to below in discussing the Labour Party proposals). However, the S.D.P. does not seem to take seriously the question of challenging in some way or another existing managerial practices. The rhetoric of partnership and co-operation slides over this fundamental issue.

THE LABOUR PARTY AND THE SUPPLY SIDE

After the defeat in the general election of 1970, there was a concerted effort by the Labour Party to formulate policies which would avoid all the errors perceived to have been committed in 1964–70. One aspect of this was the formulation of new policies which may be called supply side, usually under the heading of 'industrial strategy', though tied to a whole Alternative Economic Strategy (Labour Party, 1973). The main thrusts of the policies formulated then have remained into the 1980s.

The industrial strategy included both a diagnosis of what is wrong with Britain's economy and specific policy solutions to these problems. The diagnosis was composed both of very general formulations about the functioning of the economy and of much more specific elements. A major contribution to the arguments was Stuart Holland's work, especially his *The Socialist Challenge* (see on this, Tomlinson, 1982, ch. 6). Central to such work was the proposal of profit-seeking as the centrepiece of the capitalist economy, instead of 'social need' as a socialist objective. This provided a general rationale for state intervention in the economy, that intervention being seen as representing the imposition of social need on profit-oriented firms.

One point which emerges from this dichotomy between profit and need is that it does not recognize the possibility that profit-oriented behaviour may, one way or another, serve needs; this is the traditional argument of the 'invisible hand'. Indeed, an explicit critique of the invisible hand is strikingly absent from most Left economic argument, though such a repudiation would seem central to attacks on the profit mechanism. (On this, see Sen, 1983A). A partial attack on this notion is inherent in the view that modern capitalism is not competitive (plainly a pre-condition for the invisible hand argument) – the concept of monopoly capitalism. However, this is a very inadequate notion, because it is usually based on the view that big firms (undoubtedly very important in Britain) are monopolies. But of course size *per se* is not an index of monopoly, and indeed effective competition may be very fierce with only two or three firms in a market.

This general ideological background is normally tied to the view that the specific problem of British capitalism is lack of investment in domestic activity, especially manufacturing. The standard argument (though this is an area rich with 'variations on a theme') is that British investment is excessively short-term, oriented towards foreign assets and domestically, towards property speculation. Commonly, the analysis is tied to the view that the fault for this lies very much with the financial institutions – the City – which is both excessively foreign-oriented and excessively short-sighted and risk-averse when looking at possible investment in Britain. Thus Left-wing supply-side policies in Britain have usually included calls for nationalization or other radical reforms of Britain's financial system. (Labour Party, 1976; Thompson, 1977; Minns, 1982 and 1983), in order to raise the level of investment. This is coupled to the advocacy of a body like the National Enterprise Board, which has a similar function.

This focus on raising the level of investment is linked to the argument about the need to control the activities of large firms, leading to the policy instrument of planning agreements. Around the time of the general election of 1974, such agreements were trumpeted as the central features of the new Labour Party policies. They united the Right, who saw them (rightly) as a Crosland-inspired alternative to the nationalization they opposed, and the Left, who saw them as a stepping stone to that nationalization. They were to involve negotiation between large firms and government, resulting in an agreement which would specify the firms' intentions in investment, and especially in employment. The government, for its part, would provide aid to firms in pursuit of these objectives. Thus, one way of regarding such agreements was that they would make firms accountable for the large sums of public money they received. From the Left's point of view the major purpose was, however, to use such accountability to make sure that investment was increased.

Planning agreements were also viewed as extending the unions' role, by making them party to corporate decision-making, though the extent of their involvement was one of the many ambiguities about planning agreements (Department of Industry, 1975; Forester, 1978). Thus they could be fitted in with the rhetoric about increased industrial democracy which has also been a part of the industrial policy of the Labour Party since the late 1960s.

This framework of policy argument raises a number of questions and difficult issues. As already noted, there are very broad questions about the character of modern capitalist economies lying behind the specific policy formulations. However, in the context of this book it is appropriate to focus mainly on the more specific policy issues, though these cannot be readily detached from the general background with which they are intertwined.

First of all there is the issue of whether or not the fundamental problem of Britain's relative inefficiency is due to lack of investment, as Labour Party proposals suggest. One aspect of the argument is that this deficiency arises especially in manufacturing industry, which is seen as a privileged sector of economic activity. Why manufacturing should be seen as privileged over services or other kinds of economic activity is not always clear, though in fact a good case can be made for his.[3] This argument would rest on the fact that manufacturing has a central, irreplaceable part in Britain's exports, and equally on the links between manufacturing and overall economic growth (Williams *et al.*, 1983, pp. 2–16; Hughes, 1982).

But has lack of investment in manufacturing been crucial to its poor performance? The simple answer to this question would seem to be that low investment has played a role, but that it is far from clear that it has been crucial. If one looks at investment in manufacturing over the long run (table 5.1), then Britain does rank very low. But equally, from table 5.2 it is clear that Britain is also characterized by a low efficiency in the use of investment. Table 5.2 is based on extremely aggregated data, and the procedure of compiling such data, especially the measurement of

Table 5.1 Per capita fixed gross capital formation, 1960–77 (in sterling)

Year	U.K.	France	West Germany	Italy	U.S.A.	Japan
1960	100	121.2	141.5	69.7	219.3	61.4
1965	100	147.3	152.8	63.6	197.8	81.4
1970	100	159.6	192.0	89.7	203.3	162.3
1975	100	180.7	171.9	79.4	141.8	165.2
1977	100	203.6	219.9	86.4	190.3	229.9

Source: M. Blume, 'The Financial Markets' in R. E. Caves and L. B. Krause (eds), *Britain's Economic Performance*, Brookings, 1980, table 2

Table 5.2 Relation of investment to growth in output, 1970–7

Country	% change in per capita G.D.P.	% of G.D.P. devoted to capital formation	Ratio of column 1 to column 2
U.K.	10.0	19.4*	0.52
U.S.A.	15.6	17.6	0.89
Japan	17.3	33.5	0.52
France	25.0	23.5	1.06
West Germany	18.8	23.4	0.80
Italy	21.3	20.6	1.03

* Note that this figure is not much out of line with those of the other countries listed: this is compatible with the low absolute figures for investment (table 5.1) because of the relatively low level of G.D.P.

Source: As table 5.1, table 3

capital, is very complex and controversial. Nevertheless, it would seem to fit in with other evidence of the poor performance of British firms even when investment levels are similar to those of competitors (C.P.R.S., 1975; Pratten, 1976).

A curiosity of argument on the Left in Britain has been the focus on explaining why, rather than whether, investment has been low. (e.g. Murray, 1983; Minns, 1983). Nevertheless the argument about why has been central to the proposed reforms. By and large, the Labour Party has rejected the simplistic view that low investment has been due in a very straightforward way to low profits. This is the common view of the 'apologetic marginalist or the apocalyptic Marxist' (Williams *et al.*, 1983, p. 64), and rests on the unacceptable assumption that the 'rate of profit' is a simple, obvious category which everyone measures alike and which conveys an unambiguous meaning. As Williams (pp. 66–7) emphasizes, profits may be seen as a dependent variable of investment strategies rather than as a cause, thus reversing the common line of argument. Nevertheless, there is a general perception that low profits in British manufacturing under current conditions (including financing conditions) are part of the explanation for low investment, and cannot be ignored by 'alternative strategies'.

If lack of investment in manufacturing is not the crucial aspect of Britain's poor economic performance, this is not to say that there is no case for reform in this area; but it does call into question the priority some Left strategies give to such reform.

The character of the problem needs to be carefully defined. Britain's pattern of finance of industry has long been different from that of other advanced capitalist (O.E.C.D.) countries. Until the mid-1970s, British companies were much more dependent on ploughed-back profits than foreign competitors (Wilson, 1977, vol. 2). Within the proportion externally financed, the contribution from the banks was very small in Britain, again in comparison with competitors. But the contribution of the stock exchange was also very small, many new issues being exchanged not for new money but for the paper of other companies which were being taken over.

This dependence on internal funding has become increasingly problematic as profitability has declined. External funding has, however, increased sharply since the early 1970s, mainly from the banks. This has been accompanied by substantial changes in the banks' lending practices, which are now geared to lending for much longer periods (in any case, overdrafts could usually be rolled-over, making them in effect long-term loans). Hence the common criticism of the early 1970s, that banks lend too little to British industry and that this is because of their short-term orientation, has been to a considerable extent undermined by the events of the last dozen years.

However, the criteria of loan-giving by banks may be a more fundamental problem than the commonly asserted short-term orientation. The American banks (who in many ways pioneered the revolution in bank lending practices in Britain) have argued that the fundamental problem of most British banking is that it is concerned with the assessment of potential borrowers' liquidation value. This means that when a bank looks at a firm, its security is the saleable value of the firm's assets, not its potential as a going concern. Thus, lending money with this approach is not oriented towards the flow of funds accruing to the firm from the project for which the money is lent, leading to a financial package geared to that particular flow (American Banks Association, 1977). In a strong sense British banks do not have sufficient knowledge of British industry to make the appropriate kind of assessment of financing needs, so they commonly rely on extremely crude and conservative measures. Williams *et al.* (1983, p. 70) have also argued that this liquidation approach is conditioned by the English legal system's emphasis on giving privilege to creditors who take security as fixed assets, and by the limited disclosure of information by British companies which inhibits more flexible financial packages.

Whilst the banks have slowly reformed themselves in some, though arguably not the most fundamental, respects, radical changes have occured and continue to take place in the share market. These changes have been very diverse in their implications, but the analyses and proposals of the Left in this area are remarkable by their absence. Because of the Left's focus on financial institutions as providers of industrial finance, coupled with a general concern about ownership of capital, most discussion of the stock market by the Left has focused on the rise of the institutional investor. Today a majority of U.K. companies' shares are owned by pension funds, insurance companies and other collective bodies, who have bought most of the shares of individual shareholders over the last twenty-five years (Wilson, 1980, chs 4–6; Minns, 1980, ch. 1). This process has a number of implications, but it certainly does not seem to have led to any greater focus on the cash purchase of British industrial companies' new issues, large sums going into property, financial institutions, and especially since 1979, into foreign investment.

The rise of the pension funds has raised issues other than that of investment in manufacturing (though that has been a major focus of concern) and there are divergent approaches to reform in this area. Minns (1980, 1982, 1983) has argued that not only are the vast sums of pension funds not used in a manner which is either beneficial or accountable to their contributors and beneficiaries, but also the *de facto* control of the shares owned by these funds is mainly in the hands of the merchant and clearing banks, and stockbrokers (Minns, 1982, pp. 10–14). He uses this point to argue that the nationalization of the City institutions would therefore give control over a large part of British industry via these shareholdings.

Labour Party policy has been less radical in its proposals, advocating that pension funds be required to invest some proportion of their funds in a National Investment Bank, aimed at regenerating British manufacturing industry (Wilson, 1980, Labour Party, 1982, para. 68).

Minns has rightly stressed the importance of the practices of financial institutions to investment in manufacturing, as against, for example, Murray's simplistic emphasis on profitability, and the need to 'restructure for labour' (Minns, 1983; Murray, 1983). Nevertheless Minns's argument, though including the need for an 'alternative investment strategy' (1982, p. 84) still rests fundamentally on the presumption that the key to Britain's poor industrial performance lies in the level of investment. As already suggested, this argument is weak. Before returning to it, however, there is the very important issue of industrial democracy.

Industrial Democracy

As already emphasized, the planning-agreements systems combined an emphasis on the state's role in increasing investment, with a plan to bring unions into greater prominence in corporate planning. This reflected one aspect of the increased emphasis on industrial democracy within Labour Party (and other Left) arguments in the last fifteen to twenty years.

Industrial democracy does not necessarily have much to do with industrial policy and the supply side. Industrial democracy could be argued solely on political grounds, as an extension of workers' rights (as in Bullock, 1977, conclusions). However, while this rhetoric of rights has been employed on the Left, it has in most cases been coupled with the view that industrial democracy will enhance industrial efficiency and thus will form a crucial part of a strategy for steering Britain's economic decline. For example in the Labour Party/T.U.C. document *Economic Planning and*

Industrial Democracy, para. 6, it is argued that 'Accountability in economic decision making is not an inefficient luxury but is essential for improving our economic performance.' The argument is pursued at greater length by Hodgson (1984, ch. 9).

Two general points can be made about this coupling of industrial democracy and economic efficiency. First, it makes democracy a means rather than an end in itself. This must necessarily make the case for democracy more fragile, as it can be argued (and has in this case been argued) that industrial democracy will reduce efficiency (e.g. Chiplin *et al.*, 1977). Secondly, the link between democracy and efficiency, whilst plausible in some contexts, may well not be a universal rule. This is especially so if that democracy involves not only greater participation in existing organizations, but the development of new organizations with potentially new objectives (see Hodgson, 1984, ch. 9). Overall, the tying of industrial democracy to efficiency looks like a dubious political strategy. In addition to the above two points, it makes 'democratization' look much more like a smooth, consensual process than would appear to be justified. Radical democratization of industry would be likely to lead to new kinds of conflict and disputes not readily resolved into productivity-enhancing harmony.

The other aspect of industrial democracy in the Labour Party programme which needs to be discussed is the emphasis on the unions as the channel for that democracy (Labour Party, 1982, paras 127–8). This follows the recommendations of Bullock (1977), and for broadly the same reasons. These are three-fold, the first being that separate channels of representation 'would lead to confusion and division which would be bad for industrial relations and would enable employers to play off one group of representatives against another'. Second, they would 'remove a primary source of strength, expertise and information' provided by unions. Thirdly, they would undermine 'the objective of linking planning to industrial democracy by dividing and separating – rather than linking and strengthening – workers' input to decision-making at all the relevant levels' (Labour Party, 1982, para. 128).

Of course the commitment of the Labour Party to single-channel representation is not just a function of the strength of these arguments. It also reflects a realistic assessment that the hostile to lukewarm attitudes of most unions in Britain to industrial democracy are likely to turn into a complete refusal if unions are denied the central role (Elliott, 1978). Nevertheless, this political calculation poses a severe difficulty. For if unions are lukewarm or hostile to industrial democracy even if it is based on unions, what is likely to be their role in newly democratized companies? It is a good point to make that unions provide an organizational base for the formulation of strategies for companies and sectors. But it is far from clear that unions have either the will or the resources to use that base to advance rather than retard experiments in industrial democracy. This is especially a problem when it is noted that a great deal of union doubt about industrial democracy is based on a dislike of *any* management role for unions, whilst thoroughgoing industrial democracy would require precisely such a role.

Whilst the S.D.P. proposals on industrial democracy seem designed to legitimize existing industrial management practices, the Labour Party proposals seem likely to stifle the experimentation which a radical programme of industrial democracy should entail. Whilst the political obstacles appear almost insuperable, what seems to be required is some capacity, some agency for the formulation of alternative management strategies, which is not tied too closely to the unions, though its expertise could be 'bought in' by unions if required. Plainly, in many large manufacturing companies unions are so strong that any organization of industrial democracy would *de facto* be based on unions, but some opening needs to be preserved, so that the growth of industrial democracy (always likely to be a tender plant in British soil) is not stifled by a union monopoly. This is not to deny the scope for an enhancement of union powers, for example in relation to information disclosure; it is, however, to suggest that industrial democracy cannot just be an enhancement of traditional collective bargaining, but must provide the possibility of a qualitative break with existing bargaining practices.

Recent Labour Party policy continues the advocacy of planning agreements, although these are now retitled 'agreed development plans'. However, the policy tries to take into account the lessons of the experiments with the Labour policies of the 1970s. These are said to include the lack of support for the policies in Whitehall, the lack of leverage by governments on companies and the failure to link aid to companies with the planning procedures. Above all, however, the criticism is made that 'the role envisaged for workers and their trade union representatives was not clearly formulated' (Labour Party, 1982, para. 64).

This kind of criticism was the one forcefully made by some trade union organizations in the 1970s period of Labour government (Joint Trades Councils, 1982). Also, the enthusiasm for 'planning from below' has been enhanced by the Lucas shop stewards' attempt to formulate an alternative strategy for their corporation (Wainwright and Elliott, 1982).

It clearly was the case that the role of unions in the industrial policy was extremely ambiguous in the 1974–9 period, and became downgraded after Varley took over from Benn at the Department of Industry in 1975. Equally, the Lucas plan does represent a most interesting attempt at formulating an alternative strategy for a large corporation.

However, it is far from clear that a greater union role in planning would be as straightforward as the advocates of popular planning would suggest. First, the Lucas shop stewards were plainly atypical in being able to draw upon a wide range of 'white-collar' expertise from within their workforces, and it is far from clear that such a reservoir of talent committed to such 'alternative' projects exists in many companies. Union input into strategies in other industries, such as coal and steel, seems to have been much less imaginative and based on understandable but highly dubious plans for expansion.

This is perhaps the crux of the matter, for governments in formulating industrial strategies cannot simply accept calls for expansion all round. If the strategy is to be successful, it must involve reductions as well as expansions in some sectors. Thus no amount of incantation of democracy can obviate the need for painful measures and for, in some cases, policy to run against the wishes of the workforce involved.

This is not to deny the case for a much greater role by unions in both the formulation and implementation of industrial strategy; but it is to suggest that the idea of planning as simply the creation of a national plan from the aggregation of plans generated at each company is highly implausible. Thus, for example, the Joint Trades Council document (1982, p. 147) argues 'it is workers' industrial and social organizations which have the potential power to control and eventually socialize private capital. The role, then, of a socialist government should be to provide a back-up, a means of co-ordinating and generalizing this paper and the initiatives which it creates'. Like the Marxist arguments cited above, such a view depoliticizes planning, though in a rather different manner, by the rhetoric of democracy.

LOCAL EFFORTS

Pioneering attempts by local authorities to regenerate their local economies have been a striking feature of the early 1980s. These attempts emerge from a similar ideological stable to the broader national plans outlined above, but from a very different organizational context.

Local authorities in Britain have, since at least the Second World War, played some economic development role. But up until the early 1970s this was mainly confined to the provision of industrial sites and premises, and advertising to attract firms from elsewhere to their locality (Minns and Thornley, 1978; Boddy, 1983). Such activity was fairly low-key until the rise in unemployment forced a change of thinking in the early and mid-1970s. (Though specially created regional bodies had been playing a more direct role in Northern Ireland and the Highlands for example.) In London, Southwark in 1975, Wandsworth in 1976 and Hackney in 1977 took employment initiatives (Gough *et al.*, 1981), and a similar timing and pattern is evident in West Yorkshire (Mawson, 1983).

Most of these initiatives focused on employment retention and creation, and did not involve any overall strategy for the local economy. Such initiatives were encouraged by the Labour government of 1974–9, the Department of the Environment sending out a circular in 1977 (71/77), for the first time locating local problems as part of national economic problems, and stressing the need for co-ordinated economic activity (Young, 1983). Funding for such policies was usually derived from the very general powers given for councils to spend a 2p rate for local purposes under Section 137 of the 1972 Local Government Act. Many of the initiatives were also aided by the Inner Area Act of 1978 and Urban Programme money, money aimed at regenerating the inner cities, where many of these initiatives have been taken.

Many of these initiatives were taken by Labour authorities, both through an ideological predilection for 'interfering in the workings of the market' and because Labour dominated in the inner-city areas where unemployment, the main stimulus, rose alarmingly. However, it was not until the re-election of Labour in Sheffield in 1980, and its capture of power in London and Birmingham in 1981, that local authority initiatives achieved a high political profile. Partly this reflected the desire of those in these authorities and later others, such as Lancashire, to demonstrate that there is an alternative to the national policy of Thatcherism.

In many ways it is misleading to group these three initiatives together. The areas are very diverse: Sheffield is a traditional heavy industry area, suffering badly from the decline of iron and steel employment; London has a long history of loss of manufacturing employment within a general prosperity; the West Midlands faced almost entirely new problems resulting from the collapse of its 'modern' mass-manufacturing employment. Equally, the organization of the initiatives has been importantly different, Sheffield operating directly through a council department, the West Midlands through an Enterprise Board with a majority of county councillors, London through an Enterprise Board without such a majority but tied in a variety of ways to pursue the council's industrial strategy. (In general, see Sheffield, 1980; West Midlands, 1982; G.L.C. 1981, 1983; Metcalf, 1983; for an overview, see Boddy, 1984.)

One obvious similarity in their programmes is the emphasis on taking an equity stake in the companies aided. This reflects the belief (similar to the national policies of the Labour Party), that financial institutions are deficient in the provision of money to industrial firms, but that money provided by public bodies should provide clear accountability, with an equity stake the best method of achieving this.

Of these programmes, that of the G.L.C. is most ambitious, aiming to 'regenerate London industry', but also with aims in the employment and organizational aspects of companies. Much of the rhetoric does envisage a large-scale 'pre-figuration' of an alternative socialist strategy for the whole country (e.g. *Capital and Class*, 1982; Murray, 1983; G.L.C., 1985). Sheffield has been less flamboyant in style, with the West Midlands playing a much lower-key role.

Whatever the rhetoric, all these authorities have recognized the limits to their capacity to achieve their objectives. This derives partly, of course, from the macroeconomic climate, where job losses have made the authorities' own job creation/retention schemes like drops in the ocean. Also, the role of these bodies is plainly constrained by finance; even in London a 2p rate generates a trivial amount (£40 million) in relation to the overall level of investment. For this reason, all these authorities have been trying to find non-rate sources of funds, and have seen pension funds as the obvious source. (Though West Midlands, for example, has also co-operated with other agencies, such as the Industrial and Commercial Finance Corporation.)

Like the national strategies, therefore, local authorities have tended to focus on investment as the key to their areas' problems. In a way this is more appropriate at the local level, for there international comparisons of efficiency are not pertinent, as they are at the national level. (This does not imply that the jobs which local authorities retain/capture are likely to be at the expense of other areas in Britain, something to which they are formally opposed.) But the problem that investment does not necessarily generate (many) jobs also exists at the local level, so that employment has normally been the keystone of the assessment of the desirability of an investment.

One of the problems for these local initiatives is how far they are to act simply as agencies for bailing out failing companies. All authorities have recognized the difficulties of this – not least the political problems of being seen as supporters of lame ducks. Hence the attempt has been made to a greater or lesser extent to finance 'commercially viable' propositions, though the G.L.C. has coupled this with grant aid for specific aspects of employment creation, for example to help ethnic minorities or women.

One of the issues raised by such local initiatives is how to assess investment projects. The expression 'commercially viable' has a number of ambiguities, not only the well-known long-run versus short-run distinction. For local authorities it also raises the question of how far they should have regard to their rate base in deciding on investments. Clearly, other things being equal, a local authority will get some of the return from higher investment in the locality through higher rates. This again is precisely parallel to attempts to show at the national level the financial benefits of higher public spending, via the effects on higher taxes and lower social security payments (e.g. Rowthorn and Ward, 1981). The difficulty, as so often in such exercises, is that no one body receives and disburses all the monies involved, so that, for example, local-authority investments which increase employment may mainly reduce central government spending on social security. Thus, what may be a rational calculation in some general sense is not the basis of any particular institution's calculations.

As already noted, local authorities have attempted to gain access to pension fund money to add to their own relatively slender (and rate-capped) resources (Minns, 1982, pp. 83–106). Minns has argued for a substantial role for local bodies in channelling pension fund money into industry. His stress is on the criterion adopted by those bodies – long-term profitability – as a way of changing the investment ideology of pension funds (see Hughes, 1982). He argues that 'The City has not invested in British industry, not because it is necessarily unprofitable in the long-term, but to put it crudely, because current income is available elsewhere. The issue is the assessment of risk and security, which *is* different compared to countries like Germany and Japan' (Minns, 1983, p. 107). This is contrasted to Murray's traditional Marxist argument which simply says firms do not invest because it is not profitable to do so (Murray, 1983). Minns's criticism of this is a telling one, and Murray's argument is further weakened by a persistent confusion of abstract categories (such as money capital) and particular institutions (such as banks). Nevertheless, Murray's analysis at least switches attention away from financing, if only to refocus it on an ill-defined notion of 'restructuring', conceived in a very conspiratorial manner. As suggested above, Minns's argument is open to the objection that it focuses too much on financing, where the undoubted need for reforms seems to be confused with a panacea device.

One implication of this dispute is that there are different views as to whether pension funds should be offered guarantees by local bodies. For Minns, this defeats the whole purpose of his proposal, which is to change the ideology of these institutions, not subsidize them. For Murray 'money capital' is being perfectly rational in not investing in British industry, so will need subsidizing to do so. Plainly it can be argued that Minns's argument is not only based on a more plausible account of the financial institutions, but also politically advantageous in not turning local bodies into further sources of handouts for industry.

The other point to be noted about pension funds is that the local authority in-house funds, such as the G.L.C. staff funds, have not been easily persuaded to invest in local initiatives. The important factor which arises from this is that the G.L.C. election in 1981 'democratized' the pension fund, giving a much large role to G.L.C. workers and unions. Yet this has not produced any strong feeling amongst the pension fund's trustees that investing in locally based initiatives is the obvious policy for the fund. This is a useful example of the dangers of seeing democracy as a means to producing the policy result envisaged, rather than as a process with extremely open effects.

One obvious problem for such local authorities is how far their administrative areas are economic units. For if we can see their policies as in part 'local Keynesianism', the same issue as for national Keynesianism arises – how far will the boost to activity spill over into other areas? And for local authorities there is obviously no way of limiting such spill-over. Remarkably little seems to have been done by the authorities to look at this fairly traditional form of analysis. The superficial evidence would suggest that the West Midlands, for example, with its constellations of small firms supplying a small number of large ones, would have a much higher regional multiplier than, say, London. Such calculations would have to form part of any assessment of the overall plausibility of these local strategies.

The unit cost of any jobs created by such interventions would also possibly be a part of that assessment. At one level this would seem to be an appropriate measure, given that employment creation is central to these strategies. However, such measures are both technically and ideologically problematic. Technically, the side effects of such interventions elsewhere have to be taken into account. The argument that the rate revenue used for financing such interventions reduces employment by raising employers' costs seems to have been decisively disproved (Cambridge, 1985). Much more difficult to assess is the effect on enterprises competing with those financed. Ideologically, there has been reluctance on the part of local authorities to attempt such measures because of a concern with the quality of jobs, rather than with maximizing the number of jobs at the lowest possible price.

Nevertheless, such calculations could form part of a defence of such local interventions. Certainly the G.L.C.'s pounds-per-job-saved figure seems to have been substantially lower than that of some national schemes – £4,000 per head, as opposed to £30,000 plus. Secondly, such calculations start to open up the whole issue of calculating the costs and benefits of policies to deal with unemployment, something which would be extremely useful (Metcalf, 1984B).[4]

A problem peculiar to the local level is the kind of jobs on which to concentrate. All the bodies mentioned above have tried to move away from simply reacting to proposals brought to them, towards taking a more initiating role in intervention. This has been limited both by their financial position and by the scale of demands from collapsing companies. This has resulted in an attempt to define some overall strategy for their areas, which at least would condition their response to firms coming to them for money.

One aspect of this is the extent to which manufacturing should have a privileged place. Whilst good arguments can be made for giving such privilege at a national level, it is far from clear that this is relevant at a local level where there is no balance of payments constraint. Obviously, as the G.L.C. emphasizes, there are cases where an existing manufacturing concern can be saved by money and organizational change, and it would be absurd to argue against this. However, this is different from a general policy of trying to resist the overall trend towards fewer manufacturing jobs. London boroughs active in the employment field quickly reversed their pro-manufacturing stance, though after some agonizing (Gough *et al.*, 1981).

A further issue of some prominence has been how local authorities are to view small firms. Much of the traditional economic role of local authorities has been in the encouragement of such enterprises, in line with the general rhetoric about the demise of small firms (Bolton, 1971). Partly in reaction to this rhetoric, and noting the poor employment practices of small firms, local authorities have not been keen on focusing on this sector of their local economy.

However, it is far from clear that the category 'small' is a pertinent one for the kind of employment-encouraging role that local authorities seek to play. Small firms are put together only because of their size, and there seems no good reason why size *per se* is relevant to the issue. The one possible relevance of size to a socialist strategy on industry is the link between small size and favourable conditions for industrial democracy (Tomlinson, 1981). In fact, most of the local authorities have shown a concern to aid co-operatives, though some scepticism seems appropriate about whether all institutions called co-operatives provide the ideal framework for the 'socialist' organization of work.

Finally in this context, the local bodies have attempted something close to the planning agreements of Labour's national programme. However, they have been in many respects in a stronger position to enforce certain conditions on firms because those firms are in a weak bargaining position, and because of the equity stake which local bodies commonly take. In this sense, the very parlous nature of local firms exaggerates the general possibilities of public bodies influencing private firms' behavious.

Somewhat tenuously linked to such measures is the attempt, notably by the G.L.C., to avoid some of the criticisms of the traditional national Labour policies being repeated at local level, by creating mechanisms of 'popular planning' (G.L.C., 1983). In practice, such efforts are a useful way of encouraging initiatives from a wide range of bodies other than the official state organs. However the rhetoric of 'popular' is extremely dubious, as what is necessarily involved is specific organizations, which are always open to being labelled not really popular (e.g. Marks, 1983). Equally, as noted with national policy, planning can never be simply the sum of all 'rank and file' initiatives, but must always involve hard political choices which cannot be universally popular.

Whilst these local initiatives are politically important in keeping open the debates on alternatives to national Conservative policy, they have obvious limitations as full-bodied blueprints for altern- ative national strategies. Whilst a national strategy might well link with and learn from the work of these local bodies, there are specific constraints on national policy which have to be dealt with at the national level. Above all, national government has to cope with a balance of payments constraint, which in Britain means especially a focus on efficiency in manufacturing production; this in itself is unlikely to be employment-creating and may well in some instances reduce employment in the manufacturing sector. Such national strategies cannot just be the aggregate of local policies, however much may be learned from these.

CONCLUSIONS

This conclusion will not attempt to summarize all the points covered in the chapter, but will try to state briefly what the above arguments imply for a plausible non-monetarist supply-side policy.

First, the Left has been right to insist that manufacturing must remain a crucial part of Britain's economic activity. The U.S.A. may be able to maintain a massive import surplus on manufactures, by agricultural and other primary product exports, but this is not an option available to Britain, especially as North Sea oil dries up. However, this is definitely not the same as saying that manufacturing employment can be expanded substantially, if at all. As the Labour Party (1982A) rightly says, most employment expansion is likely to come from services and the public sector.

The need for an efficient manufacturing sector does require, again as the Left maintains, a more 'interventionist' stance by government, on the model of most O.E.C.D. countries (N.E.D.O., 1981). *Vis-à-vis* the Conservatives this is an important argument, though as suggested in chapter 1, the actions of the Conservations have, in their own fashion, been much more 'interventionist' than the rhetoric would imply.

In relation to the Left itself, the crucial argument is not on that basis, but on the character of the reforms needed to accompany such interventionist policies. The thrust of much of this chapter has been that whilst there is certainly a case for reform of the financial system, it is far from clear that this has the pivotal role that many on the Left suggest. Above all, this is because the focus on finance derives in turn from an exaggeration of lack of investment as the crucial source of Britain's poor industrial performance.

The effect of such a focus is to bypass the crucial but politically much more painful elements which affect industrial performance. Issues of work practices and work organization raise, for the Left, very difficult problems, partly because so much of the debate is couched in moralistic terms ('are the workers to blame?'). Equally, a focus on managerial practices is problematic; whilst the Left is very happy to talk of 'bad management', it runs against the grain of much Left and trade union practice to talk about what good management would look like, and how this might be aided by workers and unions.

Yet these issues will not go away, and the response of proposing an alternative 'blame the capitalists' to the 'blame the workers' view is economically vacuous and politically suspect. To put the point in a rather different way, there is a need for legitimizing management as a practice, but not, as the S.D.P. suggest, a need for legitimizing existing management forms and personnel.

This leads on to the issue of industrial democracy. One rhetoric which supports industrial democracy says that only with such arrangements can the untapped resources of workers' knowledge be put to use. Now this clearly has a lot of point to it; many forms of work organization take little account of the skills and talents of the workforces they employ. On the other hand, the argument should not be used to suggest an innate set of well-organized skills which are available as soon as the shackles of capitalist hierarchy are loosened. Especially this is the case if one is talking not of technical, production-oriented skills but of organization and management skills. Indeed, the argument about industrial democracy can here be turned on its head – a major *purpose* of such democracy would be to provide a framework for a training in these skills.

The difficult question is, given a commitment to industrial democracy of a radical kind, what relation does this have to 'industrial regeneration'? Certainly the current public rhetoric (if not always the practice) of management is not such as to encourage the co-operative reactions between unions and management which play some part in industrial efficiency. As argued in chapter 1, there is no convincing evidence that current policies have moved Britain on to some higher level growth path. Nevertheless, the belief that industrial democracy is a kind of panacea, happily combining an appealing political rhetoric of extension of rights and the solution to Britain's industrial ineffectiveness, is erroneous. The first steps to industrial democracy, a radical extension of management's accountability to workforces, may well encourage the discontinuation of inefficient management behaviour. But mechanisms of accountability, taken by themselves, cannot determine the policies of those agents who have the new powers to call management to account.

Hence, finally, the emphasis on the need for experimentation in industrial democracy. If the effects of such democracy are problematic and open; if there is no simple functional relationship between democracy and efficiency; and if the unions' role in such democracy is open to doubt; then variety and experiment are vital.

In sum, the Left's supply-side policy must accept the creation of new tensions and problems, not expect easy solutions. The easy coupling of democracy and efficiency is beguiling but potentially deluding. It does not provide the best ground for opposition to Thatcherism.

6

Public Expenditure, Taxation and the Nationalized Industries

INTRODUCTION

Central to the policies of the Conservative governments since 1979 has been the attempt to 'roll back the frontiers of the state'. The attempt to cut public expenditure in absolute terms has failed, and the target is now to reduce it as a proportion of a growing national income (chapter 1). But, beginning in 1981, and especially since 1983, this has been replaced in policy emphasis by privatization, a notion covering a number of distinct policies, but one which serves to emphasize the general hostility of the government to the public sector.

The parties opposed to the government have been divided in their response to such hostility and the measures which have flowed from it. Broadly speaking, the Labour Party and the Marxist Left have re-emphasized their support for public expenditure and the public sector, and have seen the expansion of both as a crucial part of their strategies for the economy.

In contrast, the S.D.P. has seen the public versus private dispute as essentially obfuscating the crucial issues, as part of the mould which they wish to break. This chapter attempts to assess these views by focusing on proposals in three related areas.

The first part of the chapter looks at discussion in the two areas of public expenditure and taxation, which are so closely inter-twined for many purposes as to be best dealt with together. This is especially so because a central part of the debate over public expenditure concerns social welfare expenditure, and social welfare policy is linked to taxation in a number of ways. Not only, and most obviously, is taxation the source of finance for welfare provision, but taxation impinges on the incomes of many who are the recipients of social welfare benefits.

The second part of the chapter looks at the nationalized industries and policy proposals both for the running of existing nationalized industries, and (where appropriate) for the expansion of the nationalized sector.

Whilst it seems appropriate to deal with all the issues of public expenditure and the public sector in one chapter, the diverse nature of concerns under this heading must be noted. First, public expenditure is obviously both a microeconomic and a macro-economic issue. The aggregate level of such spending and the manner of its financing are seen as crucial issues, though in different ways, by all parties. But this aspect is discussed in chapters 2, 3 and 7 and will be secondary here. Instead, the emphasis will be mainly on particular spending programmes and the microeconomic issues raised by public spending, taxation and the nationalized industries. Secondly, the time-scale of proposals in this area clearly varies considerably. For example, some proposals by the Left for nationalization are seen as part of a short-term programme for economic revival, whilst others are seen as long-term changes which will become part of the economic structure. The emphasis here will be the former arguments, although their interrelationship with longer term proposals will not be ignored.

PUBLIC EXPENDITURE AND TAXATION

The S.D.P., Public Expenditure and Taxation

An expansion of public spending plays a crucial role in the S.D.P. proposals for a rapid reduction in the level of unemployment. Public expenditure is to be used in two distinct ways. On the one hand, it is viewed as part of a traditional fiscal expansion, in combination with tax reductions. On the other, it would be used to finance 'a crash programme of special short-term measures, designed to act quickly and targeted on the most needy groups, especially the long-term unemployed and the young' (S.D.P., 1983A, p. 2). The macroeconomic aspects of such proposals have been discussed in chapter 2.

Such policies are similar to, if less ambitious than, those of the Labour Party. They represent a consensus view across a consider-able part of the British political spectrum. Much more problematic than such short-term proposals is the general place of public expenditure in Social Democrat policy.

The intellectual background to much Social Democrat thinking is the writing of Crosland (especially 1956; also 1974). Crosland's revisionist socialism was based on the argument that the primary socialist objective is social equality, and that in the context of a fully employed mixed economy, and reasonable levels of economic growth, such a policy should be pursued by higher levels of public expenditure. The focus on equality as a primary goal seems to be retained by Social Democrats (e.g. Owen, 1981, part 2). But the Crosland legacy is also criticized for its centralizing character and for underestimating 'the importance of changing attitudes, seeing changes in terms of legislative or administrative reform' (Owen, 1981, pp. 34, 35). Rather more sharply, Marquand (1982, pp. 77–8) has questioned the Crosland emphasis on state action and the capacity of state institutions actually to deliver the objectives of democratic socialism. In addition, pessimism over economic growth is seen as limiting the possibilities of continued expansion of public expenditure (e.g. S.D.P., 1982B, p. 4).

This kind of ambivalence leaves the future trend of Social Democrat policy extremely open, though there is evidence of a movement to the Right in the general rhetoric about public expenditure (e.g. Owen, 1983). This seems especially linked to the view that Crosland-style policies face an insurmountable political barrier in the hostility of lower earners to paying for public expenditure by the income tax which has increasingly been paid by them in recent years (e.g. Jenkins, 1982, pp. 52–3; for data on this, see table 6.1.).

Table 6.1 Tax threshold as a percentage of average male earnings (married couple with two children under eleven)

Year	%
1949–50	123
1959–60	104
1969–70	68
1982–3	60

Source: 'The Structure of Personal Income Tax and Income Support', *3rd Report from the Treasury and Civil Service Committee*, H.C.P. 386 1982/3, H.M.S.O.

Such a political calculation seems in part to underlie the increasing sympathy in the S.D.P. for a radical reconstruction of the tax and benefit system. This is seen as making possible a combination of lower taxation, if this is desired, with the concentration of social welfare benefits on the poorest, as well as providing a more 'rational' administrative structure (S.D.P.,

1982C). The most extended case for such a system is that by Dilnot *et al.* (1984), which is a close cousin to the S.D.P.'s proposals, but argued for at much greater length. This involves a tax credit scheme which is seen as a better alternative than either an attempt to go 'back to Beveridge', that is, the principles of the Beveridge Report of 1942, or to move towards a negative income tax scheme. 'Back to Beveridge' means basically a substantial increase and extension of National Insurance benefits to cover the contingencies of disablement, unemployment, sickness and so on more thoroughly. A negative income tax scheme means focusing on providing a minimum level of income, irrespective of contingency. It would work by paying those below a threshold a benefit and taxing all those above it. The former kind of scheme is seen by Dilnot *et al.* (1984, ch. 3) as too expensive, and not in any case doing enough for those not suffering from such contingencies, for example poor working households. The disadvantage of a negative income tax scheme is seen to be either that benefits paid are very low or there are very high marginal rates of tax.

The proposed tax credit scheme would try to combine elements of both contingency and income relatedness. It would focus the reforms on the working poor (p. 81). A tax credit system would be based on lump-sum payments linked to the circumstances of particular households, the payments being reduced as income increases. The scheme would work via the Inland Revenue, that is, it would be linked administratively with the income tax scheme.

Dilnot *et al.* give various possible versions of their scheme, some designed to maintain public expenditure, some to allow a reduction in income taxation. Whichever version is used, the major reduction in benefit paid is child benefit. 'Most current recipients of child benefit would lose entitlement; of the children to whom benefit is currently paid, 63 per cent would be in households which would receive no benefit credit whatever' (p. 123).

The overall thrust of the Dilnot *et al.* proposals is summarized thus:

> The savings we have effected are achieved by a savage, but selective, retrenchment of the benefit system. It rests on the principle that, as far as better-off households are concerned, provision for children, old age, dependent spouses, and other contingencies is a matter for those households rather than the state. It therefore abandons the last vestige of the Beveridge plan . . . [because] it is very much more cost-effective to tackle actual need. It involves an extension of means testing . . . administered through the tax system, and so poor families would in fact be subject to less,

and less demeaning, enquiry into their household circumstances than is now the case. (p. 5.)

Two general points may be made on such schemes at this stage, though the issues will be returned to below in discussing Labour Party proposals in this area. First, it must be stressed that the proposals are based on a political calculation as to what it is politically possible to pay for. Thus, although Dilnot *et al.* look at revenue neutral schemes, they focus attention in their introduction on making possible a 5p cut in income tax, and they certainly do not look at any schemes involving increased overall expenditure. The simple point to be made is that the technical apparatus deployed in the discussion should not blind us to this fundamental political calculation.

Secondly, Dilnot *et al.* have a focus which fits in with both mainstream economics and traditional British socialism. This is a focus on the vertical distribution of income, where the units in that distribution are households. In both cases there is a basic lack of concern with the intra-household distribution of income. Dilnot *et al.* are amazingly insensitive to the feminist issues raised by their child benefit proposals (see pp. 116–18). Yet the argument that women should have a separate source of income to help finance their childcare role was one of the major arguments for the movement from family tax allowances to cash child benefits.

Whilst the analytic thrust of Dilnot *et al.* is very similar to that of the S.D.P. policies (S.D.P., 1982C), there are ambiguities over the extent to which public-expenditure reductions are part of the case for such policies, and secondly over what to do about child benefit.

In the 1982 discussion document (S.D.P., 1982C) the S.D.P. view was that the transitional arrangements towards a tax/benefit credit system would involve increased expenditure, especially because of the retention and indeed increase in child benefit paid in addition to the basic benefits. The taxation of child benefit was explicitly rejected as, for most people, simply transferring income from one pocket to another (1982C, p. 9).

Hence this version of the S.D.P. strategy does not follow the logic of the rhetoric of 'concentrate help where help is needed' which was used by Dilnot *et al.* against child benefit. In addition, the proposals include increased benefits for sick, unemployed and non-industrial disabled. The same line was taken in the Alliance election manifesto (Liberal/S.D.P., 1983).

Hence, in its immediate proposals the S.D.P. in 1983 was putting forward policies not very different from those of the

Labour Party (below). The major difference was the suggestion for transitional arrangements heading towards a full tax credit scheme. But the redistributive effects of such a scheme would depend crucially on whether it displaces all other benefits (especially child benefits), as well as its own conditions of operation. The proposals of 1982/3 envisaged a lump-sum basic benefit which would give an income somewhat above existing supplementary benefit levels. The benefit would be withdrawn at the rate of 30 per cent for those without children, 45 per cent for those with, a higher rate for the latter deriving from the generous (by supplementary benefit standards) initial payment for children and the continuation of child benefit. The document notes the dilemma between a high level of withdrawal which exacerbates the poverty trap, and a low level which pays money to people high up the income scale. Its proposals were seen as a middle way (S.D.P., 1982C, pp. 7–8).

One difficulty with such a scheme is that it replaces a sharp poverty trap for a few with a 'poverty plateau' for many more (Hemming, 1984, pp. 179–82). But as already noted, abolition of the poverty trap is probably impossible under any plausible level of public expenditure.

The drift of S.D.P. policy since the 1983 election seems to have been more towards the Dilnot *et al.* kind of scheme, with less willingness to see increased welfare expenditure (Owen, 1983).

Finally, the S.D.P. takes the classic economists' view that the means of income redistribution is through the tax benefit system.[1] It maintains against the Labour Party's minimim wage arguments that this would not help most of those in poverty, and would increase unemployment. Those arguments are returned to briefly at the end of the discussion of the Labour Party's welfare proposals.

The S.D.P. view on social welfare expenditure on services in kind (such as N.H.S.. and personal social services) is that there is only limited scope for expansion with current levels of economic growth. The Social Democrats envisaged in 1982/3 the creation of 100,000 part-time jobs in the social services as part of emergency job creation. And they also envisaged an Employment and Initiative Fund as a longer term measure to try to link employment creation with the reduction of specific inequalities in the distribution of health and welfare provision (S.D.P., 1982B, p. 12). But they emphasized that in the medium term they proposed no major expansion in this area because of financial constraints (contrary to the Labour Party) nor major reorganization (contrary to the Conservatives). Their programme concentrated on localized experiments to try to relieve inequalities, whilst endeavouring to encourage voluntary action. They also stressed the preservation of the private sector on 'libertarian' grounds, though saying it should not be subsidized. This policy was defended on the grounds that 'A universal commitment to ensure equality of access for all is compatible with a pluralistic pattern of provision' (1982B, p. 23). However, the mechanisms of such compatibility are not spelt out, and indeed the present private system is seen as simply a feature of 'reality', which has to be accepted (p. 25).

Social welfare expenditure is at the centre of the debate over public expenditure, because of its large proportion of that total (see table 6.2), its interactions with the tax system, and its redistributional component. But it does not exhaust the important issues of public expenditure. Also economically significant is money spent in the trade and employment areas. Here the S.D.P. does not seem to envisage any changes in the overall level of spending (though the proposals are not costed). The proposals set out (S.D.P., 1983B) involve various kinds of financial aid – for cheap loans to aid international competitiveness, for training, for small business – which may represent a reorientation of expenditure but no drastic change in the aggregate sum (industrial policy is discussed in chapter 5).

Much more out of line with existing policy is a large-scale expansion of spending on employment measures, especially for young people, the long-term unemployed and married women (S.D.P., 1983A, pp. 14–16). However, with the exception of the policies for young people, these proposals are seen as temporary, as operating quickly before the macroeconomic measures have worked and other policies have delivered more permanent employment.

On taxation, the S.D.P. policy envisages various reforms to increase the egalitarianism of the system, for example the scaling down of mortgage interest relief, and the abolition of the ceiling on National Insurance contributions (done for employers but not employees in the 1985 budget). In addition, it accepts the anomalous position of the married man's allowance, and the sense of linking its abolition to a rise in child benefit. There is also an emphasis on reducing the arbitrary nature of tax allowance on some forms of saving and not on others, though there seems to be no consensus on moving towards an expenditure tax (Meade, 1978) which would abolish taxation on all savings. The short-run proposals of the S.D.P. are not, in fact, very different from those of the Labour Party, though there is less egalitarian rhetoric and more doubt about the efficacy of measures such as a wealth tax.

Table 6.2 Public expenditure on social welfare (£million)

Health and personal social services		13,455
of which	Health	12,822
Social security		35,119
of which major items	Pensions	15,501
	Supplementary benefit	6,367
	Family benefit	4,543
	Unemployment benefit	3,956
	Housing benefit	2,895
Other major programmes		
	Defence	17,249
	Industry, energy, trade and employment	7,007
Total public expenditure		128,111

Source: *The Government's Expenditure Plans 1985/6 to 1987/8*, Cmnd. 9428, H.M.S.O.

The Labour Party, Public Expenditure and Taxation

Labour's Programme, 1982, the most recent general and substantial policy document produced by the party, stresses that 'expansion of the public sector is central to Labour's whole economic and social strategy' (p. 18). This may stand as a statement of the central thrust of Labour's policies. It is important to note the reasons for this emphasis. On the one hand they are macroeconomic – public spending is the central feature of reflationary policies designed to reduce unemployment, and the focus in this context is on an expansion of public investment and labour-intensive public services. On the other hand, aggregate public spending should rise because of the expansion of individual programmes (especially in social welfare) not offset by cuts elsewhere.

Thus the growth of the public sector is seen as operating at two levels, the macroeconomic and the social policy, and on two rather different time-scales, the short and the medium term. What is not discussed is the long-run status of the growth of the public sector as the key to Labour's whole policy stance. In some respects this may be understandable – electoral policy-making, it may be said, operates on a relatively short time-scale and deals with specifics, not grand strategies. But the attack on public spending by the Conservatives is clearly linked precisely to a long-term plan to 'roll back the state' and this in part is based on the belief that there are both strong economic and political arguments against the growth of the public sector. Therefore, in this section some comments will be made on the general question of the expansion of the state sector before looking at the specifics of Labour's proposals.

Whilst Crosland may be seen as the major post-war proponent of the view that expanding public expenditure should be a central feature of Labour Party policy, he is not very explicit about why, given his objective of equality, it is public spending that should be seen as the major instrument of obtaining that objective. Indeed, whilst that undoubtedly is the general thrust of Crosland's argument, it is not without its ambiquities (see Crouch, 1981).

First, he argues that equality is not the primary aim of the social services, but rather the 'relief of hardship and distress' (Crosland, 1956, p. 148). Secondly, he argues that the redistributive and equalizing effects of services provided in kind (as opposed to cash benefits) are small because they are not concentrated on the poor and are financed by taxation which falls on the mass of taxpayers (1956, pp. 146–7). Finally, less fundamentally, he emphasizes the importance of high quality in public services because 'the provision of free and universally available services will not enhance social equality if they are much inferior to the corresponding private services' (p. 146).

If nothing else, Crosland's first point is a useful reminder (from a surprising source) of the dangers of using 'equality' as an all-purpose socialist objective, and reductions in inequality as the universal measure of policy success: for example, the disabling attempts within much Left argument to reduce all feminist issues to ones of 'equal opportunity' (Rose, 1980). On a slightly different plane, Sen (1983) has argued powerfully that the post-war emphasis on poverty as inequality is in crucial respects misplaced. He argues that what is at stake in discussion of poverty is commonly an absolute notion of 'capabilities', for example, avoiding shame from failing to meet social conventions, participating in social activities, and retaining self-respect. Whilst resources to do this will vary from country to country and over time, it is nevertheless an absolute standard. He points out that Townsend, usually seen as one of the key proponents of relative measures of poverty, actually uses an absolute measure, of ability 'to participate in the activities of the community', in his monumental study *Poverty in Britain* (Townsend, 1979). Following Sen, it may be right to emphasize that the problems of poverty and of inequality should be seen at least in part as issues which can be separated.

Crosland's second point – the distinctive effects of cash benefits as opposed to provision of services in kind – takes us closer to the specific programmes within Labour's policy. Crosland's point about the limited redistributive effects of the services provided in kind is the central thrust of the work of Le Grand (1982). Le Grand argues that the 'Strategy of Equality', that is, of providing such services as the central part of a drive for social equality, has failed. The basic point he makes is that the greater resources (material and cultural) of the better-off enable them to make more use of the N.H.S., education and most public transport and hence reduces or even reverses any equalizing impact. Against this 'Strategy of Equality' Le Grand proposes instead a 'direct attack' on inequality of income, with a great emphasis on attacking the ideology of inequality.

Heald (1983), in the best available overall discussion of public expenditure, has strongly criticized Le Grand's arguments. He points out that Le Grand's arguments focus only on the expenditure side, ignoring the redistributive effects of taxation. Secondly, Le Grand treats tax expenditures (especially mortgage interest relief) as if they were part of the strategy of equality, rather than strong qualifications of it. Thirdly, Le Grand conflates equality 'in general' with equality in the provision of specific services. Fourthly, Le Grand is over-pessimistic about changing the structure and functioning of these services to offset some of the effects he highlights. Finally, Heald argues, Le Grand criticizes in detail the 'Strategy of Equality' but seriously underestimates the obstacles to a much greater reliance on cash benefit transfers to the poor (Heald, 1983, pp. 141–5). It might also be noted that transfers in cash are not necessarily redistributive; this depends on how they are financed. For example, Creedy (1982) shows that most pension schemes are not redistributive.

Whilst Le Grand makes a useful corrective to some claims about the effects of such services as the N.H.S., most of Heald's criticisms seem appropriate. Indeed, in some respects they do not go far enough. Le Grand's emphasis on the 'ideological' obstacles to redistribution via cash transfer seems strangely at variance with his emphasis on the very 'material' reasons why the better-off benefit so much from public services. In addition, Le Grand's emphasis on inequality as the single measure of policy success disguises the rise in absolute standards of the health of the poor attained under the N.H.S.

On one important point, however, Heald's own argument raises a difficulty. He is right that in terms of presentation, talk of the redistributive effects of the social services should be linked to a similar analysis of the tax system. But in practice the redistributive effects of the tax system taken as a whole are extremely limited (Kay and King, 1983, ch. 14; Davies and Piachaud, 1983, p. 46). More than that, there seem to be very substantial obstacles to making it more progressive in ways which cannot be evaded by the better-off. The implications of this general point are returned to below.

For the sake of completeness, a brief comment should be offered on Crosland's third point, that the way to cope with the inequalities generated by the existence of private health care and medicine should be overcome by the improved provision of public services. As a strategy this appears Utopian. Given any plausible resources devoted to the public sector, the standards in the private sector are likely to continue to attract considerable numbers to it. Hence the current Labour Party strategy of moving towards the abolition of private education and private health (whilst recognizing the difficulties of doing so) appears quite right. Note, however, that this can be argued not only on the grounds of reducing inequalities in life chances, but also as a means of raising absolute standards in these services, by bringing to bear the powerful pressures of those currently leaving the public sector.

Very briefly, the general conclusions that may be drawn from the above discussion are that the Labour Party's emphasis on the expansion of the public sector as the centrepiece of its policies would benefit from a more explicit justification of those areas of spending which are traditionally and currently given priority. Such a case would need to be much more explicit about the goals of the Left in social welfare policy, especially the limits of equality as a criterion, and the problems of devising an effectively progressive tax system.[2]

Most of the general discussion above related to Labour's programme of social welfare expenditure. But as already noted, public expenditure in the short run is seen as predominantly a macroeconomic weapon. This comprises two major categories: public investment projects 'which make a direct contribution to creating jobs as well as providing a long-term benefit to society' (Labour Party, 1982B, p. 18) and labour-intensive public services.

In comparison with the S.D.P., Labour emphasizes increases in public expenditure rather than tax cuts as the main thrust of reflation 'since public spending has a more direct impact on demand for home produced goods' (1982B, p. 18). However, it should be noted that this difference is only a first-round effect; once those who receive the income from increased public expenditure spend it, it will go as much on imports as any other consumption expenditure. Nevertheless a continuing effect of this kind can be maintained if the expenditure is a continuing one. But this then runs up against the potential conflict between policies aimed at social priorities and those aimed at maximizing the domestic employment effects of a given increase in expenditure. Increases in expenditure on transfer payments and on labour-intensive public services, for example, may not be as useful in the latter respect as expenditure on construction projects for which many of the inputs are domestically produced.

It is instructive to contrast Labour's programme with that of the S.D.P. Whilst both agree on an expansion of public-sector capital expenditure, concentrated on housing, thereafter the packages diverge substantially. The S.D.P. package involves more focus on tax cuts, primarily because of the effects of such cuts on inflation (e.g. reduction of V.A.T.) and price restraint on the nationalized industries, with similar effects. Hence, there is a sharper distinction made by the S.D.P. between what is desirable in a reflationary programme and what is desirable as part of a social programme.

The employment aspects of these programmes are looked at in some detail in chapter 2. In the current context it is important to note that Labour's programme of public-sector expansion is much larger than that of the S.D.P., and the main difference is Labour's emphasis on expansion in the N.H.S. and education. Two problems arise in relation to this programme. First, it is far from clear that it is very efficacious as an employment programme. The presumption seems to be that because expenditure on the N.H.S. and education is labour-intensive, these sectors could be quickly used to expand employment. But these points are logically distinct, and the latter would require the ability to recruit quickly across the board people with appropriate abilities (not just unskilled workers). The capacity to do this seems administratively constrained, as well as limited by the availability of particular skills.

The second problem which arises is the old but inescapable one of priorities within social welfare expenditure. There is a good discussion of some of the economic constraints on the welfare proposals of *Labour's Programme 1982* in Davies and Piachaud (1983). They point out that in that programme there are proposals for increased spending of about £8·5 billion on the N.H.S., education and housing, and £10 billion (allowing for increased tax receipts) on social security benefits. They plausibly argue that given the likely rates of growth of the economy, and the political need for some increase in private consumption, 'The plans contained in *Labour's Programme 1982* for increased services and for larger transfer payments are not compatible. If the policy does not reconcile these aims while it has time, the foreign exchange markets will do so thereafter' (p. 60).

The implication of these points is not that there should be a total separation of reflationary measures and social welfare measures. But the general point should be made that these two things do not mesh together as easily as the Labour programme seems to imply. Secondly, if there is to be a substantial increase in social welfare expenditure as part of the reflationary package, this seems best done via enhanced social security payments which are easier to organize quickly, have direct effects on aiding those hardest hit by Thatcherism, and would seem to have no worse import consequences than increased N.H.S. and education sector employment (see Labour Party, 1981B, p. 4).

These points are largely independent of any discussion of a medium-term programme of change in social welfare expenditure. The starting point for Labour's discussion of social security is opposition to the means test (Labour Party, 1981A, p. 3 and 1983B, p. 93). The opposition to such benefits is based on 'the often degrading and stigmatising encroachment on personal privacy which they entail'; it also maintains that they are expensive to administer, contribute to the poverty trap and the problem of work incentives, and are inefficient in the sense of low take-up (1981A, p. 5).

Because opposition to the means test is so central to Labour Party arguments it is worthy of some detailed examination. Means testing in its broadest sense means the payment of social security benefit according to income not contingency, in the language of economists who analyse the social security system (Dilnot *et al.*, 1984; Hemming, 1984). This very general definition highlights the point that what seems to be at stake in Labour's opposition is mainly the mechanisms of assessing the income of claimants, rather than income measures *per se*. This emerges from the fact that Labour discussion documents seem willing to countenance means testing through the tax system, both with reference to child benefits (Labour Party 1981A, p. 19) and more generally in a tax credit scheme (Labour Party, 1981B, pp. 23–4).

Although it is not spelt out in these documents, the implication of these points is that income assessment via the Inland Revenue does not have the humiliating and degrading implications of scrutiny via the social security system. Hence, in certain respects the general notion of means testing does obstruct discussion. It does need to be noted that a tax credit system would not solve the problem of the poverty/unemployment trap; but then any plausible system which was fairly generous to those not in employment would pose this problem. And whilst they cannot be ignored, the significance of these problems seems grossly overstated by the Right (Hemming, 1984, chs 4, 5). The important point here is not advocacy of a tax credit system, but that the discussion of social welfare expenditure is not aided by vague notions of means testing.

Labour's line of thinking on social security is sharply at variance with the S.D.P./Dilnot *et al.* view, though explicit critiques are as yet limited. Piachaud (1984), whilst again deploying the anti-means-test rhetoric, at the same time focuses the arguments on specific benefits, mainly child benefit and state earnings-related pensions. And the same point could be made about Labour's stance in general: most of it is couched as a defence and calls for expansion of specific benefit where there is quite a wide consensus on particular 'target groups' who fare badly under the present system. These are families with children, one-parent families, the disabled (other than the industrially disabled) and the long-term unemployed. It also advocates generally increasing National Insurance benefits to reduce the number of claimants of supplementary benefit. (This stance, which might be called 'quasi-Back-to-Beveridge', is strongly influenced by Atkinson, e.g. 1984.)

The first of these concerns especially leads to an emphasis on a substantial increase in child benefit as the centrepiece of social welfare policy. One advantage of such a proposal is that it can, at least in part, be financed by the abolition of a tax allowance which presumbly is aimed to help families with children, the married man's allowance, but which is given indiscriminately to all married men. This proposal also reflects the feminist concern to obtain an independent source of income for those who in the vast majority of cases care for children, and who may not receive much income even in a high-income household (for examples, see Rimmer, 1980).

The other benefits seem to reflect quite a wide consensus about the priorities in social welfare expenditure, but have no such neat source of financing. This point leads naturally on to a discussion of taxation.

Traditionally, Labour Party discussion has had much more to say on social security and social welfare than on taxation. There is some evidence of a shift in this of late, partly because of the recognition that taxation has increasingly encroached on the incomes of the less well-off, to the point where now the income tax threshold is below the level of supplementary benefit. The traditional focus of Labour policy has been on increasing the progression of the system by increasing direct taxes, both on income and on wealth. But recently, it has come to be recognized that the simple idea that income tax is very progressive and indirect tax regressive is not true: 'V.A.T.'s impact on income distribution is not very different from that of income tax over most of the income range' (Labour Party, 1981B, p. 27). There seems also to be a greater recognition of the effects of tax allowances in reducing the tax base, and hence, other things being equal, raising the rate of tax. Nevertheless, thinking on the Left still seems to avoid some of the difficult problems by presuming that there are readily available sources of tax revenue which would not derive from the vast mass of taxpayers (Day and Pond, 1982, p. 157). Now, clearly there is scope without radical structural changes to increase the tax taken from higher income groups and the wealthy. But it is, of course, the case that wholesale withdrawal of tax allowances, whilst hitting the better-off harder, would also hit the majority of taxpayers. (A recognition of this seems to have been behind the distancing of the Labour Party leadership from Meacher's proposals in spring 1985. In fact these included compensation via housing and child benefit for many of those who would lose by the ending of mortgage relief.) And whilst it is right to point out the sharp decline in taxation of companies, it has to be recognized that a large part of this is accounted for by the fall in company profits, so there is no pot of gold to be readily raided.

Thus, whilst it seems right to move towards some kind of comprehensive income taxation, towards treating more of income for tax purposes as it is treated under Pay as You Earn (P.A.Y.E.) and towards reducing the scope of allowances, the Labour Party would be mistaken to delude itself into believing that such measures could provide a painless solution to tax raising.

The general point to be made is that progressive taxation as a 'strategy of equality' has not been a great success. By and large, high-income groups and the wealthy have found ways around the system, so that as Kay and King (1983, ch. 12) point out, very high nominal rates of tax are only actually paid by those who lack competent professional advice.

In the long run this failure requires some profound reassessment of the manner of financing public expenditure and of reducing income inequality. On the first point, the short-run necessity is to accept that improved social welfare provision has largely to be paid for by taxes on the great mass of taxpayers (though relieved right at the bottom end by raising the thresholds above the rate of inflation). On the second point, it has been argued that incomes inequality should be tackled 'at its source', by having a maximum wage (e.g. Pond and Popay, 1983; Cripps *et al.*, 1981). These proposals are interesting, but they raise a host of problems. They do not, of course, help the financing of public expenditure, as if implemented they would be likely in the first instance to raise the level of corporate profits rather than the revenue of the exchequer.

The Marxist Left, Public Spending and Taxation

Marxist discussion of state spending and the welfare state has three striking characteristics. First, politically it finds an easy target in the failure of Labour governments to provide an ideal level of publicly financed welfare provision. This provides a stick with which to beat those who do not recognize that under capitalism such provision will always be fatally compromised by the demands of that capitalism. Secondly, there is the attempt to found a specifically Marxist theory of state spending and the welfare state within capitalist countries. Finally, there is the striking absence of detailed programmes of reform, so that it is difficult to treat Marxist discussions in this area on a par with those of the S.D.P. and the Labour Party.

On the first point, the fundamental political argument is that it is only capitalism that constrains an optimum level of expenditure on welfare provision. The failure of Labour governments and their allies is a failure to recognize that unless they confront capitalism as a whole they will never deliver the social programmes they would like to (Kerr, 1981; Glyn and Harrison, 1980, ch. 5). In this view, any sign of a desire to control the level of public expenditure is a clear sign of reactionary intent. Thus Hall (1983, ch. 8) berates advocates of the Alternative Economic Strategy who accept the case for any control over the level of public expenditure. Such a view is in conflict with a clear but unargued for belief that any talk of a problem of financing public expenditure is tantamount to wanting to cut it (Hall, 1983, pp. 93–4). This is linked to the view that public expenditure arguments are simply a case of stressing the priority of either finance or needs. In this view, there are no problems of the diversity of purposes of public expenditure – as a means of economic management, as well as a provider of services. There is no difficulty about resources to fund industrial investment and exports (1983, pp. 88–93).

This kind of discussion is founded on a simple view that public expenditure on welfare services is a good thing, and that any talk of issues such as financing, or priorities, or divergent objectives, is simply a cover for cuts. In contrast to this, Marxist attempts to theorize the welfare state have taken a much more ambivalent view of the status of public welfare services. Indeed, the motif of such analyses is the contradictory nature of such services. This position is well summed up by Leonard (Introduction to Gough, 1979, p. ix): 'All sensitive and careful Marxist writing on the state and on the economy has to walk a tightrope between crude functionalism and starry-eyed voluntarism – at its extreme, between seeing the welfare state as wholly oppressive and seeing it as a bastion of socialism within a capitalist economy.' This tightrope provides for the possibility of a range of emphases, some of which tend towards the first view (e.g. Ginsburg, 1979) and some which tend towards the second (e.g. Hall, 1983).

Gough gives this contradiction a particular economic twist, arguing that 'A high level of state expenditure maintains demand and employment, but may reduce profits and accumulation' (1979, p. 138). In this view, the current pressure for public-expenditure cuts arises from the profits squeeze on companies, which makes them emphasize the benefits of cuts as a way of increasing profits over the lost demand such cuts entail. The assumptions of this argument are that the final source of tax revenues is plain, and that it is companies. But neither of these seems acceptable. As Kay and King stress (1983) the question of who really pays the tax is never easily resolved. Secondly, what does seem clear is that it is difficult to see tax as a major part of the profit problem of British companies. Indeed, the trend over almost all of the post-war period has been for a reduction in company taxation to offset falling pre-tax profits. Indeed, the low share of tax revenue from companies is one reason why the income tax threshold has fallen so far down the income scale.

Gough sees policies such as the social contract of the 1970s as an attempt to shift the tax burden from companies to workers, and hence as a temporary resolution of the crisis (1979, p. 149). But this is only a temporary resolution, because in the long run such policies are undermined by the slow-down of economic growth and by the conflict between trade union leaders and the rank and file. Thus, despite the specifically Marxist theory deployed, the conclusion is remarkably similar to that of Crosland – that economic growth is necessary to generate the consent to increased taxation and high public expenditure. Indeed, the overall impression of Gough's argument is that, despite the agonizing over the correct emphasis within the 'fundamental contradiction', the final result is unremarkable. Apart from the emphasis on the slow-down in economic growth and the tensions created by high taxation, the positive policies are also remarkably commonplace. The call is to 'realise in practice the ideology of the welfare state propounded in many orthodox textbooks: a system for subjecting economic forces to conscious social control and for meeting human needs' (p. 153).

As already noted, Marxist Left positive, programme statements are commonly as general as this. In a sense this is perfectly logical: if the underlying problem is capitalism, then the abolition of that system will provide the solution to all the problems of social welfare. Deacon (1981; see also 1984) spells this out when he lists the principles of socialist social policy. The first item on the list is that under socialism 'economics will be subordinated to welfare' because scarcity will be abolished by socialism (p. 63; see also Glyn and Harrison, 1980, pp. 164–74). Deacon also emphasizes the role of need in determining the level and type of service, but like other contemporary Marxist writers in the area he gives remarkably little attention to how those needs are to be specified and made effective. The discussions in this area seem to be characterized by the incantation of a few key notions – needs, democracy, anti-bureaucracy, anti-professionalism – which, un-exceptional as slogans, hardly amount to a programme. Some of this literature is delightfully naïve, for example, Deacon's asser-tion that 'Mass participation will ensure full public discussion of all policy questions' (1981, p. 63). But it is also extraordinarily silent about current discussions, for example in the specification of needs. The London/Edinburgh Weekend Return Group (1980) assumes that any opposition to cuts prefigures a superior, socialist specification of 'needs'. But the group does not support its example, opposition to hospital closures, with any discussion of the current formula for allocating health resources according to some criteria of need.[3] One may disagree with this formula, or argue that it should only take place in the context of differential rates of growth, not cuts. But nevertheless, it is one example of a specification of need, and one which has to be addressed if rhetoric is not to be a substitute for policy discussion.

The Marxist Left has generally very little to say about taxation. Any talk of financing constraint is seen (not always consistently) as either ideological camouflage for lack of willingness to confront capital, or as a problem only under capitalism. When the issue is discussed, the position is simply a stronger version of the 'pot of gold' mentality, where resources will come easily and without adverse side effects from the rich and the company sector if only the political will is there.

Conclusions on Expenditure and Taxation

The above outlines of the policies of the Left suggest that at the level of short-run programmes there is considerable agreement between the Labour Party and the S.D.P. (1983 vintage). On the expenditure side, this would involve a programme of public investment and some expansion of direct state employment, primarily for employment reasons. For social welfare, it would involve an increase in child benefit, increased benefits for the long-term unemployed, one-parent familes and pensioners. It would also include some nationalization of the benefits for the disabled.

On the tax side of the balance sheet, there also seems scope for agreement on short-run measures. Both groups would like to abolish (perhaps gradually) the married man's allowance, scale down the mortgage interest relief, abolish the upper limit on National Insurance contributions, and move towards a 'social security tax' parallel to the income tax, and hence the abolition of the National Insurance Fund.

As short-run policies these seem macroeconomically unexceptionable, and clearly superior to any policies likely to follow from the current Conservative view of the welfare state. But the longer run seems much more problematic. In the case of the S.D.P., there seems to be some movement away from the egalitarian stance of welfare policy of 1983; and the unification of the tax and benefit scheme could be used as a means of reducing public expenditure on welfare, though this is by no means intrinsic in such a unification. On the Labour Party side there is an apparent lack of any long-run policy on the occupational welfare system. For example, the rise of pension funds has been dominated in Labour discussions by the view of them as sources of current money (see chapter 5). Their implications for social welfare, beyond a vague dislike, have received much less attention (see Field, 1981).

Whilst there are plainly urgent necessities in social welfare, there is also a need for long-run thinking about the shape of the welfare state. This seems to be hindered in part by an obsession in the literature on problems such as the 'poverty trap', which appears to be a problem greatly exaggerated (Atkinson, 1984, pp. 133–4). Unfortunately, the Marxist Left appears to have little to offer such a long-run perspective because of its combination of Utopianism and easy rhetoric as opposed to programmatic discussion.

On the taxation side, there are long-run proposals such as that of Meade (1978) which are open to development. The major hindrance here, notably in the Labour Party, is the view that there is a 'pot of gold' somewhere which will provide resources. Whilst such a view prevails, any fundamental reforms seem unlikely.

NATIONALIZATION

The S.D.P., the Labour Party and the Marxist Left all say a great deal about nationalization in their programmes for Britain. But the context of the discussion differs quite markedly in each case. For the S.D.P., the context is largely one of dealing with the long-run problems of the nationalized sector, not the immediate economic crisis. In the S.D.P. view, the prime policies to deal with the latter are predominantly macroeconomic, with any kind of industrial policy playing a subordinate role. For the Labour Party, in contrast, nationalization plays a dual role as both central to the resolution of the immediate economic crisis and (more ambiguously) as a socialist objective in its own right. For the Marxist Left, both these aspects are present also, but both are dominated by the view that it is the power of capitalists which is the crucial problem and nationalization the central solution.

In looking at the discussion of nationalization on the Left, starting with the S.D.P., we necessarily pursue arguments of increasing generality. Broadly speaking, the further Left one goes, the greater significance is given to nationalization as an instrument (and indeed objective) of policy.

The S.D.P. and Nationalization

Nationalization is discussed at some length in the S.D.P. policy document on industrial strategy (S.D.P., 1983B). However, it is clear that in fact the nationalized industries have little distinctive role to play in this strategy. As already noted in chapter 5, the three predominant themes of S.D.P. industrial policy are working 'with the market', seeing increased competition as the major means to greater efficiency; reforms of research and development (R and D) policy; and reforms of education and training. The discussion of the nationalized industries focuses mainly on the first of these, that is, increasing competition where appropriate and providing substitutes for such competition for those nationalized industries where this is seen as impossible or inappropriate.

Such an approach rests on the view that the ownership of economic assets is an issue which is of secondary importance to the efficiency of its use. 'Social Democrats regard the question of ownership as of little interest in its own right, and have no desire to change the frontier between the public and private sectors of industry for its own sake' (S.D.P., 1983B, p. 26). 'The first need is to put the long and sterile debate about ownership behind us, the incessant concentration on nationalization and de-nationalization which has done so much damage to industry through the uncertainty it has created, and which has hindered the development of a creative industrial policy based on a genuine partnership between Government and industry' (1983B, p. 1).

Coupled with this line of argument is the view that Britain needs an industrial 'strategy', but not industrial 'planning' (p. 2), so there is no role for nationalization as part of a more *dirigiste* style of policy. Hence, most of the S.D.P. proposals are for incremental changes to the existing functioning of the nationalized industries along lines which have been part of discussions in this area for a number of years.

In the case of nationalized industries in competitive sectors, the S.D.P. argues that they should be restructured as Companies Act companies, have private equity capital introduced, and close down those parts of their operation which are found unprofitable in the market place (p. 27). For monopolistic firms, or ones such as British Rail where there is (and should remain) a substantial element of social obligation in their running, the market should be replaced by an Efficiency Audit Commission. This would be a permanent body, with a remit to examine the efficiency of nationalized firms not subject to the full rigours of competition, and to make its reports available to the Treasury and to parliament (pp. 28–9).

The industries would obtain greater insulation from day-to-day interference by ministers by the device of a supervisory board between ministers and the executive management of the firm. Finally, external financing limits, which should be retained for the monopoly industries, should as far as possible be separated from general government financial policy, so that the conduct of each nationalized firm should be insulated from the needs of macro-economic management (pp. 29–30).

In part, such policy proposals follow those of the N.E.D.O. proposals made in 1976 (N.E.D.O., 1976). These included the idea of some kind of continuing efficiency audit and a 'policy board', though in the N.E.D.O. proposals this would have had representatives of various interests upon it – workers, consumers,

civil servants – an idea which does not seem to form part of the
S.D.P. proposals. Both reforms seem eminently sensible.

More problematic is the attempt to insulate the functioning of
individual nationalized firms from the exigencies of macroeconomic
management. There would seem to be two distinct problems with
such proposals. On the one hand it may be a 'counsel of
perfection', as the 'New Right' have argued; as long as a
nationalized industry remains such, it is likely to be thought of as a
potential weapon in the armoury of government (Beesley and
Littlechild, 1983 and 1984). Indeed, this is borne out by the
S.D.P.'s own proposals to use controls on nationalized industries'
prices as a means of reflating the economy whilst minimizing
inflation (S.D.P., 1983A, pp. 2, 14).

The presumption of the New Right is that any such interference
will always be a bad thing, so nationalized industries should be
privatized, to make sure that the temptation to interference does
not arise. The difficulty with this line of argument is that it
presumes that any outcome produced in the 'market place' will be
superior to that produced by government. But such theory is
precisely what the S.D.P. objects to in its general rhetoric, and it
seems perfectly sensible to see nationalized industry prices as a
potential weapon of macroeconomic management, where it can be
argued that the benefits of such a policy outweigh any harms done
by interference in the functioning of nationalized industries. And
such policies are not necessarily incompatible with the dual board
structure, and the attempt to separate, to some extent, policy-
making from execution. What matters is that such macroeconomic
policies are clearly made the responsibility of government, and
their effects allowed for in the scrutiny of the performance of the
nationalized firms.

But this ambivalence in the S.D.P.'s own policies obscures a
deeper problem. Like the New Right, the S.D.P. takes it for
granted that by and large, efficiency is a function of the degree of
competition, and hence the main thrust of policy for nationalized
monopolies should be to find substitutes for such competiton. The
major analytic difference between the S.D.P. and the New Right is
that for the former it is product market competition which is
crucial for efficiency, whilst for the latter capital market competition is also vital. Hence the latter advocates privatization primarily
to create such competition (Beesley and Littlechild, 1983 and
1984). Whilst this difference is an important one, it should not hide
the similarity of the analyses which underpin the arguments.

These analyses are two-fold. The first concerns a view of the
effects of competition in the private sector; the second considers

the question of what efficiency is. Both of these issues are very broad, very complex and very important. They cannot be dealt with adequately in the context of this book. But some points must be made because the issues do seem to arise directly out of the policy proposals.

Both the S.D.P. and the New Right follow the mainstream of economic theory in seeing product market competition as the crucial determinant of efficiency in firms. In this view the market process will both drive resources into areas where consumers gain greatest satisfaction from the outputs (allocative efficiency) and towards those firms which produce given outputs at least cost (*x*-efficiency). A large part of microeconomics is concerned with elaborating on and qualifying the processes involved.

The mechanism is one of the 'survival of the fittest', where the unfit, like the Dodo, fail to adapt, and go under, the real resources being reallocated to the more efficient elsewhere. A devastating critique of this kind of argument has been made by Winter (1964 and 1971). Very broadly, he argues that the firms which the markets select to survive in one situation will simply have characteristics favourable to survival in that situation, rather than in others. And there is no reason to suppose that characteristics beneficial to survival will be the same in the two situations, nor is there a mechanism akin to genes in biology to alter characteristics as the environment alters. More empirically, it has long been argued that economics is unhelpful about the internal workings of firms which bear on their efficiency, because of the almost obsessive interest in the functioning of markets. Hence, applied economics suggests that inter-firm differences in efficiency must be explained by many factors other than the degree of product competition to which the firm is subjected (e.g. Nelson, 1982; Pratten, 1976).

Hence the view that product market competition is the be-all and end-all of efficiency seems unjustified. Partly in response to such arguments, but more probably because of the widespread absence of competition in product markets, much recent analysis has focused on competition in financial markets. Here it is broadly argued that, whatever else enters into the firm's behaviour, if it is constantly pressurized to produce profits by the threat of takeover or the need to raise finance, this will be a major stimulant to efficiency. But again, there is good evidence against the strong version of such arguments. Singh (1975) has shown how takeovers do not provide a mechanism by which the inefficient are taken over by the efficient. Rather, the takeover process is predominantly about size, which may have little or even an inverse relationship to efficiency. As for raising new funds, evidence on the criteria used seems rather thin, but again size, rather than just profitability and efficiency, would seem to be crucial (because it is seen as an index of security).

These points are not made in order to argue that monopoly is a good thing. It is accepted that competition is often one important stimulus to efficiency. The problem is using an idealized notion of the efficiency of the private sector as a guide to the conduct of nationalized firms. In particular, this implies that efficiency auditing in some form may be an appropriate policy for all firms, not just monopolies in the public sector. Such a policy might, for example, be similar to that pursued by the Price Commission in the latter days of the 1974–9 Labour government. This commission conducted a kind of compulsory management consultancy role in firms which applied for price increases. Such a policy is likely to be beneficial in almost all firms (Tomlinson, 1983A).

Related to this problem of idealizing the efficiency effects of the market is the problem of defining efficiency. In the above discussion the traditional economist's definitions of efficiency – allocative and productive – have been uncritically used. But in fact efficiency is far more complex than such notions imply. In particular those concepts are based on the assumption of full employment of resources, and secondly they focus on static not dynamic efficiency.

The first assumption is plainly invalid today. Hence the possibility must be recognized of an efficiency trade-off between employing more resources and the output per unit from such employment. A good example of one solution to such a trade-off is the Soviet Union, where a very strong pressure of demand maintains full employment of resources, but at the cost of producers always being able to sell their output, and hence providing a major disincentive to production efficiency.

In Britain such a trade-off might mean using the nationalized industries as instruments of employment policy, along with general measures, such as the Temporary Employment Subsidy. Such measures would be microeconomically inefficient if one assumed full employment, but might well be a second-best solution when such an assumption was clearly inappropriate.

The second question, that of static versus dynamic efficiency, has been touched on in chapter 5. Here it is sufficient simply to point out that if the focus is on dynamic efficiency in the form of, for example R and D, nationalized firms may again be readily available vehicles of such policy. As suggested in chapter 5, once a priority R and D has been decided upon, the best policy may be to find a firm in a relevant industry with a good management structure and to focus on that as a vehicle of the policy. The S.D.P. goes some way towards this view (1938B, p. 11) but seems to assume that this would be a private firm, and that private firms in Britain would be willing to accept the conditions attached to their use as such vehicles. Given the backwardness of much private-sector management in Britain, neither of these assumptions seems justified.

Overall, the policy on nationalized industries seems to be fairly typical of S.D.P. policy as a whole. The Social Democrats propose intelligent, gradual reforms which reflect the lessons learnt from the conduct of British policy in the last couple of decades. At the same time, the analytic framework of their discussions broadly follows that of conventional microeconomics, which in the industrial area is probably particularly conservative, with what can only be called a faith bordering on the religious in the efficacy of market mechanisms. This framework seems to inhibit putting forward policies which measure up to the S.D.P.'s own acceptance of the scale of Britain's economic problems.

The Labour Party and Nationalization

The Labour Party is committed by clause IV of its constitution to 'the common ownership of the means of production, distribution and exchange'. As far as the Labour Party is concerned this remains in place as the specifically socialist goal (1982B, p. 48), and it is this which differentiates the Labour from the Social Democratic Party, with the latter's commitment to the mixed economy (e.g. Cripps *et al.*, 1981, p. 174). Whilst this commitment remains central to Labour's view of the world, there is a widespread acceptance that the case for nationalization is not an electorally popular one. Hence Labour's programme (1982B, p. 48) argues the need to 'demonstrate the practical benefits of common ownership, showing how public enterprise can be a spearhead for innovation and new investment, making clear the benefits to both workers and consumers, and explaining the best forms of organization and different forms of common ownership'. This defensive attitude has been reinforced by recent privatization, though for some on the Left this has been seen as an opportunity to open up the issue of public/private distinction (e.g. Heald and Steel, 1984).

This posture creates a certain ambivalence about Labour's nationalization proposals. On the one hand, nationalization is a goal, an objective in its own right, politically crucial because it is seen as the one clear, defining characteristic of socialism as a political creed. On the other hand, nationalization is a means to a large variety of ends, and in principle, therefore, might be a good or a bad means.

The consequence of this ambivalence is that nationalization appears overloaded with objectives; because it is itself desirable it is seen as a solvent for almost any problem. Equally, the precise relationship between nationalization and any particular policy outcome is underspecified.

The first point has been well argued by Pollard (1979, pp. 184–5) with respect to Labour's past proposal to nationalize the banks:

> it emerged and disappeared from time to time as a component of different policy packages, without being firmly based on a tradition of its own. . . . More significant still is the discontinuity which can be observed in the justification, rather than the proposals themselves. . . . Beginning with redistributive justice and economic power, we move to efficiency, the maintenance of employment, the prevention of poverty, the control over foreign policy, the planning of industry, efficiency and low cost in banking, the prevention of fraud, the reduction in nepotism, the development of long-term investment, and many others besides from time to time.

A similar set of multiple purposes emerges from more recent proposals for common ownership. It will provide a 'means to bring greater collective control over the development of industry and a fair distribution of the wealth that is generated' (Labour Party, 1982B, p. 39); it has 'a vital part to play in rebuilding the economy and creating an efficient and democratic industrial structure' (1982B, p. 48). Also, 'public ownership can play a dynamic and enterprising role, leading economic recovery and supporting industrial planning' (p. 49); it will be 'a major source of technical innovation' (1983A, p. 12), and will have a major role in 'returning to full employment' (1982A, p. 18).

Thus the Labour Party's proposals for nationalization operate at at least three different levels. First, there is what may be called the traditional socialist objective of nationalization, as a means to wealth redistribution and greater accountability. Secondly, there is nationalization as a means of attaining the macroeconomic purpose of full employment. Finally, there is the microeconomic aspect, with nationalization as a central part of an industrial strategy involving an extension of planning and the nationalization of firms in 'key sectors'.

The first of these levels of argument plainly raises a host of issues which can only be sketched out here. Nationalization as a means to wealth redistribution has never been argued at any length by the Labour Party. Partly, this is because, being committed to 'proper' compensation of private owners, Labour's acts of nationalization have not functioned as a means of redistribution, as expropriation would. Secondly, the act of nationalization by itself does not redistribute personal wealth, but simply replaces one asset in the hands of the previous owner with another. To change the distribution via nationalization would seem to require using the nationalized assets in such a way as to allow workers and consumers to accumulate greater wealth from higher incomes. But this would seem to cut across other aims commonly linked to nationalization.

It may be objected that what is meant by wealth redistribution is not such a narrow notion of wealth, but the idea that nationalization will remove control of wealth from a small minority of owners to the public in general, in other words, the issue is really one of accountability, not personal assets. Unease within the Labour Party with the existing nationalized industries has to a considerable extent derived from a belief that the Morrisonian form of public corporation has reduced their accountability almost to vanishing point. Against this trend there are demands for much greater democracy and accountability within the public sector (Labour Party, 1982B, p. 50). This policy involves the creation of industrial democracy within nationalized industries, and greater accountability 'upwards' to the new planning apparatus.

The last Labour government did, in fact, initiate extensions of industrial democracy in the public sector, notably in British Steel (Brannen *et al.*, 1976) and the Post Office (Batstone *et al.*, 1984). Whilst both of these experiments were important attempts to give form to the common calls for democracy in industry, they were not, for a whole host of reasons, resounding successes. More important in the current context, they could at best form only one part of an overall strategy of democratization. In other words, they would have to be linked to mechanisms of democratization and accountability 'to the nation'. In the most naïve version, such accountability is achieved by having a minister responsible for the industry who is answerable for its conduct to parliament. One has to be far gone indeed in 'parliamentary cretinism' to believe that such a system amounts to effective means of accountability, even with the addition of a select committee to provide more detailed scrutiny.

Debates in this area of the relation between nationalized industries and the political process have come to be dominated not by questions of effective accountability but by the mechanisms necessary to give nationalized industries more autonomy. An exception to this generalization is the N.E.D.O. report (1976), which, as already noted, suggested a policy council for each industry, on a representative basis, providing a strategy which a lower tier board would execute. The S.D.P. has endorsed a version of this proposal. The Labour Party (as opposed to Labour governments) has not played much part in discussions in this area. The whole emphasis has been on democracy *vis-à-vis* the work-force. Whatever the merits of the proposed accountability via planning mechanisms as a form of 'industrial policy' (see further below) it is far from clear that such proposals take the arguments about accountability any further. They involve a new role for government ministries (and unions) in the nationalized sector, but it is not clear how, if at all, this extends the scope of accountability rather than just complicating ministerial responsibilites.

Much less general is the idea of using the vehicle of the nationalized industries as a means of expansion, that is to say, as instruments of macroeconomic policy. If this means simply that a public-sector firm should 'give top priority to the part it can play in helping to fulfil the overriding objective of a return to full employment' (Labour Party, 1982A, p. 19), this seems reasonable as a broad injunction. But, of course, it does not help much in looking at the unavoidable issues on which the expansion of industries should be focused, and in turn it is far from clear that being part of the nationalized sector should itself be a reason for expanding an industry. Overall, it is not clear that it is very helpful to see nationalized industries as potential macroeconomic instruments, the pertinent considerations being such things as the employment intensity and import intensity of expenditures, rather than ownership *per se*. Nationalized industries are not homogeneous with respect to such considerations.

The most detailed discussion of nationalized industries in recent Labour Party proposals has been regarding their function as a vehicle for industrial policy. Newly created or expanded existing public firms are seen as central to the Labour Party's policies to regenerate the British economy. Such policies involve a substantial expansion of nationalization, as well as a renationalization of those assets privatized under the Conservatives.

The emphasis of such proposals differs from the traditional nationalizations of 1945–51. For a diversity of reasons, those measures largely embraced whole sectors of the economy, not individual firms. Such policies could be rationalized by socialists as giving control of the 'commanding height', and by economists as reflecting the need for public intervention where natural monopolies and/or substantial externalities existed. But these kinds of arguments now play little role in Labour Party discussions, and the focus is on individual firms as vehicles for raising the efficiency of the economy's manufacturing base.

This focus on individual firms originated on the Right of the Labour Party, in the attempt to make nationalization a means to specific ends rather than an end in itself (Crosland, 1956). It was taken up by Holland (1976), and became part of Labour's official policies from 1973. Holland's emphasis was on the need to create public firms which would break up the cosy, non-competitive environment in which most British firms were argued to operate. More recent discussion has emphasized their role in both technical innovation and planning (Labour Party, 1983A), or where a firm is 'pivotal' (1982B, p. 45).

Some comments on the nature of planning in the Labour Party programme have been offered in chapter 5. One point that was made there needs to be reiterated in the current context. If industrial policy involves attempting to expand particular firms as a means of expansion of a specific sector, then some means is needed of choosing the firm. This involves, above all, a scrutiny of the firm's management structure, and hence its likely capacity to deliver the efficient expansion desired by government. This dimension seems to be lacking from Labour Party discussion. If the intention is to nationalize an individual firm in order to lead the expansion of a sector, then choosing the firm is crucial. A simple assertion that a firm is 'pivotal' seems wholly inadequate. Equally, if the emphasis is on the expansion of technical innovation it is vital to attempt to assess a company's capacity to absorb and deploy R and D resources – a particularly problematic area in Britain (Smith, 1984, ch. 4).

'Picking winners' involves picking both firms and sectors. On the latter, the Labour discussion is rather general. There is the obligatory mention of the 'new technology', in which, indeed, INMOS, the originally publicly owned microchip company is important (Labour Party, 1982B, pp. 45–6). But beyond this there seems less certainty. The 1982 programme jumbles together 'electronics, pharmaceuticals and health equipment; the construction industry and building materials; the private road haulage industry; major ports, forestry and timber' (1982B, p. 49). This looks more like a combination of 'commanding heights' (such as transport) and other policy purposes (pharmaceuticals), rather than the basis of a sustained expansion of key manufacturing sectors. The election manifesto of 1983 seems to retreat from such specific commitments, but does commit Labour to expansion of existing public enterprise activity in steel, shipbuilding and aerospace (1983A, p. 12). These sectors also do not look like obvious candidates for expansion, and aerospace in particular looks precisely like one of the industries where Britain has greatly overcommitted itself in terms of R and D expenditure in the past (Smith, 1984, ch. 4; Freeman, 1979).

Overall, the specific policy proposals for nationalization in the industrial sector seem insufficiently argued. In the context of the economic condition in which Britain is likely to be by the late 1980s, it does seem appropriate to see nationalization mainly as a possible instrument of industrial policy. But as already suggested in chapter 5, industrial policy is a very problematic area for the Labour Party. Until some of the ambiguities in that area are clarified, nationalization as an instrument appears to be a secondary issue.

Equally, the conduct of existing and future nationalized firms seems to be an area where a ritual incantation for more democracy and accountability and less bureaucracy has taken the place of serious policy discussion. Here, perhaps, more attention to the 'traditional' Social Democratic case for nationalization would be one element of a more helpful discussion (e.g. Lipton, 1976; Nove, 1973).

One exception to this general neglect of the specifics of the functioning of nationalized industry has been the desire to free nationalized industry funding from the constraints of the P.S.B.R. (Labour Party, 1982B, p. 50). This proposal is similar to that of the S.D.P.; but it raises the same ambiguity. Whilst it is undoubtedly right to reject the current government's fetishism about the P.S.B.R., it needs to be accepted that a complete severance of nationalized industry financing and macroeconomic management is not attainable: the nationalized industries are too important for that. And, conversely, it would be curious for socialists to argue that nationalized industries could not sometimes be used as instruments of macroeconomic policy, a view based on the rejection of such a severance. So once again, the full implications of an initially sensible policy are not worked through.

One proposal for nationalization which the Labour Party has recently entertained, though it is not in the manifesto for 1983, is that of nationalizing a clearing bank (Labour Party, 1976 and 1982B, pp. 52–3). The context of the proposals, which in addition to nationalizing a bank include the creation of a National Investment Bank, is one of finance for industry. As noted in chapter 5, Labour Party discussion of Britain's economic problems is dominated by the view that it is low investment which is crucial, and that the major reason for that low investment is inadequate finance. As argued there, this seems extremely problematic.

The other side to this obsession with the financial system as a source of funds for industry is a neglect of its other roles. As Thompson (1977) has noted, the whole issue of credit control, the macroeconomic aspect of the financial system, is absent from the discussion. Linked to this is a neglect of the whole complex issue of the relation of dependence between state financing and the financial system. Finally, the focus on banks obscures the financial role played by other institutions, building societies for example, which in Labour Party discussions appear as related solely to housing policy, despite being the largest institutions in the flow of funds in Britain. As with industrial nationalization, the priority seems to be first to clarify the policy objectives and policy instruments in the area before assessing how far nationalization is a pertinent measure.

The Marxist Left and Nationalization

For the Marxist Left, nationalization is crucially important because it deprives capital of its control over the means of production.[4] Thus critiques of the Alternative Economic Strategy from the Left (e.g. Militant, 1981A; Glyn and Harrison, 1980; Harrison, 1982) argue that its fundamental weakness is its evasion of the need to nationalize a large proportion of private industry, in order to prevent capital from sabotaging the strategy.

In this view, nationalization is fundamentally a source of power over the economy. 'There is nothing sacrosanct or magical about the figure 200 – 150 or 300 would achieve fundamentally the same effect; the state would control the major share of production. The takeover of 150 or more companies would deprive capital of the main levers of economic power. Meeting the A.E.S. target of 20–25 would not' (Glyn and Harrison, 1980, p. 165).

In essence, this view is one which is based on the naïvest kind of reasoning about the functioning of organizations. It sees firms as organizations in which there is an unambiguous seat of power, and that power can simply be wrenched from one set of hands and placed in another (the workers' or the state's – this is ambiguous). Such a view treats the firm as a totalitarian organization which has a 'goal' which is realized without any problems. The difficulty for socialists is simple to displace its rulers, and hence acquire the ability to displace one goal by another (production for profit by production for social need).

The naïvety of such a view is apparent if one asks who controls existing capitalist enterprises. The obvious answer is the board of directors. But it is well known that these boards are often 'rubber stamps' for decisions made elsewhere. And, as Marxists know, workers and their organizations also affect the policy of enterprises. But it is not simply that organizations are complicated places. When a board of directors decides, for example, on an investment project, its decision will be affected by the means of finance available, the forms of calculation employed, the time horizons considered appropriate, and so on. There will be a decision, but that decision will in turn be an effect of dozens of other decisions made elsewhere and by different agencies. So the notion of some simple agent who controls the enterprise is unhelpful to a serious analysis of firms and their functioning (see also Tomlinson, 1982 and 1984; Thompson, 1982).

Secondly, and related to this, is the notion of capital. In the Marxist Left's arguments the body of (never specified) persons who really control enterprises is a homogeneous, self-conscious body able to act in unison on an agreed programme. Now plainly there are bodies which seek to articulate what might be construed as the views of capital, for example the Confederation of British Industries (C.B.I.) or the Institute of Directors. But these bodies have all the problems of calculating where interests lie, of deciding issues of representation and legitimacy, which are so much better known in the case of socialist parties and trade unions. The capacity of such bodies to articulate a policy line does not mean that they are homogeneous entities, with a single, well-thought-out view, any more than it does in the Labour Party. Indeed, in recent years the C.B.I. has floundered partly because of the increasing difficulty of articulating a view acceptable to all its members in the face of the depredations of 'Thatcherism'.

Overall, the scenario conjured up by the Marxist Left of a simple showdown where the state either nationalizes or gives in to capital is theoretically crude and politically inadequate. Equally, the presumption seems to be that once nationalization has taken place in a truly socialist manner, the problems of organization, of competing objectives and all the other traditional concerns, will be rendered obsolete by a transcendent political consciousness.

Conclusions on Nationalization

Arguments about nationalization are arguments about the ownership status of companies. The difficulty is to demonstrate any unambiguous consequences of different forms of ownership. For the S.D.P. this is not much of a problem, because the policies they wish to pursue are based on displacing questions of ownership from a central role in arguments about the economy. But even for the S.D.P. there is a dogmatic insistence on the maintenance of a mixed economy, which is in effect an insistence on a particular mix of ownership. (And this poses difficulties for the S.D.P. when, as now, that mix is being sharply altered.)

One advantage of the recent emphasis on democracy in the rhetoric of the Left has been its influence in at least partially opening up the problems of treating private and public ownership as polar opposites. In the discussion above, nationalization and public ownership have been treated as interchangeable terms. But in Labour Party discussions there is now some awareness of the alternative versions of ownership which differ from classically 'private': 'We believe that common ownership through public enterprise and co-operatives has a vital part to play in rebuilding the economy and creating an efficient and democratic industrial structure' (Labour Party, 1982B, p. 48). Thus the programme has a number of proposals to build on which greatly encourage the expansion of co-operatives (1982B, p. 51).

Apart from the political arguments for co-operatives as alternatives to private firms, their return to the agenda of the Labour Party will, one hopes, have useful analytic effects. The development of co-operatives has the potential to open up issues about the organization of firms which the focus on ownership has functioned to obscure. The dominant socialist tradition has seen the capitalist enterprise as a stage upon which preconstituted interest groups (workers: managers/capitalists) fight out their battles. Every aspect of the firm's functioning – technology, organizational forms, payment systems, accounting practices – can then be viewed as a more or less straightforward expression of one interest or the other. In consequence, the Left has generally been strikingly ignorant about issues of corporate organization, and in particular about the diversity of effects which those forms of organization generate.

Through the slogan of nationalization, the Left has rightly raised the issue of the disposition of corporate assets. But any progress on that issue requires jettisoning much of the Left's intellectual baggage. And this is not just an ideological problem of the proper definitions of socialism. It impinges directly on issues of a return to full employment, which the Left rightly stresses. The character of these links is taken up in chapter 7.

7
Some Strategic Issues

This chapter offers an overview of some of the major themes of the policy proposals discussed in the previous six chapters. It does not attempt to offer a comprehensive overall strategy for the British economy. Partly this is for banal reasons of personal incapacity: no one person could sensibly hope to know enough about the British economy, let alone the context in which future policies might operate, to offer such a comprehensive view. The other reason is more substantive.

The very notion of strategy can be unhelpful if it conjures up an image of a coherent, well-articulated set of policies which can both derive from a common source and be put into practice simply on command of some central agency. This is to picture economic policy as like a (naïve) view of military strategy, in which armies are deployed on the ground in exact accordance with the battle plans for the general staff, via the mechanism of an unquestioning military hierarchy. (This is the imagery which often seems to lie behind the notion of 'Thatcherism', which gives to current Conservative policy a much more coherent and much less contingent character than seems justified.)[1]

Against such a view should be stressed the unavoidably contingent nature of economic policy, most especially in an open economy like Britain – a dependence on unforeseeable events. Secondly, policy is necessarily incoherent, in the sense that it is unimaginable that such a policy will not involve stresses and direct contradictions between different components. Indeed, one may say that successful policy-making is characterized by the management (but not resolution) of such tensions.

This chapter attempts to highlight and develop certain themes already touched on in the previous chapters, and gives some comments on points of stress and contradiction which policies based on such themes are likely to entail. To return to the military metaphor for a moment: battles are never the replication on the ground of the paper plans of the general staff. But what such plans should do is bring out certain objectives to be obtained to secure victory: powerful counterforces which will have to be out-manoeuvred or destroyed, and the weakness of one's own forces which will have to be overcome. In the same way, 'strategic' may be a term deployed in discussions of economic policy for the process of recognition and assessment of how to deal with both the strength of one's 'opponents' (constraints on policy) and the weaknesses of one's own forces. (The problem of 'strategy' is taken up from a rather different perspective in the final section of this chapter.)

AREAS OF AGREEMENT AND DISAGREEMENT

As should be apparent from the previous chapters, there are several areas where, at the level of broad concern, anti-Conservative forces are united.[2] There is agreement that employment should be a central goal of policy, and not just a rhetorical concern. This agreement was indicated by the launch of the Employment Institute in April 1985, a potential focus of anti-Thatcher policies on employment. There is agreement too that a revival of manufacturing output is crucial, though it is widely accepted that this is because of problems with the balance of payments at anything approaching full employment (especially as North Sea oil runs out), rather than as a direct source of employment. There is also agreement that an extension of industrial democracy/workers' control is central, though here the meanings given to such a phrase are extremely diverse. For the S.D.P., as suggested in chapter 5, industrial democracy would be mainly a new form of legitimation of management, whilst for the Marxist Left anything short of full workers' control (a concept not easy to define) is likely to be seen as inadequate. Nevertheless, it is worth noting the convergence of rhetoric in this area, which opens up the possibility of significant reforms.

Of the topics where much less consensus is apparent, that of the scope and character of the public sector is undoubtedly the most important. As noted in chapter 6, on reform of the social security system there is some convergence of the S.D.P. and Labour Party lines, and no obvious reason why the character of these changes should be unacceptable to the Marxist Left. However, on broader questions of the general position of public expenditure and the public sector, much less agreement is apparent. Within the S.D.P. there seem to be strong pressures for viewing quite large parts of recent privatization as desirable, and as something to be retained by post-Thatcher governments. On the other hand, the Marxist Left still seems to retain a belief in the expansion of the public sector as a necessary if not sufficient basis for its objectives. Between these views, the Labour Party seems to be forced into a largely defensive posture, of renationalization of assets privatized by the Conservatives, but with no clear picture of how the public sector as a whole is to be organized.

In part, as already suggested in chapter 6, the problem is the overloading of the public sector and public expenditure with objectives, and the unavoidable disappointments and conflicts when these cannot all be realized. Amongst such issues, public expenditure is likely to force itself onto the agenda fairly quickly for any post-Thatcher government.

The panic over public expenditure in the mid-1970s was compounded of a real but limited problem of expenditure control under specific inflationary and political circumstances, with an absurd exaggeration of this in a rhetoric of world-threatening danger (see Tomlinson, 1985, ch. 6). In retrospect, what is worrying is the incapacity of the government of the time to distinguish and cope with these two different components.

A lesson of this episode is that cash limits must be one part of control of public expenditure. For macroeconomic purposes, such instruments are unavoidable, however much they might, for example, be opened up for negotiation rather than imposed unilaterally by government. Part of these negotiations could be about the relation between these cash limits, their real resource implications and their links to the policy objectives which the expenditure is supposed to finance. (The whole area of the relation between public expenditure and policy objectives is one crying out for reform (see Cockle, 1984.)

Whilst the panic of 1975–6 was in large part the result of those of bad political faith taking advantage of an apparent opportunity, this does not mean that there are not long-term upward pressures on public expenditure to be taken seriously. Above all, the increasing longevity of the population and the very powerful pressures towards higher health standards do pose problems which are not just a figment of the expenditure-cutting Right. There is no obvious reason why the increased taxation to finance such expansion should not be relatively easily and consensually obtained, if the issue is dealt with appropriately. But 'appropriately' must embrace not only an acceptance of the need for clear priorities in public expenditure, but also a giving-up of the 'pot of gold' attitude to taxation.

CONSTRAINTS ON REFLATION

The Left is united, and rightly so, in believing that there is substantial scope for a reflation of demand in the British economy. Not only does the evidence suggest that since 1979 the deflationary policies of the government have been a major cause of the rise in unemployment, but their own 'supply-side' objectives, even if attained (for example, lower interest rates), are likely to make little difference if overall demand is depressed. Recent American experience has shown once again that high real interest rates are no great hindrance to investment if demand is buoyant.

Whilst such a line of argument cannot, perhaps, be too often stated in the context of Conservative policies, advocacy of reflation must take seriously the constraints it would face. Here, it would seem, is where S.D.P. policy discussion is most persuasive. A realistic appraisal of the strengths of the constraints on macroeconomic policy is the starting point of the S.D.P. programme, even if, as has been suggested, the means of dealing with those constraints are in some respects less convincing.

Central to those constraints is the capacity of financial markets to translate their view of a country's economic policy into financial pressure on that country. The leverage of such markets operates both via government debt sales, and via the buying and selling of foreign exchange. In the classic case of Britain in 1976, the unfavourable view taken of government policy led both to a 'gilt strike' and a run on the pound which forced a sharp reversal of policy.

There is some scope for reflation in Britain which would probably do very little damage to international financial confidence, given that Britain's policies have been particularly deflationary for the past few years in comparison with those of the other advanced capitalist countries (see table 1.4). But the combination of a non-Conservative government, and a reflationary package which went beyond simply bringing Britain up to the O.E.C.D. average in fiscal stance, would undoubtedly lead to a 'loss of confidence'.

One unavoidable response to such a constraint is caution in the scale and speed of reflation. This the S.D.P. rightly emphasizes. What is much more in need of policy development is the scope and means for offsetting the effects of any such constraints, that is, reducing the leverage of financial markets on economic policy. This involves two separable issues – government debt policy, and policy on the exchange rate.

Debt Policy

On debt policy the Labour Party and much of the Left have focused too much on the intellectual absurdity of using nominal P.S.B.R. as a sensible guide to, and measure of, policy. They have given less attention (though apparently more than the S.D.P.) to how, given that this magnitude is taken seriously by financial markets, the sales to finance that borrowing can be a less potentially powerful lever on government policy. This is not just an issue of interest rates. The evidence of 1976 suggests that even higher interest rates may not attract buyers if government policy is perceived as reprehensible enough.

Revell (1983, p. 161) has pointed out that Britain is out of line with many other countries in the way it finances its public borrowing. 'In many countries the government ensures the fulfilment of its borrowing requirements by imposing obligations on banks and other financial institutions to hold certain quotas of government bonds, but this is a method that is practically unknown in Britain, many of the obligations imposed on savings banks having been relaxed.' Given the considerable leverage of government over financial institutions, this is one obvious way of reducing the potential difficulties of open market sales of debt. Equally, other institutions, notably pension funds, could also be required to hold some proportion of government debt in their portfolio. Such policies, in addition to development of the Conservatives' use of index-linked securities, could help at least to reduce the scope for financial market leverage on policy.

Exchange Rate Policy

Debt sales have not, in fact, been a problem for the current Conservative government – it has had no trouble in selling its debt at prevailing interest rates. But even a highly 'responsible' Conservative government has had difficulties with loss of confidence in sterling, which bodes ill for hopes of easy management of the exchange rate for any government less committed to the canons of 'sound finance'.

Any fully comprehensive system of exchange controls, able to discriminate sensibly between necessary and speculative exchange purchases, looks like a pipe-dream. But this is definitely not a reason for giving up all forms of such control, even though all of them look more likely to be more effective over the medium term than in offsetting short-run pressures. Again, the portfolios of institutions such as pension funds look like an obvious target for regulation in terms of proportion of foreign assets. (The whole area of pension funds is in need of a radical reform of its regulatory framework.)[3] As Hattersley (1985) has stressed, there has been a marked shift in the composition of the funds' assets since 1979 which shows no sign of stabilizing, and fiscal measures (that is, loss of tax privileges) would be one way of regulating this. Such measures would be quite compatible with seeking some international framework for greater exchange rate stability, as discussed in chapter 3.

More complex still are problems in relation to the money supply. Here the S.D.P. has again stressed that this cannot simply be ignored as an 'ideological camouflage' as much of the rest of the Left suggests. The issue is two-fold. On the one hand, there is what may be called the 'expectational' aspect. If the money supply (however exactly defined) is taken seriously by economic agents (and this is much more plausible for financial markets than for wage bargainers), can any government afford simply to ignore the issue? The other question is the 'instrumental' aspect. Given that a government has to have a monetary policy, is it not sensible for that policy to focus on instruments which are more readily controllable than the money supply has proved to be, and therefore on things which can more sensibly be called instruments? This would seem likely to mean much more attention being given to interest rates and the whole range of credit sources, rather than to the money supply.[4]

Possibly these potentially conflicting demands on policy can best be coped with by announced exchange rate targets, given that financial markets are sophisticated enough to calculate the scale of domestic expansion implied by this. These targets would then be pursued by whatever instruments seemed efficacious, which are likely to include a combination of traditional monetary instruments such as interest rates and credit controls, working in concert with direct instruments of exchange control.

As argued in chapter 4, the case against seeing import controls as a central weapon in an alternative policy appears a powerful one. Whilst the case for selective import controls as a support for industrial policy looks more persuasive, the need here would seem to be to look much more analytically at the costs and benefits of various methods of subsidy of whatever sectors/firms are to be favoured by such polices. (The general issue of industrial policies is returned to below.)

In chapter 2 no discussion was offered of the correctness of the Left's focus on unemployment, except to attack those who suggest that such a focus is inappropriate because of the alleged inescapability of mass technological unemployment. But this focus does raise very general 'strategic' issues which need to be considered in looking at overall policy positions.

A major reason why unemployment deserves the central place in the Left's policies is its effects on the incomes of those who suffer from lack of a job. The average household receives only approximately half of its work income in unemployment benefit. It is obvious that, at least for the foreseeable future, some such a link between work and income levels will remain. For this reason, the best way of reducing income loss from unemployment is to reduce unemployment. Few, perhaps would disagree with this. But the comments above about reflation suggest that any reduction in unemployment will be a slow process – certainly slow in comparison with some of the claims made in the general election of 1983.

The implications of any large-scale reduction in unemployment are spelt out in rather a different manner by Metcalf (1984A, pp. 65–6). He points out that to reduce unemployment by one million over a five-year period would mean the creation of two million new jobs, allowing for increased labour supply (resulting both from demographic change and the encouragement of those who have currently given up a fruitless search for work). This implies new jobs being created at a rate of 1,150 per day – a figure with a precedent only in the 1930s.

Not only is this aggregate figure sobering, but the problems are made more apparent by looking at likely sectors of employment growth. Expansion of employment in manufacturing looks extremely unlikely. Expansion of services looks more plausible, as the government stresses, but not on anything like the scale required, even if reflation boosted output growth. In short, it is difficult to see a plausible strategy of employment creation, even on the 'moderate' scale of a reduction in unemployment of one million over five years, which does not involve a major expansion of public-sector employment. Plainly, this raises a whole host of issues in relation to the Conservatives. But the point to be stressed here is its implications for the Left. For what such an expansion focuses on is the need for a redistribution of income from the currently employed to the unemployed.

This is inescapable, because either unemployment falls rapidly, which involves a major expansion of public expenditure – and taxation, given the constraints on public borrowing; or unemployment falls more slowly, and income has to be redistributed in the form of higher benefits for the unemployed. So whatever the plausible pace of reflation, there is no 'free lunch' solution to unemployment. It involves a substantial redistribution of income.

As argued in chapters 2 and 3 in a slightly different context, the real (take-home) wage cannot be used as an index of correct policy in the current British economic policy situation.

INCOMES POLICIES

Nothing in the discussion of macroeconomic policy within the Left is as contentious as incomes policies. This may even have led in some quarters to an excessive emphasis on the centrality of such a policy. But it is difficult to see how it can be argued that without some effective control on the growth of money wages, a reflationary effort is likely to be successful in reducing unemployment in anything but the shortest run. One point to be stressed in this argument is the advantage of posing the issue as a direct one of employment, not inflation. Given the constraints imposed by financial markets, inflation – and hence the scale of reflation – can and must be controlled by the use of traditional fiscal and monetary policies. The incomes policy is, then, the means by which as much as possible of the expansion in demand is translated into jobs. Put in this way, the issue at stake in a discussion of incomes policy is the Left's willingness to forgo many of its traditional doctrines and policy stances in pursuit of its proclaimed central goal of reducing unemployment.

What needs to be seen as the strategic issue for the Left is not whether or not to have an incomes policy, but what form such a policy should take to be most favourable to the Left's other policy desires. This is plainly a complex issue, because incomes policies impinge on so many other facets of policy.

There is much to be said for Wootton's (1974) proposal for an income gains tax, to be levied on increases in personal income above some specified norm. As Hirst (1981) points out, such a scheme has the explicit advantage of building in a strong egalitarian aspect, as the tax rate is graded according to the absolute level of the base income, lower incomes being subject to a lower tax rate. Such egalitarianism would fit in with the policy objectives of the Left, and the need to create consent and support for incomes policy.

The problem with such a policy would seem to be this. If it is accepted, according to the arguments made in chapter 3, that strong trade unionism is itself an objective of Left policy, then incomes policy of any type threatens this, given British unions' traditional role in collective bargaining over wages. Hence the argument that a radical extension of industrial democracy must accompany the introduction of incomes policy, to provide an alternative focus for union activity. But if this industrial democracy is to lead (though no doubt slowly and unevenly) to changes in task organization, production processes and the like, that is, changes in the division of labour for which the Left has long argued, there is a serious problem. For such 'organizational' changes to make sense, changes in wage structures and wage differentials would also be involved, which would cut across any individualized wage policy such as an income gains tax.

The combination of incomes policy and a radical form of industrial democracy would seem to be best allied in a Layard- and S.D.P.-style incomes policy, based on taxing corporate rather than individual income. This leaves great scope for autonomy in organizational and wage structures within the overall regulation of average wage levels.

A number of problems arise with such an argument. First, the issue at stake here is in part the traditional one of centralization, seen as a condition of egalitarian policy, and decentralization, seen as most compatible with effective democratic structures. The argument is that if industrial democracy is to be taken seriously, it must involve a considerable degree of autonomy for individual enterprises, and the acceptance that this will always mean actual or potential clashes with other policies the Left might want to pursue – both egalitarian and others. This definitely does not mean that the enterprise would be 'completely autonomous'. Such a concept can have no meaning in a complex economy, where the enterprise is in part a creation of a central agency, in other words the legal system, and where its practices are inextricably interwoven with supra-enterprise agencies, ranging from labour markets to the whole field of state regulation. (The issue of the regulatory regime within which enterprises function is returned to below.)

The specific issue which a Layard-type incomes policy poses for such centralization/de-centralization arguments is that of wages. There are strong grounds for arguing that an egalitarian element in incomes policy can be combined with a framework of this sort via a minimum (and maximum) wage that would override the regulatory focus on the average wage. And there is no reason why such a strategy should not be combined with a strengthening of the law on employment discrimination against women and ethnic minorities. (On women, it has been argued that even the current legal position could be better exploited, both in respect of claims of indirect discrimination, and the 1983 introduction of an 'equal pay for equal value' clause into the Equal Pay Act; see O'Donovan and Szyszczak, 1985; Szyszczak, 1985.)

Such an egalitarianism is important both for its direct effects and its capacity to win support for the policy. But it is also important as a recognition that industrial democracy is a mechanism with no certain policy outcomes. Rather, it will create new arenas for policy formation and new agents participating in existing arenas, but the decisions of these arenas will not be predetermined by their democratization. It is worth emphasizing the point that industrial democracy could lead to extremely disadvantageous consequences from a Left viewpoint, and this is such an important issue that it needs expanding (see section on industrial democracy, below).

Another major problem of incomes policies is what to do about the high profits of those firms which could easily afford wage increases above the norm, but which because of the policy are able to pay wages which increase profits. Such a problem would still occur under a Layard-type scheme, though some of the 'excess profits' might be used to finance 'above norm' wage increases and the consequent tax penalties.

The S.D.P. has suggested that in such cases, workers should be allowed at least some part of the benefits of these profits indirectly, via a share distribution; this would not be simply wages by another name because the shares would not be resaleable immediately. Such a scheme obviously ties in with the considerable emphasis in S.D.P. policy on encouraging individual workers to own shares in their employing enterprise.

From a socialist point of view such a scheme would appear to have little to offer. Individual share ownership on the scale envisaged by the S.D.P. seems not so much undesirable as irrelevant to the issue of firms' efficiency. In addition, it would not offer any plausible benefits in the form of control over the enterprise, given that small shareholders are effectively dis-enfranchised precisely by the dispersion of shareholdings, and worker shareholders would be in no different a position. Also, socialists would presumably take the view that the revenues accruing to such enterprises should not be seen as the property of the workers in the enterprise, and hence should not be distributed solely to those workers.

A much more attractive model is that offered by Sweden, including the recent beginnings of a form of collective share ownership (Hashi and Hussain, 1985). The context of this development is precisely one of a long-established incomes policy (agreed by the equivalent of the T.U.C. and C.B.I.) yielding a windfall gain to some firms, which threatens the policy of wage solidarity, quite successfully pursued until now. The recent collective capital fund scheme in Sweden creams off some of these profits and allocates them to a share-owning fund run by unions on a regional basis. These nationally financed funds focus on investment in their local region, but there is also a ready mechanism for redistributing revenue in that the income of the fund accrues to a national pension scheme.

Plainly, such a scheme would not readily translate into the British institutional context, even allowing for the prior construction of an incomes policy. There is no 'solidaristic' wage bargaining in Britain, nor indeed the kind of strategic calculation which allows Swedish unions to accept that such a policy must entail a high degree of job mobility, so that the less profitable firms lose workers to the more profitable. In addition, there is no parallel to the national pension scheme of Sweden, Britain's pensions above the state minimum being based on many separate occupational schemes. (A national pension scheme was once seriously discussed in the Labour Party, but never translated into legislation except as the residual State Earnings Related Pensions scheme; see Crossman, 1972.)

Neither of these features of British institutional arrangements looks very desirable from a socialist viewpoint; but equally, neither appears a likely object of rapid reform. But what is potentially translatable is the idea of some kind of collective capital fund, financed by an earmarked profits tax, and used mainly to fund investment. Some of the returns on these investments could in turn be used to finance forms of collective consumption. This would combine an egalitarianism in distribution with potential investment 'clout' for a worker/union-based institution.[5]

Finally on incomes policy, there is the question of non-wage income. This is probably less of a problem for corporate-derived income than income from self-employment. For dividends from corporations there could be exactly the same norm as for wages with the same tax rates. For capital gains from corporate shareholdings the remedy is an effective capital gains tax with the rates the same as those for income tax. Probably much more difficult is the taxation of self-employment income, as plainly this is in many areas a form of tax avoidance (with great potential for tax evasion). The only path here seems to be greatly to narrow the scope of self-employment tax, and to bring the rules of the taxation for those with that status into line with the P.A.Y.E. system.

INDUSTRIAL DEMOCRACY

Both the S.D.P. and the Labour Party see a happy convergence between the desirability of industrial democracy and its positive consequences for efficiency. This is problematic as an argument on two grounds. First, it makes too sweeping a presumption about the relations between democracy and efficiency. Whilst it is true that many attempts at increased participation have increased productivity,[6] these have usually been in the context of fairly limited changes within fixed strategic frameworks of decision-making. In a context of a radical measure of industrial democracy, where such a framework would at least potentially be at issue, these consequences may not follow.

More fundamentally, basing the case for industrial democracy on its alleged consequences for efficiency is dangerous as a strategy because it reduces democracy to a means, rather than an end in its own right. Against viewing it as a means to a clear end, one could argue that (industrial) democracy is desirable because it is a *principle* of social organization which socialists favour, but that its consequences will be diverse and affected by circumstances which cannot be predetermined by any particular mechanism of that democracy.

One reason why there has been so much focus on the efficiency effects of industrial democracy is that this avoids the problem of the short-run inverse relation between wage and profit levels. If it is perceived that profits must rise to encourage and finance investment, but that a reduction in real wages is inconceivable, then postulating a rapid rise in productivity means that such a zero-sum game problem can be avoided. Thus Hodgson argues this line, and suggests that 'substantial reforms can be accommodated by increases of productivity in the transitional period' (Hodgson, 1982, p. 61). As suggested several times in the other chapters of this book, it would be better if the Left faced up to, rather than evaded, the consequences of its presumption that the movement of real wages is an index of the degree of 'goodness' of a policy.

Whilst the S.D.P. and the Labour Party agree on this way of arguing for industrial democracy (and the short-run attractions of doing this are apparent), their views about what such democracy means are far apart. For the S.D.P. the parallel is with political democracy – industrial democracy is a form of political representation in another sphere of activity. In consequence, universal suffrage within the enterprise is the only truly democratic form.

In contrast, Labour Party and other socialist versions of industrial democracy usually see it as an extension of collective bargaining, rather than a form of political representation. This is why, for example, discussions of industrial democracy from this viewpoint emphasize the need to make sure it does not conflict with other, more traditional, forms of collective bargaining. The major policy implication is the advocacy of union-based, 'single-channel', representation, as proposed by the T.U.C. and endorsed by the Bullock Committee.

It is possible to argue that the former type of analysis ignores the fact that any form of democracy will not be pure representation, but, depending on its form, will advance the likelihood of one outcome as against others (Hirst, 1981). Certainly the S.D.P. line of argument is one which looks likely simply to give greater legitimacy to existing management, rather than provide much of a challenge to its strategies and practices. (This conforms to the S.D.P. view that it is the ideological divisions in the economy, as in the state, which *per se* are a major hindrance to efficiency). On the other hand, any system of industrial democracy which is not based on universal suffrage is likely to suffer severe legitimacy problems with all but committed trade union supporters of the idea. Given this problem, the absence of universal suffrage is likely gravely to inhibit a radical extension of industrial democracy being launched, let alone its success once established.

The other difficulty with single-channel forms of representation is that, given the lukewarm-to-hostile attitudes of many British trade unions to industrial democracy, they may effectively preclude bold experimentation in such democracy. Because of the diversity of company size, organization and hence appropriate forms of representation, plus the many different kinds of objective which might be deployed within such structures, experimentation seems crucial.

Whilst unions have tended to see a single channel of representation as crucial to their acceptance of industrial democracy, it is far from clear that it makes much difference to the role of unions. In West Germany, where forms of representation are not single channel, representative posts in unionized firms are dominated by trade unionists. So in certain respects the issue of single channel versus universal suffrage may not be as crucial to outcomes as British debates have tended to suggest.

But the case for not having a single-channel form of representation can be put more positively. Like the closed shop, single-channel representation means that unions do not have the same incentive to do what is wanted by their members in order to maintain their support. Hence both practices can be seen as harmful to processes of democratization, even if other arguments can be made in favour of such arrangements.

The balance of advantage would seem to lie with a compulsory and substantial element of worker-directors, but below that level much should be left to codes of practice rather than law. Of course, whatever the symbolic importance of worker-directors, their appointment may reinforce the board of directors as a merely 'rubber-stamp' body. But symbols are not to be disregarded, and it seems impossible to so police the internal administration of firms as to guarantee the location at which decisions are made.

PLANNING AND COMPETITION

A movement towards a 'wages fund' for enterprises and a radical extension of industrial democracy would be a step on the road to what might be called a form of 'market socialism'. Plainly, any further movement along such a road would require a necessarily prolonged process of attenuation of the 'control rights' aspects of equity, so that the long-run objective of reducing the role of external finance in the enterprise to a purely funding function could begin to be achieved. Curiously, Labour Party proposals for reform of companies have not taken up this issue seriously, but have tended to focus on the industrial democracy aspect or on tighter legal regulation of company affairs (Labour Party, 1974).

Such a market socialism would involve the continuation of labour markets, but tend towards regarding them as something of a last resort. The emphasis would be an encouraging voice within the enterprise, rather than an exit from it (Hirschman, 1970). The efficiency consequences of this, whilst not pre-given, seem plausibly favourable. A great deal of the more interesting work on employment relationships has recently stressed the beneficial effects of long-term labour contracts and the trust relations which such contracts engender (Williamson, 1984; Dore, 1983; Fox, 1974).

Any talk of market socialism fits ill with the currently dominant programmatic statements of the Left. Crudely, one might say that the S.D.P. now largely abjures any interest in socialism, whilst most socialists have little positive concern with markets.

In fact, both groups show considerable ambiguity in this area of policy. The S.D.P. document (1983B) on industrial policy stresses that the party does not favour planning, and sees competition as vital to efficiency. But it does propose a programme of quite 'interventionist' policies, focusing on three main areas. These are finance – the provision of cheap credit to favoured projects; R and D – the government subsidization of this on a selective basis; training – a focus on industrially oriented learning both as a path to efficency and to high-wage employment, especially for the young.

In contrast, some economists otherwise close to the S.D.P. analysis (Cairncross *et al.*, 1982) have criticized the idea of such industrial policy, specifically mentioning the N.E.D.O. advocacy which is close to the kinds of argument advanced in the S.D.P. official paper. They argue that

> a more purposeful industrial strategy, along the lines now widely advocated, is likely to do more harm than good. The emphasis in industrial policy needs to be shifted in the opposite direction, away from discretionary and protectionist instruments and towards more general and impersonal measures – for example, competition policies, the establishment of a more liberal trade regime, and policies to raise the quality of management – which would help to create an environment more favourable to innovation and change. (1983B, p. 95)

If the S.D.P. position may be crudely summarized as embodying an ambiguity about how far competition *per se* can generate industrial efficiency, the ambiguity of Labour policy is on the scope and character of planning. This is two-fold. On the one hand there is an ambiguity about the scope of planning *via-à-vis* market relations; on the other hand, there is ambiguity in the proposed combination of planning and industrial democracy.

The Left's views on planning are often linked to rather vague rhetoric along the lines: 'the free market is an irrelevance in a modern and complex society' (Labour Party, 1982A, p. 6) and a very ambitious view of what planning can deliver (Hare, 1983). On the other hand, the most recent proposals by the Labour Party in this area do spell out in detail the proposed institutions of planning (Labour Party, 1982A), and in doing so suggest what the purposes of planning would be. Thus the following summary of the objectives of planning is offered (1982A, p. 12):

> encourage companies to adjust plans to bring them into line with the plan for expansion;
> ensure that sectors of future growth where British industry stands a real chance of success are encouraged;
> sustain vital industries and provide alternative employment to ease the decline of those which have a limited future;
> improve the balance of industry and employment between regions;
> encourage the introduction of new technologies while reducing the social costs of technological and industrial change;
> ensure that necessary industrial investment is not hindered by lack of appropriate finance;
> provide a structure in which the initiatives of workers at the enterprise level can have a real impact;
> achieve a closer match between the pattern of output and social needs.

The striking feature of this is its generality. Planning, rather like nationalization, becomes the means of achieving all the good things desired by the Left.

What is needed, as Hare powerfully argues, is clarity 'about the reasons for planning since this will help to delineate the appropriate scope of the plan, both in space and time: that is, we should be able to determine what activities should be subject to the plan, and what time period such a plan should cover' (Hare, 1983, p. 225). In such a task the experience of both past planning in Britain and that in existing planned economies need to be brought to bear, along with analysis of the specific shortcomings of markets which make planning desirable. Together these would discourage both the windy rhetoric about the possibilities of planning and the shortcomings of market mechanisms, and hence encourage less ambiguity in programmatic pronouncements on planning.

As already noted in chapter 5, the Labour Party proposals seek to combine (workers') democracy and planning, via mechanisms which essentially aim at the extension of collective bargaining 'upwards' to both corporate and national policy. (The latter also embraces the National Economic Assessment with respect to macroeconomic policy.) For industry, this approach would involve, amongst other institutions, the creation of a ministry of Economic and Industrial Planning, and the negotiation of 'agreed development plans' with major companies. These plans are central to the industrial democracy aspect of the planning proposals, because they would be negotiated with both management and unions in the companies concerned.[7] This would be coupled with a substantial democratization of the internal regime of the company (Labour Party, 1982A, pp. 22–5).

The ambiguity of such proposals is that, as stated, they would provide a major stimulus to growth in worker/union involvement in company-level decision-making, but would appear to do much less in coming to grips with the general objectives of growth and full employment, insofar as these are related to enterprise practices. The actual policy mechanisms which will impinge on company performance are in fact a modernized version of traditional post-war industry policy – investment grants and financial aid; they differ mainly by being conditional on the negotiation of an agreed development plan.

In contrast to the view of those who would see the policies of the Labour Party in this area as gross concessions to 'statism' as against 'real industrial democracy' (Green and Wilson, 1982), the policies seem better described as fairly radical proposals for industrial democracy mixed with a very conservative view of what needs to be reformed in company practices. (This issue is returned to in the section Inside the Company, below.)

The case against any form of industrial policy can be made by reference to well-known failures in this area in the past (Cairncross *et al.*, 1982). But in a more systematic sense the case against relying on competition as the main force for efficiency seems a powerful one. Both in the case of product and capital markets, there are good grounds for believing that competition is not the mechanism for separating the sheep from the goats which it is commonly claimed to be. In the case of both kinds of markets the competitive mechanism works via profits. In the case of product markets there are long-standing theoretical arguments that profit levels have no *long-term* relation to efficiency over different states of the world, so that the profitable and efficient firm in one situation may survive into a situation in which it is less profitable and less efficient (Winter, 1964). On financial markets, more empirical work has suggested that neither the take-over process nor the direct provision of stock-exchange funds strongly favours the efficient at the expense of the inefficient (Whittington, 1974, p. 11–13; Singh, 1975).

Of course such arguments are not arguments against competition, nor indeed against, for example, stronger anti-merger and anti-monopoly policy. But they do provide a basic rationale for some form of industrial policy, in the sense of policy aimed at encouraging private companies to behave differently than they would otherwise do.

The official programmes of the S.D.P. and the Labour Party concur in arguing that such 'intervention' should be focused on encouragement of investment via financial provision to companies, and aid for expanded research and development efforts.

On finance, the S.D.P.'s main policy proposal is for an 'industrial credit scheme', based on state subsidy via existing financial institutions to agreed investment projects (1983B, pp. 8–10). The Labour Party stresses the need for a new institution, a National Investment Bank, to channel funds into long-term industrial investment (Labour Party, 1982E, pp. 57–65 and 1982B, p. 52).

As already suggested in chapter 5, the Left, and particularly the Labour Party, have exaggerated the role of low investment by itself in reducing the efficiency of the British economy. There is plenty of evidence not only via low profitability, but also direct measures of capital output ratios, that British companies use investment very inefficiently. (See tables 5.1 and 5.2.)

Nevertheless, it is important not to collapse the argument into one of 'supply versus demand' as happened at the time of the Wilson report (1980). Here one side (broadly the Left) contended that financial institutions were under-financing industry, whilst others (broadly the Right and Marxists) argued that the problem was simply a lack of profitable investment opportunities. What needs to be stressed is that one aspect of the calculation of the profitability of a project is the terms on which it is financed, and hence the lending practices of financial institutions do matter, although they are far from the be-all and end-all of investment levels.

In this light, the S.D.P. proposals appear inadequate precisely because they accept the existing lending practices of financial institutions and focus solely on the rate of interest on loans. But lending is not just a matter of interest rates, but of term, collateral and forms of monitoring the use of funds, all of which will impinge on the calculations of the borrowers. Hence the case for some kind of National Investment Bank, funded partly by the state and partly by institutions, seems a powerful one. But this should be qualified by two points. First, the capacity of any financing body to raise by itself the level of investment must not be exaggerated. Secondly, what is at stake in such a bank's development are the detailed terms of lending and not just the quantity of funds lent.

The other major thrust of industrial policy, especially as advocated by the S.D.P., is research and development. A number of issues are intertwined in this policy debate. At the most general level the focus on R and D is based on an acceptance that investment *per se* is not the central problem in Britain.

> In an economy in which relatively slow growth and declining manufacturing competitiveness are a century-old problem, spread across almost every sector, it is tedious but necessary to find out what has gone wrong market by market, and to direct policy to the recapturing of demand. Investment has its place in the vicious circle of slow growth, but it is not the right place to *break into* the circle when the productivity of existing capital is low. (Stout, 1979, p. 103)

Such a view chimes in more with S.D.P. opinions than with those of the Labour Party, precisely because it plays down the investment aspect.

R and D is also focused on because of the perception that Britain's problems lie in the area of 'non-price' competitiveness, which includes many areas related to R and D – not just invention and innovation, but also design and marketing of products. Whilst Labour Party policy seems to have accepted this general starting point in talking about international economic policy (chapter 4) there is less evidence of such acceptance when talking about industrial policy. Rather, Labour policy focuses on certain 'high-tech' areas which are important but are far from embracing all that is involved in R and D – much of which is development as well as research (see references in Labour Party, 1982B).

Policy discussion on R and D is strongly influenced by the view that much of Britain's past R and D effort has been misdirected, away from commercially productive areas. The Science Policy Research Unit at Sussex University has pushed this argument a great deal, and pointed at the focus of British R and D effort on aircraft, military electronics and defence products more generally, and on nuclear reactors (Freeman, 1979; Pavitt, 1980; Smith, 1984, pp. 87–94). This misdirection has been coupled with an absolutely low level of R and D expenditure by British companies, which by itself reinforces the case for a government role, but away from the areas traditionally favoured by government.

Smith (1984) has recently argued at considerable length that the key problem for Britain is that of R and D. This leads to the advocacy of a Japanese-style industrial policy, with government encouraging, financing and co-ordinating a mammoth R and D effort. Much of the general argument deployed by Smith seems persuasive, but the discussion of it seems to share a feature common to industrial policy discussion on the Left – a failure to get 'inside the company'.

INSIDE THE COMPANY

In the burgeoning literature on R and D deficiencies in Britain there is recognition that the level, direction and success of such R and D is in part a function of the practices of the firms themselves. Plainly there are many ways of analysing such practices. A common one seems excessively 'sociological' – a focus on the social and educational background of managers as an explanation of firms' performance (e.g. Swords-Isherwood, 1980). More helpful is the focus on the calculative framework within which R and D and other investment activities take place (Rothwell, 1980).

However, such problems go far beyond the issue of R and D. For it should be argued that other policy objectives – full employment for example – also need to address the issues of company organization, management practices, forms of calcula-ion and so on, which are indeed the mainstay of the literature of managerial science but rarely find their way into discussions of public policy by economists.

At the most general level, the neglect of such issues by the Left can be linked to certain ideological predispositions – a view of the corporation as essentially exploitative, a suspicion of management *per se*, a concern with issues of equity rather than production and efficiency. Hence, in part, the focus on industrial democracy is seen by and large as an extension of collective bargaining, but one whose effects on the internal regime of the firm remain largely unexamined.

The discussion in this area has not been aided by the notion of the entrepreneur, a shadowy figure whose main function is to obstruct sensible argument about enterprise strategies (Williams, 1984, p. 493). A much more useful starting point would be to focus on what have been called the 'national conditions of enterprise calculation' (Williams *et al.*, 1983). This approach is particularly helpful because it takes institutional factors very seriously without collapsing the argument into a general account of social and cultural conditions. In particular, the argument focuses on

1 management control over the labour process;
2 market structure and the composition of demand;
3 relation of the enterprise to financial institutions like the banks and stock exchange;
4 relation of the enterprise to the state (pp. 29–30).

Without following the argument of Williams *et al.* in any more detail, it should be apparent that their focus is on how 'external' institutional arrangements impact on the practices of firms. The argument does not reduce enterprise practices to their environment, but neither does it allow a voluntarism in which, given the right strategy, any firm can 'succeed'.

Starting from these general points, it is useful to look at one policy issue in more definite terms. The obvious one seems to be employment, given that this is central to the Left's programmes.

As already discussed in chapter 3, part of a plausible strategy for a reduction in unemployment would be a tax on 'above the norm' wage increases. This would affect enterprise calculation directly; by focusing on the average wage it would give an incentive for measures which lowered this average, such as more part-time work, less overtime, employment of the unskilled and lower paid. Thus the enterprise calculations would be biased towards (but not determined by) policy.

Secondly, investment[8] decisions are taken at the level of individual companies and it is a striking feature of these entities that in the U.K. they are constructed legally as essentially autonomous, sovereign bodies subject to very few restrictions over the use and disposal of their funds and resources. However, Swedish practice gives one example of how the behaviour of private companies may be biased in favour of national economic objectives such as full employment. In Sweden, a company establishes an investment reserve by debiting the profit and loss account and crediting the investment reserve account. The allowance for this reserve is deductible for tax purposes, provided a part of it (a fraction marginally less than the rate of corporate tax) is deposited at the Swedish central bank. No interest is received on this deposit. It may be viewed as a tax payment, which is refundable *under certain conditions*. In order to utilize the investment reserves, a permit is usually required from the Swedish Labour Market Board. These permits enable the Board to effect a measure of control over the timing, content and location of investment financed from investment reserves (see Johanssen, 1965; Mukherjee, 1972). Swedish practice thus contrasts sharply with the way depreciation allowances, for example, are treated in the U.K.; the tax relief arising from the latter provides an *unconditional* increase in company cash flow.

It is possible to take this example somewhat further. The 1977 U.K. White Paper 'The Conduct of Company Directors' proposed changing company law so that directors would be required to take into account the interests of employees as well as shareholders (Department of Trade, 1977, paras 5 7). Such a change in company law could, for example, be coupled with an accounting regulation which would require a certain amount to be debited from the profit and loss account and credited to a labour reserve account before determining distributable profits. This reserve could be earmarked for expenditures aimed, say, at improving working conditions, generally enhancing the quality of working life and facilitating the employment of the disabled through investment in work reorganization and redesigned production and administrative systems.

These policies are intended as examples of what might be entailed by policies getting 'inside the company'. Plainly, they are at best very illustrative of policy options in one policy area, that of employment. But what they may serve to illustrate about policy more generally is that getting 'inside the company' involves consideration about the general regulatory framework within which companies function, this framework already exists in the form of company law, industrial relations law, the Health and Safety Executive, Stock Exchange Rules, the Equal Opportunities Commission etcetera, all of whose activities to a greater or lesser extent necessarily bias enterprise calculation and conduct in various directions. So what is at stake in policy is not the unhelpful dichotomy 'to intervene or not to intervene' but the individual and collective consequences of different regulatory regimes.

REGULATORY REGIMES

The Equal Opportunities Commission, the Accounting Standards Committee and the training section of the Manpower Services Commission provide instances of one form of already existing external scrutiny of enterprise practices which appear to have little to offer in terms of their organization. The action of such bodies is subject to very restricted forms of accountability, and the 'public interest', in the name of which they claim to act, is frequently conceived dogmatically in terms of the discourses of particular professional groups. One challenge for socialists is to design agencies more open to public inspection, with extensive account-ability provisions, governed by elected representatives of the relevant constituencies and organized on the basis of decentralized processes of decision-making.

In addition there is a need for new, or revived, regulatory functions. One example is that of the Price Commission. Current Labour policy is for such a commission to have a major role in the controlling of inflation. As argued in chapter 7, this looks implausible. But one way in which the Price Commission of the late 1970s did serve a useful function was that it subjected firms who asked for price increases to a form of compulsory manage-ment consultancy. This could potentially be a useful form of efficiency audit, which is in effect also what many Monopoly Commission enquiries do, but which would seem to have a useful general role in encouraging the spread of 'best practice' manage-ment. In the late 1970s such activities were bitterly resented by many managements, but the extension of industrial democracy could be seen as functional to a more favourable reception to such procedures at company level.

Again, such points are intended only as examples of a way of thinking about policy. The two interconnected aspects of that way are the emphasis on enterprise level practices, and the regulatory regime within which they function. The relation between these is conditional, not deterministic. Its positive advantages would seem to be two-fold. On the one hand, it would open up internal issues about the enterprise which the Left largely ignores. Secondly it would avoid posing the problem as one of workers/government getting 'real power' over the enterprise so that it can do as they will. Such a concept ignores the point that no complex organization has a single site of 'power', from which it may simply be subordinated to the will of whoever obtains that power.[9]

CONCLUSIONS

If it is accepted that national economic management is an appropriate concern of the policy of the Left (and plainly the argument of this book is that it should be), then the detailed policy arguments can link to a well-established field of macroeconomic policy discussion. If one sets on one side the neo-classical macroeconomics of the Right, and accepts the case for economic management at all, then the options are relatively plain in existing literature. This does not mean they are not controversial, and in particular the notion of constraints on such management raises serious analytical as well as practical difficulties; but the field is not riven by fundamental conceptual problems.

By contrast, with microeconomic or industrial policies, the field of argument is riven by fundamental conceptual difficulties in and around which circulate all kinds of ideological disputes. In particular, various dichotomies such as plan/market, public/private, control of capital/workers control continue to thrive as the ultimate benchmarks against which many still judge policy. A general conclusion of this book is that such dichotomies serve little useful purpose in organizing argument on the Left.

Of course, such a generalization is subject to qualification. The recent British discussions of market socialism are very important. In particular, Nove (1983) deploys (eclectic) economic theory and profound knowledge of Eastern European economies to demolish the fantasies of those who, even if as only an ultimate goal, hanker after a completely planned economy. Nevertheless, once this point is made, the meaning of 'market socialism' becomes less clear. One can make argue this in two rather different ways. In the most abstract sense the meaning of 'market' is extremely unclear, and often seems to carry overtures of a natural phenomenon, a principle of human action making itself felt whenever the state turns its back. Against this, one can argue that markets are always constructed from definite forms of calculation, themselves part of differentiated organizational forms. Hence it is unclear that the notion of *the* market as a general principle is very illuminating.

More concretely, whilst all forms of market socialism involve a degree of autonomy for individual enterprises, the nature and scope of this autonomy is extremely varied. This is the basis of the argument about regulatory regimes. In Nove's model of 'feasible socialism' this autonomy is quite strictly controlled in one crucial domain, that of investment, where it would seem that the central planning mechanism and central bank would play a very large role in investment decisions (Nove, 1983, pp. 221–2).

This links to a final point about market socialism. The force of the argument for such a system (and, one might say, its attractiveness to economists) depends a great deal on its acceptance of the allocative advantages of the price mechanism. This concern with allocative efficiency is by no means to be derided. But plainly it rather understates the importance of the dynamic aspects of economic activity, the problems of growth and structural change which, it can be argued, are the vital issues for Britain in the 1980s. The role of the price mechanism is much more problematic in such a dynamic context, and hence the notion of market socialism in the simple sense appears less pertinent.

Such dichotomies as plan/market and so on ultimately rest on ill-specified Utopian fantasies about what true socialism would look like. They also serve to undercut the discussion of the principles which might be seen as central for the Left, and the policies appropriate to those principles. Discussion of principles takes us back to where this chapter began, the question of strategy.

The starting point of the discussion of strategy was that as commonly employed, the notion of strategy implies a much more close-fitting and coherent set of policies than is plausible. Of course, the baby must not be thrown out with the bath water. The idea of strategy as trying to take a long view, of trying to foresee obstacles before they arise, of trying to stay one jump ahead of the constraints on policy, is crucial. But what needs to be stressed is that strategy cannot involve any easy reconciliation of the divergent and often contradictory pressures on policy.

In the attempt to cope with such divergence and contradiction, principles are crucial. For example, in making strategic judgements about industrial democracy, principles should provide some basis for decision; equally with discussions of policy on employment. But this is an area where intellectual work is clearly required. One has only to state what might be considered Left and socialist principles – democratization, accountability, egalitarianism, co-operation – to recognize how inchoate the discussion of these principles is. Yet without such discussion the twin devils of Left policy – Utopianism and servile pragmatism – will remain triumphant.

The discussion of principles is only one amongst several areas of intellectual failure of the Left. Whilst one must beware the rationalist fallacy – that the best arguments win political disputes – it is appropriate here to stress those intellectual failures, given that current discussion on the Left focuses on the sociological dimensions of the Left's failures.

As Dunn (1984, p. 92) has recently written, 'The failures of democratic socialism in the West over the last ten years have been predominantly intellectual failures, failures in comprehension and not in intrepidity or the capacity for evocative, non-rational persuasion.' Such a diagnosis seems apposite in discussing economic policy. Economic policy, no more than any other policy area, is never simply idea made flesh. (The cynic might say, it is well that it is so.) But unless these ideas are sorted out, little else seems possible. The aim of this book has been to provide at least some guidelines and pointers to this end.

Notes

INTRODUCTION

1 There are clearly considerable overlaps between S.D.P./Alliance and Conservative 'Wet' policies, but this is not an issue for discussion here.
2 This link is a fairly transparent one in the case of the Clare Group, which is made up of economists who wished to 'counteract the increasing polarisation that was appearing in discussions about economic policy in this country', and who wanted to assert the continued relevance of Keynesian analysis of the macro economy, and neo-classical analysis of markets (Matthews and Sargent, 1983, Preface).
3 The Falklands War belied this point for the Conservatives in 1982 – an eventuality hardly to be relied on for repetition.

CHAPTER 1

1 For a very useful summary of macro policy under Thatcher, see Buiter and Miller (1981) and (1983), and for other aspects of policy as well as macro, see Thompson (1985).
2 In Britain the P.S.B.R. includes borrowing by local and central government and the nationalized industries. It is linked in an accounting sense to sterling M3, in that the increase in sterling M3 = P.S.B.R. minus non-bank lending to the government, plus bank lending to the private sector.
3 As Beckerman points out, this fall in commodity prices means that the price of deflation in the O.E.C.D. has been paid not only by the unemployed in those countries, but also by the third-world countries whose incomes have been radically reduced.
4 As a general point such an argument may concede too much to the efficacy of market mechanisms in 'weeding out' the inefficient, as opposed to the illiquid and the unlucky (a point I owe to Graham Thompson).

CHAPTER 2

1 For a brief summary of the arguments for making unemployment a top priority see Tomlinson (1983B); for a more extensive analysis, see Sinfield (1981), Jahoda (1982), Hakim (1982).
2 See Tomlinson (1985), chs 1 and 6.
3 Some of them, e.g. the importance of the real net nominal national debt, would be agreed to by supporters of a purer form of monetarism than the current government's – Friedman (1980).
4 The irrationality of policy-makers was a major thrust of Keynes's whole analysis of policy, e.g. in relation to public-work policy in the 1920s and 1930s. See Keynes and Henderson (1929). For comments see Tomlinson (1981B, ch. 5).
5 Keynes, despite his emphasis on rationality and the scope for persuasion towards more 'intelligent' policy, seems sometimes to have regarded financial markets as incorrigible, hence his advocacy of a 'socialization of investment' to overcome the effects of the stock exchange.
6 Marxists confuse the argument by talking most of the time about profits in a standard accounting sense, but then (unsuccessfully) trying to reconcile profits defined in this way with profits defined in Marxist terms. The analytical helpfulness of such an attempted reconciliation is unclear, though obviously it is an attempt to assert the viability of the Marxist theory of value – see Glyn and Sutcliffe (1972).
7 Before November 1982 the unemployed were all those who registered at employment offices. Since that date only those who claim benefit are counted, hence the figure has been 'massaged' down by around 375,000 (Metcalf, 1984A, p. 59).
8 A more common version is perhaps that Keynes accepted the need for a fall in real wages, but argued that politically this was best achieved not by nominal wage cuts but by price increases, e.g. via devaluation.

CHAPTER 3

1 Hahn's main purpose is, in classic Keynesian fashion, to argue that the doctrine behind government policy is incoherent, in stressing the importance of reducing inflation but using theories which suggest inflation is not seriously harmful. For a more policy-oriented discussion of the Left and inflation, see Ormerod (1981).
2 A feature of the arbitration as proposed by Meade would be that the arbitration body could choose as its award only the last claim of the union or last offer of the employer. This is seen as an incentive to 'reasonableness' by the two parties.
3 The Liberal Party has, in fact, been an advocate of such a policy for some years. See Pardoe (1974).
4 The explicit, but dubious, assumption being that greater democracy will lead to more 'reasonable' (less militant) union behaviour.

5 'The fact that the labour market is divided into largely non-competing occupation groups does not mean that it is inflexible. A part of the flexibility is achieved through changes in the supply of labour, by expansion or contraction of the fraction of the population seeking work, by variations in hours worked and multiple job-holding, by migration, interindustry shifts, education and training. Among those people already in the labour force, flexibility is achieved by lower tiers serving as resources of labour for higher tiers and as safety nets for workers displaced downwards' (Tarling and Wilkinson, 1982, p. 41).

6 For example Freeman and Medoff (1979); Williamson (1984); Malcolmson (1982).

7 For example, Hay and Morris (1979), ch. 2.

8 Tony Lane of Liverpool University has impressed on me how far free collective bargaining, whatever its doctrinal basis, is tied to the tactical rather than strategic outlook of trade unions, within a context of highly fragmented and sectionalized bargaining.

9 Though such arguments are not confined to the Left, e.g. Middlemass, 1979. For a more extended discussion of Left versions of the corporatism thesis, see Tomlinson (1981A).

CHAPTER 4

1 Note, however, that modern trade theory is by no means a simple assertion of the benefits of free trade but 'is concerned in particular with providing rigorous rankings of alternative policies (including protection) when one or other of the perfectly competitive assumptions (including full employment) breaks down' (Lal, 1979, p. 24).

2 See also Emerson (1979) and comments by C. Allsopp (Fishman, 1980).

3 Used by Switzerland and West Germany in 1978–9, though not very successfully (Lomax and Gutmann, 1981).

4 For some discussion of the financing decisions of multinationals, see Caves (1982, pp. 177–83); Gilman (1981).

5 Note that these figures are for flows, not stocks of assets. Broadly, foreign assets now make up 15 per cent of institutional stocks of assets, compared with 5 per cent in 1979 (Hattersley, 1985).

6 These rather sweeping statements are argued in more detail in Tomlinson (1982).

7 This reference here is to Labour Party doctrine, not to the policy of Labour governments, which have tended to be as enthusiastic as any in trying to induce multinational investment in Britain.

CHAPTER 5

1 As always, such a sharp dichotomy as micro/macroeconomic ultimately breaks down. For example, the Conservatives' macroeconomic

policies of reductions in government spending are supposed to have micro effects, via the alleged impact of lower taxation on individual work effort.

2 A unitary notion of the enterprise sees it as a 'functionally integrated and normally harmonious system which is directed towards the attainment of a set of goals that all its members hold in common' (Child, 1969, p. 12).

3 In Marxist versions, this privileging arises from the privileging of certain kinds of labour as 'productive', though it is not clear in Marx's terms that this label can be used as synonymous with manufacturing.

4 It would mitigate against, for example, the use of 'uneconomic' as if its meaning were unambiguous, as happened to an astonishing extent during the miners' strike of 1984–5. Obviously the usage of this term by the National Coal Board and government was partly facilitated by the National Union of Mineworkers' ultimately absurd slogan of 'no closure of uneconomic pits'.

CHAPTER 6

1 Solow, (1980, p. 8) offers a nicely ironical comment on this view: 'While we think it is usually a mistake to fiddle the pure system to achieve distributional goals, we realize that the public and the political process are perversely more willing to do that than make the transfers we prefer. If we oppose all distorting transfers, we end up opposing transfers altogether.'

2 Heald(1983) has many good qualities, but reflects much Left literature in having little to say on taxation issues.

3 The Resource Allocation Working Party of the Department of Health and Social Security (D.H.S.S.) reported in 1976. Their report formulated proposals for a more egalitarian geographical distribution of N.H.S. resources. These were to be allocated to regions on the basis of needs, measured by standardized mortality rates multiplied by the population. Both Labour and Conservative governments have broadly followed their proposals.

4 Marxist discussion of the existing nationalized industries is very thin. One exception is Fine and O'Donnell (1982) in which all the problems of such industries are dissolved into the effects of their being in a capitalist economy.

CHAPTER 7

1 In this, if in little else, one can agree with those who wish to re-assert the role of 'class politics' (Fine *et al.*, 1985). A striking feature of this pamphlet is how little is done with this insight to analyse positive policy issues.

2 This agreement does not, of course, extend to feminists. Phillips

(1983) provides a useful feminist critique of these priorities. These issues cannot be discussed at length here. All that may be asserted is that if management of the national economy is what is at stake, then it has to be accepted that some of the policy debates are unavoidably indifferent to both socialist and feminist concerns, e.g. over plausible levels of public borrowing or exchange rate management. Equally, full employment delivers neither socialist nor feminist objectives; but it does deliver buoyant public revenues, expanding output and incomes, which provide a better basis on which these objectives can be fought for. Finally, scepticism about a male, trade union-dominated industrial democracy opens up precisely the issues of the meaning of such democracy and its problems discussed in chapter 5 (and later in this chapter). Again, industrial democracy of itself guarantees neither socialist nor feminist objectives.

3 For example, Wilson (1980), ch. 23.
4 This assumes, as accords with the evidence, that there is no stable relation between the P.S.B.R. and M3.
5 Even if, in the long run, such a purpose would be undermined by the attenuation of the 'control' aspect of shareholdings.
6 See Hodgson 1984, ch. 9.
7 There would also be a tripartite National Planning Council, advising the Department of Planning.
8 This section owes a great deal to direct discussion with Stuart Burchell.
9 Tomlinson 1982, ch. 7.

Bibliography

Aaronovitch, S. (1981): *The Road from Thatcherism*, Lawrence and Wishart.

Aaronovitch, S. and Smith, R. P. (1981): *The Political Economy of British Capitalism*, McGraw Hill.

American Banks Association (1977): *Evidence to the Wilson Committee*, H.M.S.O.

Armstrong, P., Glyn, A. and Harrison, J. (1984): *Capitalism Since World War Two*, Fontana.

Artis, M. J. (1982): *Memorandum and Evidence on International Monetary Arrangements*, Treasury and Civil Service Committee International Monetary Arrangements, H.C.P. 21–II, 1982/3, H.M.S.O.

Artis, M. J. and Currie, D. A. (1981): 'Monetary Targets and the Exchange Rate: A Case for Conditional Targets', *Oxford Economic Papers*, 33, suppl., 176–200.

Artis, M. J. and Posner, M. (1984): 'The British Economy and the International Scene, 1984', *Midland Bank Review*, Autumn, 8–15.

Atkinson, A. B. (1984): 'Taxation and Social Security Reform', *Policy and Politics* 12, 107–18.

B.E.Q.B. (1981): 'The Effects of Exchange Control Abolition on Capital Flows', *Bank of England Quarterly Bulletin*, 21, 369–73.

B.E.Q.B. (1984): 'Company Profitability and Finance', *Bank of England Quarterly Bulletin*, 24, 353–9.

Barker, K., Britton, A. and Major, R. (1984): 'Macroeconomic Policy in France and Britain', *National Institute Economic Review*, 110, 68–84.

Barker, T. (1982): 'Long-Term Recovery: A Return to Full Employment?', *Lloyds Bank Review*, 143, 19–35.

Batstone, E., Ferner, A. and Terry, M. (1984): *Unions on the Board: an Experiment in Industrial Democracy*, Blackwell.

Beckerman, W. (1985): 'How the Battle Against Inflation was Really Won', *Lloyds Bank Review*, 155, 1–12.

Beesley, M. and Littlechild, S. (1983): 'Privatisation: Principles, Problems and Priorities', *Lloyds Bank Review*, 149, 1–20.

Beesley, M. and Littlechild, S. (1984): 'Reply to Williamson', *Lloyds Bank Review*, 151, 47–8.

Beveridge Report (1942): *Social Insurance & Allied Services*, Cmd 6406, H.M.S.O.

Boddy, M. (1983): 'Changing Public–Private Sector Relations in the Industrial Development Process' in K. Young and C. Mason (eds), *Urban Economic Development*, Macmillan, 34–52.

Boddy, M. (1984): 'Local Economic and Employment Strategies', in M. Boddy and C. Fudge (eds), *Local Socialism*, Macmillan, 160–91.

Bolton (1971): *Report of the Committee of Inquiry on Small Firms*, Cmnd 4811, H.M.S.O.

Brannen, P., Batstone, E., Fatchett, D. and White, P. (1976): *The Worker Directors*, Hutchinson.

Brech, M. J. and Stout, D. K. (1981): 'The Rate of Exchange and Non-Price Competitiveness: A Provisional Study with U.K. Manufacturing Exports', *Oxford Economic Papers*, 33, suppl., 268–81.

Brittan, S. (1984): 'The Politics and Economics of Privatisation', *Political Quarterly*, 55, 109–28.

Brooks, S. J. (1979): 'The Experience of Floating Exchange Rates' in R. Major (ed.), *Britain's Trade and Exchange Rate Policy*, Heinemann, 200–13.

Brooks, S. J. and Henry, S. G. B. (1984): 'Simulation Exercises with the Complete Model' in A. J. Britton (ed.), *Employment, Inflation and Output*, Heinemann, 121–32.

Buiter, W. H. and Miller, M. (1981): 'The Thatcher Experiment: The First Two Years', *Brookings Papers in Economic Activity*, 2, 315–74.

Buiter, W. H. and Miller, M. (1983): 'Changing the Rules: Economic Consequences of the Thatcher Regime', *Brookings Papers in Economic Activity*, 2, 305–79.

Bullock (1977): *Report of the Committee of Enquiry into Industrial Democracy*, Cmnd 6706, H.M.S.O.

Cmnd 9189 (1984): *The Next Ten Years: Public Expenditure in the 1990s*, H.M.S.O.

Cmnd 9829 (1985): *The Government's Expenditure Plans 1985/6 to 1987/8*, H.M.S.O.

C.P.R.S. (1975): *The Future of the British Car Industry*, Central Policy Review Staff.

C.S.E./L.W.G. (1980): *The Alternative Economic Strategy*, C.S.E. London Working Group.

Cairncross, A. (1982): *Evidence to Treasury and Civil Service Committee, International Monetary Arrangements*, H.C.P. 1982/3, 21–II, H.M.S.O.

Cairncross, A., Henderson, P. D., and Silbertson, Z. A. (1982): 'Problems of Industrial Recovery' in R. C. O Matthews and J. R. Sargent, *Contemporary Problems of Economic Policy*, Methuen, 88–95.

Callaghan, J. (1976): *Speech to the 1976 Labour Party Conference*, Labour Party.

Cambridge (1985): *The Effect of Business Rates on the Location of Employment*, Cambridge University, Dept of Land Economy.

Cambridge Economic Policy Review, Vols 1–8, 1975–82, Gower.

Capital and Class (1982): 'A Socialist G.L.C. in Capitalist Britain', *Capital and Class*, 18, 117–33.

Caves, R. E. (1982): *Multinational Enterprise and Economic Analysis*, Cambridge University Press.

Child, J. (1969): *The Business Enterprise in Modern Industrial Society*, Macmillan.

Chiplin, B., Coyne, J. and Sirc, L. (1977): *Can Workers Manage?*, Institute of Economic Affairs.

Coakley, J. and Harris, L. (1983): *The City of Capital*, Blackwell.

Cobham, D. (1984): 'French Macroeconomic Policy under President Mitterand: An Assessment', *National Westminster Bank Quarterly Review*, February, 41–51.

Cockle, P. (1984): *Public Expenditure Policy 1984/5*, Macmillan.

Coutts, K., Cripps, F. and Ward, T. (1982): 'Britain in the 1980s', *Cambridge Economic Policy Review*, 8, 4–17.

Creedy, J. (1982): *State Pensions in Britain*, Cambridge University Press.

Cripps, F., Griffith, J., Morrell, F., Reid, J., Townsend, P. and Weir, S. (1981): *Manifesto: A Radical Strategy for Britain's Future*, Pan.

Cripps, F. and Ward, T. (1983): 'Government Policies, European Recession and Problems of Recovery', *Cambridge Journal of Economics*, 7, 85–99.

Crosland, A. (1956): *The Future of Socialism*, Cape.

Crosland, A. (1974): *Socialism Now*, Cape.

Crossman, R. (1972): *The Politics of Pensions*, Eleanor Rathbone Memorial Lecture, Liverpool University Press.

Crouch, C. (1981): 'The Place of Public Expenditure in Socialist Thought' in D. Lipsey and D. Leonard (eds), *Crosland's Legacy*, Cape, 158–85.

Currie, D. A. (1982): 'The Volatile Pound and Exchange Rate Policy', *Socialist Economic Review*, Merlin, 231–45.

Currie, R. (1979): *Industrial Politics*, Clarendon Press.

D.E./D.T.I. (1983): *Draft European Community Directives on Procedures for Informing and Consulting Employees. Draft European Communities Fifth Directive on the Harmonisation of Company Law*, Department of Employment/Department of Trade and Industry.

Daniel, W. (1981): 'Influences on the Level of Wage Settlements in Manufacturing Industry' in F. Blackaby (ed.), *The Future of Pay Bargaining*, Heinemann, 148–62.

Daniel, W. and Milward, N. (1983): *Workplace Industrial Relations in Britain*, Heinemann.

Davies, G. and Piachaud, D. (1983): 'Social Policy and the Economy' in H. Glennerster (ed.), *The Future of the Welfare State*, Heinemann, 40–60.

Day, L. and Pond, C. (1982): 'The Political Economy of Taxation and the Alternative Economic Strategy', *Socialist Economic Review*, Merlin, 157–74.

Deacon, B. (1981): 'Social Administration, Social Policy and Socialism', *Critical Social Policy*, 1, 5–17.

Deacon, B. (1984): *Social Policy and Socialism*, Pluto.

Department of Industry (1975): *The Contents of Planning Agreements*, H.M.S.O.

Department of Trade (1977): *The Conduct of Company Directors*, Cmnd 7037, H.M.S.O.

Dilnot, A. (1984): 'The Impact of the 1984 Budget on the Household Sector', *Fiscal Studies*, 5, 57–62.

Dilnot, A., Kay, J. and Morris, C. (1984): *The Reform of Social Security*, I.F.S./Oxford University Press.

Disney, R. (1979): 'Recurrent Spells and the Concentration of Unemployment in Great Britain', *Economic Journal*, 85, 109–19.

Donovan (1968): *Report of the Royal Commission on Trade Unions and Employers' Organisations*, Cmnd 3623, H.M.S.O.

Dore, R. (1983): 'Goodwill and the Spirit of Market Capitalism', *British Journal of Sociology*, XXXIV, 459–82.

Dunn, J. (1984): *The Politics of Socialism*, Cambridge University Press.

Elliott, J. (1978): *Conflict or Co-operation?: The Growth of Industrial Democracy*, Kogan Page.

Emerson, M. (1979): 'The United Kingdom and the European Monetary System', in R. Major (ed.), *Britain's Trade and Exchange Rate Policy*, Heinemann, 66–81.

Fforde, J. (1983): 'Setting Monetary Objectives', *Bank of England Quarterly Bulletin*, 23, 200–8.

Field, F. (1981): *Inequality in Britain: Freedom, Welfare and the State*, Fontana.

Fine, B. and O'Donnell, K. (1981): 'The Nationalised Industries', *Socialist Economic Review*, Merlin, 265–85.

Fine, B., Harris, L., Mayo, M., Weir, A. and Wilson, E. (1985): *Class Politics: An Answer to its Critics*, Leftover Pamphlets.

Fishman, D. (1980): 'A Radical View of the European Monetary System', *Politics and Power*, 1, 175–84.

Flanders, A. (1970): *Management and Trade Unions*, Faber and Faber.

Forester, T. (1978): 'How Labour's Industrial Strategy got the Chop', *New Society*, 6 July, 14–17.

Foster, J. (1976): 'The Redistributive Effect of Inflation on Building Society Shares and Deposits 1961–74', *Bulletin of Economic Research*, 28, 68–75.

Fox, A. (1974): *Beyond Contract: Work, Power and Trust Relations*, Faber and Faber.

Freeman, C. (1979): 'Technical Innovation and British Trade Performance' in F. Blackaby (ed.), *De-Industrialisation*, Heinemann, 56–73.

Freeman, R. and Medoff, J. (1979): 'The Two Faces of Unionism', *Public Interest*, 57, 69–93.

Friedman, M. (1977): 'Inflation and Unemployment', *Journal of Political Economy*, 85, 51–72.

Friedman, M. (1980): *Memorandum of Evidence to Treasury and Civil Service Committee: Monetary Policy*, H.C.P. 720, H.M.S.O.

G.L.C. (1981): *A Socialist Policy for the GLC*, Labour Party.
G.L.C. (1983): *Jobs for a Change*, Popular Planning Unit, G.L.C.
G.L.C. (1985): *An Economic Plan for London*, G.L.C.
Gardiner, J. and Smith, S. (1982): 'Feminism and the Alternative Economic Strategy', *Socialist Economic Review*, Merlin, 31–45.
Gill, K. (1981): 'Incomes Policy: The Trade Union View' in R. Chater, A. Dean and J. Elliott (eds), *Incomes Policy*, Clarendon Press, 180–92.
Gilman, M. (1981): *The Financing of Foreign Direct Investment*, Frances Pinter.
Ginsburg, N. (1979): *Class, Capital and Social Policy*, Macmillan.
Glyn, A. (1978): *Tribune's 'Alternative Strategy' or Socialist Plan*, Militant.
Glyn, A. (1982): 'The Cambridge Economic Policy Group and Profits', *Socialist Economic Review*, Merlin, 251–60.
Glyn, A. and Harrison, J. (1980): *The British Economic Disaster*, Pluto.
Glyn, A. and Sutcliffe, B. (1972): *British Capitalism, Workers and the Profits Squeeze*, Penguin.
Gough, I. (1979): *The Political Economy of the Welfare State*, Macmillan.
Gough, J., North, D., Escott, K. and Leigh, R. (1981): 'Local Authority Policies in Inner London', *Local Government Studies*, 7, 53–63.
Gould, B., Mills, J. and Stewart, S. (1981): *Monetarism or Prosperity?*, Macmillan.
Green, R. and Wilson, A. (1982): 'Economic Planning and Workers' Control', *Socialist Register*, 21–46.
Grubb, D., Jackman, R. and Layard, R. (1982): 'Causes of the Current Stagflation', *Review of Economic Studies*, XLIX, 707–30.

H.M.S.O. (1984): *Autumn Statement 1984*, H.C.P. 12, 1984/5.
Hahn, F. (1980): *Memorandum on Monetary Policy*, Treasury and Civil Service Committee, Monetary Policy, H.C.P. 720, 1979/80, H.M.S.O., 79–85.
Hakim, C. (1982): 'The Social Consequences of Unemployment', *Journal of Social Policy*, 11, 433–67.
Hall, D. (1983): *The Cuts Machine*, Pluto.
Hare, P. (1980): 'Import Controls and the C.E.P.G. Model of the U.K. Economy', *Scottish Journal of Political Economy*, 27, 183–96.
Hare, P. (1983): 'The Precondition for Effective Planning in the U.K.,' *Socialist Economic Review*, Merlin, 221–42.
Harrison, J. (1982): 'A Left Critique of the Alternative Economic Strategy', *Socialist Economic Review*, Merlin, 117–26.
Hashi, R. and Hussain, A. (1985): 'Employee Investment Funds in Sweden', unpublished, Keele University.
Hattersley, R. (1985): Speech to Teesside Fabians, 13.1.85 (summarized) *Sunday Times*, 13.1.85).
Hay, D. A. and Morris, D. J. (1979): *Industrial Economics: Theory and Evidence*, Oxford University Press.

Heald, D. (1983): *Public Expenditure: Its Defence and Reform*, Martin Robertson.

Heald, D. and Steel, D. R. (1984): *The Privatisation of Public Enterprise, 1979–83*, Royal Institute of Public Administration.

Hemming, R. (1984): *Poverty and Incentives*, Oxford University Press.

Henderson, P. D. (1983): 'Trade Policies: Trends, Issues and Influences', *Midland Bank Review*, Winter, 8–19.

Higham, D. and Tomlinson, J. (1982): 'Why Do Governments Worry About Inflation?', *National Westminster Bank Quarterly Review*, May, 2–13.

Hindess, B. (1981): A Left Strategy for Disaster: A response to Peter Hain, *Politics and Power*, 4, 323–8.

Hindess, (1983): *Parliamentary Democracy and Socialist Politics*, Routledge and Kegan Paul.

Hirschmann, A. O., (1970): *Exit, Voice and Loyalty*, Harvard University Press.

Hirst, P. (1979): 'The Necessity of Theory', *Economy and Society*, 8, 417–45.

Hirst, P. (1981): 'On Struggle in the Enterprise' in M. Prior (ed.), *The Popular and the Political*, Routledge and Kegan Paul, 45–75.

Hodgson, G. (1982): 'On the Political Economy of the Socialist Transformation', *New Left Review*, 133, 8–18.

Hodgson, G. (1984): *The Democratic Economy*, Penguin.

Holland, S. (1975): *The Socialist Challenge*, Quartet.

House of Commons (1980): *3rd Report from the Expenditure Committee: Monetary Policy*, Appendices, H.C.P. 713, H.M.S.O.

House of Commons (1983): *3rd Report from the Treasury and Civil Service Committee: The Structure of Personal Income Tax and Income Support*, H.C.P. 386, 1983/84, H.M.S.O.

Howson, S. (1975): *Domestic Monetary Management 1919–39*, Cambridge University Press.

Hughes, J. (1982): 'Putting Pension Funds to Work', *New Socialist*, 3, 48–9.

Huhne, C. (1984): 'Tax Cuts are no Help to the Jobless', *Guardian*, 13 December.

Jackson, P. (1980): 'The Public Expenditure Cuts: Rationale and Consequences', *Fiscal Studies*, 1, 66–82.

Jahoda, M. (1982): *Employment and Unemployment*, Cambridge University Press.

Jenkins, P. (1982): 'The Crumbling of the Old Order' in W. Kennett (ed.), *The Rebirth of Britain*, Weidenfeld & Nicolson, 33–60.

Johanssen, S. E. (1965): 'An Appraisal of the Swedish System of Investment Reserves', *International Journal of Accountancy*, 351–402.

Joint Trades Councils (1982): *State Intervention in Industry: A Workers' Enquiry*, Coventry, Liverpool, Newcastle, N. Tyneside Trades Councils.

Jones, D. (1983): 'Productivity and the Thatcher Experiment', *Socialist Economic Review*, Merlin, 27–45.

Jones, D. (1984): 'The People's Profits', *New Statesman*, 7 December, 15–16.

Kay, J. and King, M. (1983): *The British Tax System*, 3rd. ed., Oxford University Press.

Kay, J. and Silbertson, Z. A. (1984): 'The New Industrial Policy: Privatisation and Competition', *Midland Bank Review*, Spring, 1–16.

Kennett, W. (ed.), (1982): *The Rebirth of Britain*, Weidenfeld & Nicolson.

Kerr, H. (1981): 'Labour's Social Policy', *Critical Social Policy* 1, 5–17.

Keynes, J. M. (1936): *The General Theory of Employment, Interest and Money*, Macmillan.

Keynes, J. M. and Henderson, H. (1929): 'Can Lloyd George Do It?' in *Keynes (1972) Collected Writings, Vol. IX: Essays in Persuasion*, Macmillan.

King, M. (1975): 'The U.K. Profits Crisis: Myth or Reality?', *Economic Journal*, 85, 33–54.

Labour Economic Policy Group (1982): *Memorandum and Evidence*, Treasury and Civil Service Committee, International Monetary Arrangements, H.C.P. 21, 1982/3, H.M.S.O.

Labour Party (1973): *Labour's Programme*, Labour Party.

Labour Party (1974): *The Community and the Company*, Labour Party.

Labour Party (1976): *Banking and Finance*, Labour Party.

Labour Party (1977): *International Big Business*, Labour Party.

Labour Party (1981A): *Socialism in the 1980s: Social Security*, Labour Party.

Labour Party (1981B): *Socialism in the 1980s: Taxation*, Labour Party.

Labour Party (1982A): *Economic Planning and Industrial Democracy*, Labour Party.

Labour Party (1982B): *Labour's Programme 1982*, Labour Party.

Labour Party (1982C): *Britain on the Dole*, Labour Party.

Labour Party (1982D): *The City: A Socialist Approach*, Labour Party.

Labour Party (1983A): *New Hope for Britain, Labour's Manifesto 1983*, Labour Party.

Labour Party (1983B): *Partners in Rebuilding Britain*, T.U.C.– Labour Party Liaison Committee.

Lal, D. (1979): 'Comment' in R. Major (ed.), *Britain's Trade and Exchange Rate Policy*, Heinemann, 24–36.

Laury, J. S. E., Lewis, G. R. and Ormerod, P. A. (1978): 'Properties of Macro-economic Models of the U.K. Economy', *National Institute Economic Review*, 83, 52–72.

Layard, R. (1980). 'Wages Policy and the Redistribution of Income' in D. Collard, R. Lecomber and M. Slater (eds), *Income Distribution: the Limits to Redistribution*, Colston Society, 123–34.

Layard, R. (1982): *More Jobs and Less Inflation*, Grant McIntyre.

Layard, R., Basevi, G., Blanchard, O., Buiter, W. and Dornbusch, R.

(1984): 'Europe: The Case for Unsustainable Growth', *Centre for European Policy Studies*, Paper 8/9.

Layard, R. and Nickell, S. J. (1984): *The Causes of British Unemployment*, Centre for Labour Economics, L.S.E., Working Paper No. 642.

Layard, R. and Nickell, S. J. (1985): 'The Causes of British Unemployment', *National Institute Economic Review*, 111, 62–85.

Layard, R., Piachaud, D. and Stewart, M. (1978): *The Causes of Poverty*, Background Paper No. 5, Royal Commission on the Distribution of Income and Wealth, H.M.S.O.

Le Grand, J. (1982): *The Strategy of Equality*, Allen & Unwin.

Liberal/S.D.P. (1982): *Back to Work: Interim Report of the Liberal/ S.D.P. Alliance Commission on Employment and Industrial Recovery*, S.D.P.

Liberal/S.D.P. (1983): 'Working Together for Britain', General Election Manifesto, in *The Times, House of Commons*, Times Books.

Lipton, M. (1976): 'What is Nationalisation For?', *Lloyds Bank Review*, 121, 33–8.

Lloyd, J. (1978): *Conflict or Co-operation: The Growth of Industrial Democracy*, Kogan Page.

Lomax, D. F. and Guttman, P. T. G. (1981): *The Euromarkets and International Financial Policies*, Macmillan.

London Edinburgh Weekend Return Group (1980): *In and Against the State*, 2nd ed., Pluto.

Lydall, H. (1984): *Yugoslav Socialism: Theory & Practice*, Clarendon Press.

Malcolmson, J. (1982): 'Trade Unions and Economic Efficiency', *Economic Journal*, Conference Papers, 50–64.

Major, R. (ed.) (1979): *Britain's Trade and Exchange Rate Policy*, Heinemann.

Manson, R. J. (1984): 'French Socialists March to the Right', *Challenge* 27, 37–42.

Marks, S. (1983): 'Making London Work', *New Statesman*, 1 April, 8–10.

Marquand, D. (1982): 'Social Democracy and the Collapse of the Westminster Model' in W. Kennett (ed.), *The Rebirth of Britain*, Weidenfeld & Nicolson, 63–83.

Matthews, R. C. O. (ed.) (1982): *Slower Growth in the Western World*.

Matthews, R. C. O. and Sargent, J. R. (eds) (1983): *Contemporary Problems of Economic Policy*, Methuen.

Mawson, J. (1983): 'Organising for Economic Development: The Formulations of L.A. Policies in West Yorkshire', in Young and Mason (eds), *Urban Economic Development*, Macmillan, 79–105.

Meade, J. E. (1978): *The Structure and Reform of Direct Taxation*, Institute for Fiscal Studies, Heinemann.

Meade, J. (1981): 'Note on the Inflationary Implications of the Wage Fixing Assumptions of the C.E.P.G.', *Oxford Economic Papers*, 33, 28–41.

Meade, J. (1982): *Stagflation: Vol. 1: Wage Fixing*, Allen and Unwin.

Mendis, L. and Muellbauer, J. (1983): *Has There Been a British Productivity Breakthrough?*, Centre for Labour Economics, L.S.E., Discussion Paper 170.

Metcalf, D. (1983): 'How Good is GLEB', *New Society*, 63, 508–9.

Metcalf, D. (1984A): 'On the Measurement of Employment and Unemployment', *National Institute Economic Review*, 109, 59–67.

Metcalf, D. (1984B): 'Employment and Industrial Assistance' in A. Jacquemin (ed.) *European Industry: Public Policy and Corporate Strategy*, Clarendon Press, 84–98.

Metcalf, D. and Nickell, S. (1985): 'Jobs & Pay', *Midland Bank Review*, spring, 8–15.

Metcalf, D. and Richardson, R. (1982): 'Labour' in A. R. Prest and D. J. Coppock, *The U.K. Economy: A Manual of Applied Economics*, 9th ed., Weidenfeld and Nicholson.

Militant (1981A): *What We Stand For*, Militant.

Militant (1981B): *Import Controls or Socialist Planning?*, Militant.

Minford, P. (1983): *Unemployment: Cause and Cure*, Martin Robertson.

Minns, R. (1980): *Pension Funds and British Capitalism*, Heinemann.

Minns, R. (1982): *Take Over the City*, Pluto.

Minns, R. (1983): 'Pension Funds: An Alternative View', *Capital and Class*, 20, 104–15.

Minns, R. and Thornley, J. (1978): *State Shareholding: The Role of Local and Regional Authorities*, Macmillan.

Moore, B., Rhodes, J., Tarling, R. and Wilkinson, F. (1978): 'A Return to Full Employment?', *Cambridge Economic Policy Review*, 4, 22–6.

Mukherjee, S. (1972): *Making Labour Markets Work*, Political and Economic Planning.

Murray, R. (1983): 'Pension Funds and Local Authority Investments', *Capital and Class*, 20, 89–102.

N.E.D.O. (1976): *A Study of the U.K. Nationalised Industries*, National Economic Development Office.

N.E.D.O. (1977): *International Price Competitiveness, Non-Price Factors and Export Performance*, National Economic Development Office.

N.E.D.O. (1981): *Industrial Policies in Europe*, National Economic Development Office.

Neild, R. (1979): 'Managed Trade Between Industrial Countries' in R. Major (ed.) *Britain's Trade and Exchange Rate Policies*, Heinemann, 5–23.

Nelson, R. (1981): 'Research on Productivity Growth and Productivity Differences', *Journal of Economic Literature*, XIX, 1029–64.

Neuberger, H. (1984): *From the Dole Queue to the Sweatshop*, Low Pay Unit, Pamphlet No. 30.

Nickell, S. J. (1979): 'The Effect of Unemployment and Related Benefits on the Duration of Unemployment', *Economic Journal* 89, 34–49.

Nickell, S. J. (1982): 'The Determinants of Equilibrium Unemployment in Britain', *Economic Journal* 92, 555–75.

Nickell, S. J. (1984): *A Review of Minford (1983)*, Centre for Labour Economics, L.S.E., Discussion Paper No. 185.

Nove, A. (1973): *Efficiency Criteria for Nationalised Industries*, Allen & Unwin.

Nove, A. (1983): *The Economics of Feasible Socialism*, Allen & Unwin.

O'Donovan, K. and Szyszczak, E. (1985): 'Indirect Discrimination – Taking a Concept to Market', *New Law Journal*, 135, 15–18 & 42–4.

Ormerod, P. (1981): 'Inflation and Incomes Policy', *Socialist Economic Review*, 177–90.

Owen, D. (1981): *Face the Future*, Cape.

Owen, D. (1983): 'Agenda for Competitiveness with Compassion', *Journal of Economic Affairs*, 4, 26–33.

Panitch, L. (1976): *Social Democracy and Industrial Militancy*, Cambridge University Press.

Panitch, L. (1982): 'Hard Pounding', *New Socialist*, 7, 18–21.

Pardoe, J. (1974): *We Can Conquer Inflation*, Liberal Party.

Pavitt, K. (ed.) (1980): *Technical Innovation and British Economic Performance*, Macmillan.

Phillips, A. (1983): *Hidden Hands: Women and Economic Policy*. Pluto.

Piachaud, D. (1984): 'The Means Test State', *New Socialist*, 20, 53–4.

Pissarides, C. (1978): 'The Role of Relative Wages & Excess Demand in the Sectoral Flow of Labour', *Review of Economic Studies*, 45, 453–67.

Polan, A. J. (1984): *Lenin & the End of Politics*, Methuen.

Pollard, S. (1979): 'The Nationalisation of the Banks: The Chequered History of a Socialist Proposal' in D. Martin and D. Rubinstein (eds), *Ideology and the Labour Movement*, Croom Helm, 167–90.

Pond, C. and Popay, J. (1983): 'Tackling Inequalities at their Source', in H. Glennerster (ed.), *The Future of the Welfare State*, Heinemann, 103–23.

Pratten, C. (1976): *Labour Productivity Differentials within International Companies*, Cambridge University Press.

Purdy, D. (1980): 'The Left's Alternative Economic Strategy', *Politics and Power*, 1, pp. 55–80. ·

Purdy, D. (1981): 'The Social Contract and Socialist Policy', in M. Prior (ed.), *The Popular and the Political*, Routledge and Kegan Paul, 76–112.

Purdy, D. (1981A): 'Government–Trade Union Relation: Towards a New Social Contract', *Socialist Economic Review*, 191–208.

Reddaway, W. B. (1968): *U.K. Direct Investment Overseas*, Cambridge University Press.

Revell, J. (1983): 'Efficiency in the Financial Sector' in D. Shepherd, Z. A. Silberston and J. Turk, *Microeconomic Efficiency and Macroeconomic Performance*, Philip Allan, 137–179.

Rimmer, L. (1980): *The Intra-Family Distribution of Income*, Study Commission on the Family.

Rose, N. (1980): 'Socialism and Social Policy: The Problems of Inequality', *Politics and Power*, 2, 111–35.

Rothwell, R. (1980): 'Policies in Industry', in K. Pavitt, (ed.), *Technical Innovation and British Economic Performance*, Macmillan, 299–309.

Routh, G. (1980): *Occupation and Pay in Great Britain 1906–79*, Macmillan.

Rowthorn, R. (1977): 'Conflict, Inflation and Money', *Cambridge Journal of Economics*, 1, 215–39.

Rowthorn, R. (1981): 'The Politics of the Alternative Economic Strategy', *Marxism Today*, January, 4–10.

Rowthorn, B. and Ward, T. (1979): 'How to Run a Company and Run Down an Economy: The Effects of Closing Down Steel-Making in Corby', *Cambridge Journal of Economics*, 3, 327–40.

S.D.P. (1982A): *Democracy at Work*, Green Paper No. 6, S.D.P.

S.D.P. (1982B): *Fair Treatment: Social Democracy in the Health and Social Services*, Green Paper No 5, S.D.P.

S.D.P. (1983A): *Economic Policy*, Policy Document No. 1, S.D.P.

S.D.P. (1983B): *Industrial Strategy*, Policy Document No. 2, S.D.P.

S.D.P. (1983C): *Industrial Relations 1. Trade Union Reform*, Policy Document No. 3, SD.D.P.

S.D.P. (1983D): *Industrial Relations 2. Industrial Democracy*, Policy Document No. 4, S.D.P.

S.D.P. (1984): *Policies for Competitiveness*, Green Paper No. 17, S.D.P.

Saunders, C. T. (1980): 'Changes in Relative Pay in the 1970s', in F. Blackaby (ed.), *The Future of Pay Bargaining*, Heinemann, 191–211.

Sen, A. K. (1983A): 'The Profit Motive', *Lloyds Book Review*, 147, 1–20.

Sen, A. K. (1983B): 'Poor, Relatively Speaking', *Oxford Economic Papers*, 35, 153–69.

Sheffield, (1980): *Employment Department: An Initial Outline*, Sheffield City Council.

Sinfield, A. (1981): *What Unemployment Means*, Martin Robertson.

Singh, A. (1975): 'Takeovers, Economic Natural Selection and the Theory of the Firm', *Economic Journal*, 85, 497–515.

Singh, A. (1977): 'U.K. Industry and the World Economy: A Case of De-industrialisation', *Cambridge Journal of Economics*, 1, 113–36.

Smith, K. (1984): *The British Economic Crisis*, Penguin.

Solow, R. M. (1980): 'On Theories of Employment', *American Economic Review*, 70, 1–11.

Stewart, M. (1983): 'Relative Earnings and Individual Union Membership in the U.K.,' *Economica*, 50, 111–25.

Stout, D. (ed.) (1979): 'De-Industrialization and Industrial Policy' in F. Blackaby, *De-Industrialization*, Heinemann, 171–96.

Swords-Isherwood, N. (1980): 'British Management Compared' in K. Pavitt (ed.), *Technical Innovation and British Economic Performance*, Macmillan, 88–99.

Szyszczak, E. (1985): 'Pay Inequalities and Equal Value Claims', *Modern Law Review*, 48, 139–57.

T.U.C. (1967): *Trade Unionism: The Evidence of the T.U.C. to Royal Commission on Trade Unions and Employers' Associations*, T.U.C.

T.U.C. (1979): *The Role of the Financial Institutions* (Evidence to the Wilson Committee), T.U.C.

T.U.C. (1981): *Annual Economic Review*, Trades Union Congress.

Tarling, R. and Wilkinson, F. (1977): 'The Social Contract: Post-War Incomes Policies and their Inflationary Impact', *Cambridge Journal of Economics*, 1, 395–414.

Tarling, R. and Wilkinson, F. (1982): 'Inflation and Unemployment: A Critique of Meade's Solutions', *Cambridge Economic Policy Review*, 8, 39–43.

Thompson, G. (1977): 'The Relationship between the Financial and Industrial Sector and the U.K. Economy', *Economy and Society*, 6, 235–83.

Thompson, G. (1982): 'The Firm as "Dispersed Social Agency" ', *Economy and Society*, 11, 233–50.

Thompson, G. (1985): *Mrs Thatcher's Economic Experiment*, Croom Helm.

Tomlinson, J. (1981A): 'Corporatism: A Further Sociologisation of Marxism', *Politics and Power*, 4, 237–48.

Tomlinson, J. (1981B): *Problems of British Economic Policy 1870–1945*, Methuen.

Tomlinson, J. (1981C): 'Socialist Problems and the Small Business', *Politics and Power*, 1, 165–74.

Tomlinson, J. (1982): *The Unequal Struggle? British Socialism and the Capitalist Enterprise*, Methuen.

Tomlinson, J. (1983A): 'Regulating the Capitalist Enterprise: The Impossible Dream?', *Scottish Journal of Political Economy*, 30, 54–68.

Tomlinson, J. (1983B): 'Does Mass Employment Matter?', *National Westminster Bank Quarterly Review*, February, 35–45.

Tomlinson, J. (1984A): 'Economic and Sociological Theories of the Firm and Industrial Democracy', *British Journal of Sociology*, 35, 591–605.

Tomlinson, J. (1984B): 'Incomes Policies and Women's Wages', *M/F*, 9, 45–59.

Tomlinson, J. (1985): *British Macro-Economic Policy Since 1940*, Croom Helm.

Townsend, P. (1979): *Poverty in Britain*, Penguin.

Treasury (1985): *The Relationship between Employment and Wages*, H.M.S.O.

Vernon, R. (1972): *The Economic Environment of International Business*, Prentice Hall.

Wadhwani, S. (1984A): *Inflation, Bankruptcy, Default Premia and The Stock Market*, Centre for Labour Economics, L.S.E. Discussion Paper 194.

Wadhwani, S. (1984B): *Inflation, Bankruptcy and Employment*, L.S.E. Centre for Labour Economics, L.S.E. Discussion Paper 195.

Wadhwani, S. (1985): *The Effects of Aggregate Demand, Inflation, Real*

Wages & Uncertainty on Manufacturing Employment, Centre for Labour Economics, L.S.E.

Wainwright, H. and Elliott, D. (1982): *The Lucas Plan*, Allison and Busby.

Ward, T. (1981): 'The Case for an Import Control Strategy in the U.K.', *Socialist Economic Review*, Merlin.

West Midlands (1982): *W.M.E.B. Ltd.*, West Midlands Enterprise Board.

Whittington, G. (1974): *Company Taxation and Dividends*, Institute for Fiscal Studies.

Williams, K. (1984): 'Made in U.S.A.', *Economy and Society*, 13, 484–509.

Williams, K., Williams, J. and Thomas, D. (1983); *Why Are the British Bad at Manufacturing?*, Routledge and Kegan Paul.

Williamson, J. (1984): 'Is There an External Constraint', *National Institute Economic Review*, 109, 73–7.

Williamson, O. E. (1984): 'Efficient Labour Organisation', in F. H. Stephen (ed.), *Firms, Organisation and Labour*, Macmillan, 87–118.

Willman, P. (1982): *Fairness, Collective Bargaining and Incomes Policy*, Clarendon Press.

Wilson (1977): *Evidence to the Committee on Financial Institutions*, H.M.S.O.

Wilson, H. (1980): *Committee to Review the Functioning of Financial Institutions: Report*, Cmnd 7937, H.M.S.O.

Winter, S. G. (1964): 'Economic Natural Selection and the Theory of the Firm', *Yale Economic Essays*, 4, 225–72.

Winter, S. G. (1971): 'Satisficing, Selection and the Innovating Remnant', *Quarterly Journal of Economics*, 85, 237–61.

Winters, L. A. (1982): *The Consequences of Devaluing Sterling*, Treasury and Civil Service Committee. International Monetary Arrangements, H.C.P. 21–III, 1982/3, H.M.S.O.

Wootton, B. (1962): *The Social Foundations of Wage Policy*, (2nd edition 1962), Unwin University Books.

Wootton, B. (1974): *Incomes Policy: An Inquest and a Proposal*, Davis and Poynter.

Worswick, G. D. N. (ed.) (1984): *Education and Economic Performance*, Gower.

Wren-Lewis, S. (1984): 'The Roles of Output Expectations and Liquidity in Explaining Recent Productivity Movements' *National Institute Economic Review*, 108, 42–53.

Young, K. (1983): 'The Problem of Economic Strategy', in Young and Mason (eds), *Urban Economic Development*, 106–30.

Index